FREEDOM
of the PRESS
The War on Words (1977–1978)

FREEDOM
of the PRESS
The War on Words (1977–1978)

AHFAZ UR REHMAN

Translated by IMTIAZ PIRACHA

OXFORD
UNIVERSITY PRESS

OXFORD
UNIVERSITY PRESS

Oxford University Press is a department of the University of Oxford.
It furthers the University's objective of excellence in research, scholarship,
and education by publishing worldwide. Oxford is a registered trade mark of
Oxford University Press in the UK and in certain other countries

Published in Pakistan by
Ameena Saiyid, Oxford University Press
No.38, Sector 15, Korangi Industrial Area,
PO Box 8214, Karachi-74900, Pakistan

ISBN 978-0-19-940733-0

Typeset in Baskerville
Printed on 80gsm Local Offset Paper

Printed by Mas Printers, Karachi

Contents

Preface

Time flies. A mountain pops up in a blink and then memories abandon me. Torrents of mist lash over the mind and past events begin to play hide-and-seek. The picture that once glittered in the mirror of my heart is not vivid anymore but the moments that moved through the garden of affection will probably never abandon me. Sometimes such memories start radiating in an instant as if it happened just today.

I experienced this more often than not while writing this book.

Years went by and the memories of a historic struggle, perhaps the greatest by Pakistani journalists, moved along.

'You have to write its account,' insisted my friends.

I hesitated in taking this up, letting some time pass. My requests to Minhaj Barna to do this and his promises to begin the task soon consumed more time. Barna was the leader of this movement. Now he has left us for his heavenly abode and I have also entered the twilight of my life. While sifting through old documents one day, I discovered a considerable amount of material on the memorable movement of 1977–8. My wife, Mehnaz, managed to retrieve all of the newspapers and magazines locked up in the attic for years. A flash of hope struck my mind. I thought that the onerous task of writing the account of the 1977–8 Freedom of the Press Movement could probably be done. I met Wahab Siddiqui, the editor of the weekly *Al Fatah*. Its publisher and chief-editor, Irshad Rao, and editor, Wahab Siddiqui, were pivotal to the movement and their participation to uphold democratic values was aggressive. *Al Fatah* played a central role in keeping the public informed despite the extreme hardships of Zia ul-Haq's rule. During the movement, Siddiqui courted arrest in Lahore and Karachi. He was exiled from Punjab and eventually forced out of the country. Irshad Rao was also imprisoned several times. On one occasion, he was sentenced to two and a half years' imprisonment on charges of rebellion and treason which compelled the International Human Rights Commission to declare him a prisoner of conscience.

Siddiqui has returned after remaining in exile in the Netherlands for 18 years. Save for some physical ailments, he is in a robust mental and intellectual condition. Siddiqui also insisted that I return what I owe. He handed me numerous magazines published under the banner of Al Fatah Publications. The military government repeatedly banned *Al Fatah* but the fearless publisher did not give up. He went around buying declarations for another publication when one was banned. Altogether, twelve magazines under different names were published. Siddiqui also helped me refresh past events and we retrieved various articles written during the movement by my colleagues and myself. Masood Qamar's autobiography was obtained from Facebook. Shehnaz Ahad sent several write-ups from *Mayar* which remained steadfast in those difficult times. Its editors Mehmood Sham, Ashraf Shad, and other staff members played a prominent role in the struggle waged by journalists against tyranny.

When I read these articles, I found it impossible to proceed any further with writing the book without them. I could pick and choose special events and memories from these narratives; however, I decided to include them in full length. After all, what could be a better way of recreating scenes from a conscientious battlefield than including the narratives of all its participants? Fresh contributions for this book were sent by Aurangzeb from Lahore and Shabbar Azmi from Karachi. Aurangzeb also sent a passionate essay about the 1974 movement which is included in the book.

I do not harbour any high hopes about the possibility of this book becoming an important archive or the journalist community learning any lessons from it. However, it is important to mention an interesting fact. Numerous books have been written about freedom of the press and the 'press [being] in chains' in Pakistan, some of which also earned fame. Nevertheless, several enlightened individuals—Minhaj Barna being one of them—were flabbergasted about the cursory mention merited in these accounts regarding the biggest struggle for a free press waged in 1977–8. There can hardly be any justification for this oversight.

The oft-quoted is Zameer Niazi's *Press in Chains* in which he writes the following:

> The central theme of this book is the persecution of newspapers and punitive actions taken against dissenting journalists. The first chapter deals with the one and three-quarters of a century of the ruthless repression and suppression under foreign domination. The rest deal with the four distinct phases of our chequered history and offer an objective account of the captivity of the press, roles of various regimes and agencies, including proprietors of newspapers, editors, working journalists, their associations and unions.

In its entirety, it is a valuable book; however, several serious omissions are visible too. It is necessary to point this out in order to keep the record straight because readers can be misled about some issues and events owing to these omissions. Since the subject of this book is the 1977–8 movement, I will restrict myself to it and some other important points.

Thousands of journalists and press workers took part in this movement (in its third phase, students, farmers, and labourers also joined it). They courted arrests in Karachi and Lahore, suffered extreme physical and mental torture, were sentenced to rigorous imprisonments and horrible flogging by military courts, and jailed

in fourteen prisons of Sindh and Punjab. For long, they continued
to bear the agony of expulsions and unemployment. I don't know
why Zameer Niazi touched only the surface of these issues. He did
not take active part in the movement at any stage even though he
was witnessing everything.

The first problem in Niazi's account pertains to the movement
of 1974 which is discussed at length in his work. About the 1974
movement, Niazi writes: 'Never in the history of Pakistan were so
many journalists and newspaper workers arrested, as they were
by the government of Punjab during the chief-ministership of
artist and journalist Mohammad Hanif Ramay.' He continues,
'Altogether, 145 journalists courted arrests, including several office
bearers of PFUJ [Pakistan Federal Union of Journalists], regional
unions, and the Union of Active Calligraphers.'

Undoubtedly, this was a large and commendable movement but
in 1978, 168 journalists and newspaper workers were arrested in
Lahore. In Karachi, the number of journalists and press workers
who courted arrests swelled to 300. The interesting bit to observe
with regards to the 1978 movement is that, in less than two
months, more than 150 journalists were arrested. About the fifth
columnists within PFUJ's ranks, he evocatively writes, 'Meanwhile,
the government succeeded in persuading a "section" of journalists
and press workers—who had accepted its conditions under which
the arrested journalists were to be released—to end the agitation.'
In other words, Niazi is falling short of outrightly declaring those
journalists who betrayed the cause and formed a parallel PFUJ
'traitors'. Instead of naming an organization, referring to 'a section
of the organization' as being 'persuaded to end the agitation',
indicates a conspiracy and it should have been mentioned as such.

Niazi presents a fragmented account of the 84-day Karachi
movement in only six or seven lines. His inattention to such
important details is evident from the incidents mentioned in
this book. The Karachi movement went on from 18 July to 18

October in which numerous colleagues from across the country were sentenced to imprisonments besides being physically tortured in horrific ways.

This book presents, in some detail, the first person accounts— that are merited only a cursory mention in *Press in Chains*—of my colleagues. In his work, Niazi records the history of the Karachi movement in the following manner:

> The Action Committees of PFUJ and APNEC had decided to re-launch the movement from Karachi. The decision was well-received in different segments of population. Meanwhile, the government issued arrest warrants of 19 leaders of the movement, including a woman journalist Lalarukh Hussain. She was arrested on the morning of 14 August 1978 along with her child and locked in Karachi Jail. They were released after about a fortnight. On 17 September 1978, the information secretary, Lt. General Mujeeb-ur Rehman, invited PFUJ president Nisar Usmani for talks. Soon after, all the arrested journalists and other individuals (numbering about 200) were released unconditionally.

Even in this brief statement few things are incorrect while some very important events are omitted which will constrain any general reader in understanding the scope and significance of the movement.

First of all, altogether 300–325 colleagues were arrested and not 'about 200'.

In addition to this, Niazi fails to address several important aspects relevant to the movement. For instance, the dates of the movement's beginning and culmination have not been mentioned. The disturbing fact that Karachi Press Club remained under police siege for days has been entirely overlooked. The harsh treatment that the activists had to put up with during imprisonment has not been discussed either. The particular accounts of frightening manhunts which would often result into the activists' homes being raided and their families being harassed do not form part of Niazi's larger narrative. Apart from the press clubs, several activists courted arrests elsewhere but neither this nor their plight as prisoners has been highlighted. It was equally important to mention specific places where the arrested activists were locked up all across Sindh; however, much to the reader's dismay, Niazi fails to include this. Where did the fast-until-death protest start and how far had it spread before the government was compelled into talks is another point that he has not addressed.

Finally, it is important to mention that Lalarukh was kept under house arrest and besides her, Tamkinat Ara from Lahore (wife of late senior journalist Shafqat Tanveer), Farkhanda Bukhari (wife of famous poet Shuhrat Bukhari), Asifa Rizvi and Hameeda Ghangro (belonging to Jamhooriat Pasand Khawateen) from Karachi, and Nasreen Zahra (from National Students Federation) also courted arrest. It is imperative for the students of journalism and common readers to know these facts.

Some individuals, including Naecm-ul-Hassan, have also done research on this struggle for press freedom in Pakistan. Undoubtedly, it is a commendable effort. However, these works are devoid of a lot of important facts because the newspapers were censored during the period when the movement was active. Moreover, in order to please the martial law government several newspaper owners persuaded many working journalists to stand against the movement. They were definitely mistaken. This was a demonstration of ignorance on their part because they failed to recognize the elephant in the room.

The *Times of India* commended the movement for press freedom in Pakistan in these words: 'Had there been organizations like PFUJ in India, it would not have been possible for Indira Gandhi to impose emergency rule.' The massive support and appreciation that we—the journalists who stood for press freedom—were able to garner reinforces that we were a force to reckon with, and those who distanced themselves from the struggle were wrong in their judgment.

It is better not to be hopeful about the impact of this account on modern-day journalists. Even though one must always believe in the principle to persevere and hope for the best, the analysis of some of my veteran colleagues is also not very different. There is a sense of loss; as if something crucial has vanished because a lot is going astray. The PFUJ has become fragmented and divided, thus losing its former glory. A great deal has gone and slogan-mongering persists. The code of conduct for journalists is in tatters. The owners of media houses and newspapers have never been its adherents because they are essentially self-centered but now a section of working journalists is also fast losing its integrity.

On the one hand, there is a serious dearth of professional ability, adequate knowledge, and the urge to learn more, while on the other, corruption is eating away their character. We were taught to behave and act gracefully. If we failed to conduct ourselves properly it was considered akin to bringing disgrace to the entire journalist community. We were very conscious of not letting down the masses who believed in us. Nowadays, journalistic ethics are degenerating and professional journalists are becoming rare. Sensational journalism has become the norm. News reports have astonishing volumes of errors. Numerous errors of language, diction, syntax, spelling, and expression have seeped in. The essential elements of news are absent from stories which also lack logical coherence and solid arguments. The only thing that remains is the first person—'I'.

These days, journalists in sizeable numbers openly say that they want to get rich as soon as possible. Consequently, networking with rulers, authorities, the wealthy and powerful, and flattering them has become habitual for them.

Let me make it clear, the courage to struggle emanates from a spotless character. Those who offer sacrifices in the war for freedom of the press don't fall prey to pelf and privileges. They do not become obsessed with fame and fortune or resort to gimmicks. They may lack wealth but their hearts beat with the agonies of the people. How can a heart that is neither tender nor free of greed fight wars?

There was a time when journalists' unions served as models. Their leaders used to be devoted to the cause of press freedom. Upholding the principles of trade unions, they remained active to mobilize people from other professions. The low morale among journalists can be gauged by the fact that they hold 'protests' in front of press clubs instead of going out in the streets. Such protests are filled with loud slogan-mongering, boisterous claims, and fantastic rhetoric: 'We are the ones who end up in jails and never surrender even after being flogged!' Their crowd constitutes of hardly thirty or forty participants. One wonders when they were imprisoned or bore whiplashes? How long are they going to capitalize on the 1977–8 movement? Seventy to eighty hundred-thousand rupees are spent on a single event. Is there someone to inquire about the source of these funds?

It is no secret that when a media house earns the wrath of the rulers, it falls in love with journalists' bodies. Journalists are showered with money so that their 'agitation power' can be exploited. The user exploits and the used is taken advantage of. One could justify it perhaps had it been an unselfish union.

A surge in the number of television channels is also giving rise to ugly consequences. The owners of media houses were advised against it by senior journalists when they were laying the foundation of this trend. However, in addition to the owners, several working journalists and anchorpersons viewed this development as an easy path to fame and riches and rode the current. Where do they stand now? There are loud calls from all over to rein in these journalists as they are dishonest and divisive. Millions are watching this pathetic sight which is further eroding whatever little is left of the reputation of the press. On the other hand, journalists who present critical points of view are being chased and shot.

Through this book, I am addressing only those dedicated journalists who love their profession. Indeed, even in these dismal times, such journalists are present in large numbers. If the incidents narrated in this book can motivate them to further strengthen their character, I will consider my effort to have borne some fruit. During the black rule of Zia ul-Haq, hundreds of journalists, press workers, labourers, farmers, and students courted arrests on the call of the Joint Action Committee of the PFUJ and All Pakistan Newspaper Employees Confederation (APNEC), in the biggest and historic war for freedom of the press. They voluntarily offered themselves for arrest in the streets and squares of Karachi and Lahore, received rigorous imprisonment sentences from summary military courts, and became targets of torture at the hands of so-called law enforcement agencies, but never bowed. Everyone's story is interesting, educative, and inspiring, especially of those volunteers who came from far-flung areas to Karachi and Lahore so that they could contribute their share in the democratic struggle against the military dictatorship. Apparently, they had no link with the struggle of journalists but they knew that the struggle for freedom of the press was actually a struggle for the restoration of democracy. This book offers real-life accounts of several peoples who were arrested, sentenced by summary military courts, and then spent several days and nights in jails across the country. It was an impossible task to gather so many stories; however, I have done my best to accurately portray the whole situation. My wife, Mehnaz Rehman, son, Rameez Rehman, and some friends posted parts of this book on Facebook and an online blog which received surprisingly wide encouragement that in turn motivated me to enrich this narrative.

Initially, I intended to only include my personal impressions in this book. Then luckily I gained access to writings by other colleagues which I felt duty-bound to include. With the inclusion of their narratives, it becomes easier to understand Zia ul-Haq's repressive era, the struggle waged by the oppressed classes, different phases

of journalists' movement, their arrests, the mechanical functioning
of the military courts, and the situation inside the jails. In this
respect, this is an autobiography as well as a biography. Keeping
this point of view in mind, I personally contacted many comrades
in various cities who were fervent activists. I have included all those
impressions as received; therefore, this book is divided in two parts.
The first part includes my personal observations and experiences
and the second consists of what other colleagues wrote during that
period. It also includes some of my articles. The reader will observe
that the articles in the latter section portray a whole picture of Zia
ul-Haq's dictatorial era and the oppression that he unleashed.

As mentioned earlier, I received requests from several colleagues
from far and wide to write a book on this subject but somehow the
matter lingered on. One of the main reasons for this inordinate
delay could be laziness but then some new factors emerged that
helped in materializing this project. One was the access to a sizeable
written matter with statistics and photos. The other was the support
of several diligent and competent associates.

My wife, Mehnaz, who was an active colleague in the movement,
frequently insisted that I compile all the happenings in the form of
a book. She also suggested making an audio recording and letting
someone else write it. Then the same request started to pour in
from my workplace. An extremely competent colleague at the daily
Express, Iqbal Khursheed, had been insisting for a long time that I
make an audio recording which he would write down for my final
editing. Khursheed is not only an exemplary journalist, he is also
a very intelligent short story writer. His journalistic writings are
also admired for their attractive style. In short, if you find yourself
reading this book, it is because of the sincere assistance and hard
work of this intelligent young man. To acknowledge his help with
a formal word of thanks would be unjust. His sincerity is etched
on my heart.

When I was reading old issues of *Al Fatah*, I deeply missed Wahid

Basheer, Irshad Rao, Wahab Siddiqui, Naeem Arvi, and all of my other friends associated with the magazine. They were lovers of democracy, offering to sacrifice their lives for freedom of the press; a crazy lot undeterred by power and authority. The enthusiasm about the singular role of *Al Fatah* in advancing the unparalleled movement of 1977–8 was also reignited. However, some other magazines and newspapers were also very active on the publishing front. Not only that, Rao and Siddiqui rendered selfless help in connecting with colleagues in other cities when we were operating underground. During Raqeeb's and my hiding, Rao mostly took care of the dangerous and sensitive task of arranging different hideouts. I called Rao in Islamabad who had earlier suffered a severe paralysis. He survived it but it was not possible for him to write. In my view, the most suitable person for writing the foreword of this book was Rao's confidant, Siddiqui. I am extremely grateful for the earnestness and zeal with which he wrote it.

As far as the photographs are concerned (most captions were incomplete and many faces are not recognizable now; there was no option but to include them as is), those of the arrests in Lahore were not available. A photo received from Ahmed Khalid from Islamabad has been included. My colleague in Karachi and a senior photographer, Zahid Hussain, sent several photos that are included in the book and for which I am grateful. The rest of them have been printed in weekly *Al Fatah*, daily *Musawat*, daily *Hilal-e-Pakistan*, and daily *Sadaqat*, and are reproduced here. There was no credit line tagged to these photos. The ever adorable Khawar Naeem Hashmi has also sent several photos and articles. It feels so formal to be thanking Khawar. He was a young kid when he came to Karachi and Mehnaz and I have held him dear ever since. I am also grateful to Shehnaz Ahad and Dr Jaffar Ahmed for their help in obtaining old issues of *Mayar*.

In the all-encompassing, successful movement of 1977–8, a decisive role was played by the unshakeable leadership of Minhaj

Barna, Nisar Usmani, and Hafeez Raqeeb, who were the office
bearers of PFUJ and APNEC. At the same time, numerous selfless
and passionate volunteers from Peshawar to Karachi and their
gruelling sacrifices should not be forgotten. However, it is difficult
to write about the individual contribution of each one of them.
Similarly, it is not possible to individually mention those numerous
respected and senior journalists and distinguished personalities
from other walks of life, who voluntarily courted arrest. These
include conscientious labourers, farmers, students, and others who
provided moral support, including those generous individuals who
provided shelter during our hiding. I wish a comprehensive list of
their names could be prepared.

Some of our comrades in Karachi included farmers, labourers,
and students, and they were also ruthlessly tortured. They were also
asked foolish questions, for instance, how much money were they
paid by the Pakistan People's Party (PPP) for protesting? Jamaat-e-
Islami backed editor of daily *Jasarat*, Maulana Salahuddin, wrote a
defamatory article titled *Movement for the Protection of PPP Newspapers*
in order to bring a bad name to our struggle. The response to
these attacks by conscientious and courageous journalists Hussain
Naqi and Abdul Hameed Chapra is included in this book. Several
journalists from Karachi were offered to be released if they disclosed
my whereabouts but they contributed to the collective struggle for
truth in a historic movement by remaining steadfast. Through this
book I want to personally salute them.

A movement backed by selfless and conscientious followers
cannot be defeated. Despite the horrible punishment at the hands
of martial law authorities, the daring workers of PFUJ and APNEC
held the flag of press freedom high in various cities. I am proud of
my colleagues Khawar Naeem Hashmi, Masoodullah Khan, Nasir
Zaidi, and Iqbal Jafri, who persisted in the face of the military
court's arrogance. There was not even the slightest shadow of fear

in their eyes when they were tortured. Their heads remained high, our movement remained intact, and the dignity of our profession was protected. When we received news of our victory, I went to an isolated spot in Karachi Press Club's backyard and wept under a tree. Perhaps my other colleagues did the same and regretted not being with our suffering comrades. I bow my head again in honour of my four colleagues.

This relationship of shared pain travels like a whiff of fragrance through human beings. It gives the courage to stand up to tyranny and injustice. It provides the emotion to fight for the destitute and the downtrodden, and teaches one to seek truth and light. This relationship creates the picture of true happiness and declares that we will never allow life to be extinguished. Even death cannot destroy this emotion.

If this book can fortify the passion to fight for life in the reader's heart and inspires him to keep the longing for freedom of expression evergreen, I would assume that the tale of our struggle is still effective.

Ahfaz ur Rehman
Karachi, 20 May 2017

Foreword I

By Wahab Siddiqui

This book covers three movements during the government of General Zia ul-Haq. It is written by Ahfaz ur Rehman, who was the general-secretary of Karachi Union of Journalists (KUJ) and secretary-general of Joint Central Action Committee of the PFUJ and APNEC during 1977–8. He was jailed during the movements of December 1977 and April 1978 and was exiled from Punjab for six months.

Before the movement began in July 1978, several organizational decisions had been made already. One of them was that PFUJ secretary, Nisar Usmani, APNEC secretary general, Hafeez Raqeeb, and Ahfaz ur Rehman would avoid getting arrested at all costs and run the movement from hiding. Ahfaz was from Karachi while the other two were from Lahore. He played a fundamental role in remaining in touch with newspaper workers, labour leaders, and student organizations; therefore, the book under review is an authentic historical document.

General Zia's military government first struck at Minhaj Barna, bureau chief of *Pakistan Times* in Karachi, and also president of the PFUJ and chairman of APNEC. He was fired from his job and the reason cited for the termination of his services was that he regularly wrote articles for the weekly *Al Fatah*. This periodical supported regional groups and propagated their rights—an ideology that negated the military government's policy. His second 'crime' was

that in his recent article, he had demanded the rescinding of the
Press and Publications Ordinance and disbanding National Press
Trust.

Previously Ayub Khan had nationalized the Progressive Papers
Limited (PPL) on the advice of Qudratullah Shahab who had
prepared the draft for the takeover. Following the same precedence,
Zia's government took over the Peoples Foundation Press (PFP)
which was owned by the Bhuttos, instead of directly banning its
subsidiary, the daily *Musawat* in Karachi. The nationalized PFP
served a notice to the management of the daily *Musawat* to stop
printing. It also stated that the no objection certificate (NOC)
required to resume printing would only be issued after *Musawat's*
administration cleared all of its outstanding dues. No printer in
Karachi agreed to publish *Musawat* without the NOC because they
were also under the government's pressure.

The PFUJ and APNEC started a movement against the closing
down of *Musawat* (Karachi) in December 1977. First, Barna went
on hunger strike at Karachi Press Club along with eight workers
from different cities. The same night, twenty-two press workers
were arrested including those eight. This was followed by a series
of regular arrests; however, the military government had to give
in after a few days. *Musawat* was restored and the arrested press
workers released.

Lt. General Mujeeb-ur-Rehman was the federal secretary
information at the time. He was a self-styled expert on psychological
warfare and repeatedly attacked newspapers and magazines.
Musawat (Lahore) was banned in early 1978. The leaders
representing journalists held talks with him and demanded the
restoration of *Musawat* (Lahore), which was rejected. During the
early days of the Lahore movement, some energetic press workers
who reached the city to court arrests were exiled from Punjab.
Barna, Ahfaz, Johar Mir, and I were arrested and externed from
Punjab with a six-month restriction on our return. With each

passing day, the military administration's policy became sterner. Summary military courts started awarding sentences of rigorous imprisonment to press workers, and finally awarded whiplashes to four journalists. Three of them were flogged the same day.

The military administration had presumed that whiplashes would scare the journalists and force them to abandon their struggle. On the contrary, this punishment intensified their passion and the movement rose to new heights. The Lahore movement went on for about a month and the military government was checkmated. *Musawat* (Lahore) was restored and the arrested journalists released.

When the military administration could not suppress the movement, it resorted to the methods it had learnt from the East India Company and British colonial masters. This entailed the creation of the Mir Jaffars and Mir Sadiqs through collusion and coercion, which in turn, created rifts between the PFUJ and APNEC. Naseem Usmani and Rasheed Chaudhry from Karachi, and Rasheed Siddiqui and Mahmood Jafri from Lahore created a parallel PFUJ and APNEC.

Even though all arrested newspaper workers were released and the publication of *Musawat* was resumed, the leadership of the newspaper workers did not feel at ease after this success. Barna was certain that the military government would strike again. He understood that the government's anti-worker moves could only be defeated by demonstrating exemplary unity and mobilizing people all across the country. He wanted to form a confederation consisting of trade unions from all the industries in the country, similar to Trade Union Congress in Britain, Federation of the Netherlands Trade Unions in Holland, and All India Trade Union Congress in India. To achieve this end, he called a meeting of different workers' organizations in Karachi as the chairman of APNEC. It was agreed that cooperation, partnership, and contact between different workers and organizations would be promoted. For this purpose, a coordination committee was formed and Ahfaz ur Rehman was appointed its secretary general. Barna travelled to various cities of Sindh and held talks with organizations of farmers, labourers, and students. I also accompanied him twice to Hyderabad. Our endeavours bore fruit and a 'struggle committee' was formed. The progressive labour, student, and farmer organizations were its members.

Then what we had feared happened: Zia regime banned *Musawat* (Karachi). The Central Action Committee of the PFUJ and APNEC met in Karachi and all aspects of the issue were discussed in detail. Barna was in favour of starting a movement while Nisar Usmani was against it. Eventually, the majority voted in favour of the movement. Since Usmani possessed a democratic temperament in its true sense, he accepted the decision and presented very convincing arguments in favour of launching the movement in his speech at Karachi Press Club the same evening. Barna had to start his hunger strike from the first day of the movement; therefore, PFUJ secretary general, Nisar Usmani, APNEC secretary general, Hafeez Raqeeb, and KUJ general secretary, Ahfaz ur Rehman were assigned the responsibility of running the movement from underground. Shamim Alam and Altaf Siddiqui were appointed couriers for this committee. The responsibility to distribute information to workers in other cities, news agencies, and newspapers was given to *Al Fatah*. Its owner and chief editor Irshad Rao's fingers moved fast on the telephone dial and he had a photographic memory for numbers. He would call all over the country, exchange information, convey instructions from the leadership, and report the day's activities to one of the leaders in hiding by evening.

Barna started the hunger strike with eight workers from different cities on 18 July 1978 and all of them were arrested the same night. The hunger strikes continued till 4 August. Police would arrest the protesting workers at night, sentence them in the morning, and then send them to jail. Afterwards, the decision was made to move out of the press club and set up base at Regal Chowk in Saddar, Karachi. The following day, five volunteers led by Johar Mir courted arrest at Regal Chowk. The next day, I led the renowned Sindhi nationalist poet, Mujrim Laghari (who was the daily *Ibrat's* correspondent in Jhudo), Ghulam Mohammad Jatoi (Sukkur correspondent for *Hilal-e-Pakistan*), Mohammad Azeem of *Musawat* (Lahore), Malak Haq Nawaz of Labour Organizing Committee, and Yaqoob Kirano of Sindhi Hari Committee to a protest where all of us were swiftly arrested. This led to a surge in the series of protests and arrests in various parts of the city on a daily basis. The military conducted summary trials and sentenced people to rigorous imprisonments for up to seven months. While this was going on, Barna announced that he would fast till death in Khairpur Jail where he was incarcerated. Upon hearing this, the farmers, students, and workers in the jail also declared to fast until death. Almost daily, three to four volunteers would come forward to join the movement in every jail. This continued for about the next three weeks. Eventually, the military government had to retreat once again. The publication of *Musawat* (Karachi) was restored and those under arrest were released.

After finally announcing the general elections in December 1970, when General Ayub Khan allowed political activities in January 1971, the information minister, Nawabzada Sher Ali Khan, newspaper owners, and rightist political parties (particularly Jamaat-e-Islami), planned to purify the newspapers from 'unwanted elements and Reds'. This was done by refusing to give provisional assistance as granted by the Second Wage Board Award. A campaign was launched against the PFUJ when it protested the decision. Weekly *Zindagi* started a series of articles against the PFUJ. They demanded the termination of K. G. Mustafa and Minhaj Barna by declaring them 'communists'. When the newspaper owners association, All Pakistan Newspapers Society (APNS), refused to pay provisional aid, the journalists were left with no option but to go on strike.

Before the strike, the PFUJ conducted a referendum in which 97.6 per cent members voted in favour of the strike. As a result of the strike, no newspaper was published in East Pakistan from 15–24 April; except for *Nawa-e-Waqt* and *Mashriq* (Lahore), no paper was published in West Pakistan. Just one brave journalist from *Mashriq* (Lahore), Altaf Qureshi, participated in the strike and suffered the consequences for doing so. There was no unit of Punjab Union of Journalists in *Nawa-e-Waqt*. Just one journalist from this paper took part in the strike, whose service was later terminated by the exploiters of 'Pakistan Ideology'. In Karachi, only an eveninger of Dawn group, the daily *Star*, violated the strike. The daily *Star* hit the stalls on the afternoon of 24 April but with a new name as its editor because the incumbent editor refused to leave the strike. The same evening, all Islamist newspaper journalists broke the strike and resumed work. By 10 pm, the PFUJ announced the end of the strike.

No journalist was fired for going on strike in East Pakistan because Sheikh Mujibur Rahman and Maulana Bhashani had strictly forbidden the owners to do so. However, in West Pakistan, about 150 journalists lost their jobs. Zulfikar Ali Bhutto promised to restore all these journalists after he was elected. The unemployment of journalists gave birth to many tragedies, for instance, district editor of *Mashriq*, Paiker Naqvi, could not pay for the treatment of his ailing son who died later.

The PPP came to power in December 1971. It kept its promise by pressurizing newspaper owners to reinstate terminated journalists; however, some well-known media houses refused to comply. A few days later, Maulana Kausar Niazi replaced Abdul Hafeez Pirzada as information minister. He put the matter of restoration of the terminated journalists in cold storage.

After the formation of Bangladesh, Barna was elected the president of the PFUJ. He was an experienced and radical trade unionist. He had immense adoration and respect for workers. His respect and value among the journalist community can be gauged by the fact that when he served as a correspondent for *Pakistan Times* in Dacca, the East Pakistan Union of Journalists helped him to be elected as the secretary of the PFUJ. The election of a West Pakistani in this position was quite surprising considering that the Six Points of Sheikh Mujib had become public and Bengali nationalism was at its peak. Two years later, he was elected on West Pakistan's quota to the same position because he had been transferred to Lahore.

Barna never compromised on principles. The daily *Azad* did not pay salaries to its various employees and journalists for several months on the pretext of running on loss. When it did not pay the salaries of its employees despite the PFUJ's intervention, Barna cancelled the PFUJ membership of some directors even though they were his friends. An unforgettable feat of Barna's was the formation of APNEC which united all newspaper workers on one platform. Several senior journalists were against the formation of APNEC including former PFUJ president Asrar Ahmed but Aziz Siddiqui, I. H. Rashed of *Pakistan Times*, Majeed and Mohammad Ali Siddiqui of *Dawn*, and Zafar Siddiqui of *Jang* favoured its creation. Barna was elected the first chairman of APNEC.

To the dismay of several people, Bhutto abandoned the politics of the poor after coming to power. The PPP government followed in the footprints of its predecessors. The enforcement of PPO, Defence of Pakistan Ordinance, Press Advice, and the employment of newsprint and official advertisements as bribe became the practice. It should be noted that after the nationalization of key industries, banks, and the insurance sector, the government had become the largest employer and advertiser. Within a few months of coming to power, the weekly *Punjab Punch*, weekly *Zindagi*, and a monthly Urdu digest were banned under a martial law order. Their editors were not only jailed but disqualified to edit any publication for ten years. Despite the fact that in the past, these publications had levelled serious allegations against the PFUJ, it strongly protested against the bans imposed on them and the imprisonment of editors. Ultimately, the restrictions on these publications were lifted and the release of its editors was ordered by Lahore High Court through the petitions filed. However, the government did not learn its lesson; it banned *Zindagi* once again. One after the other, Shami launched five publications which were all banned by the government. Official advertisements for *Nawa-e-Waqt*, *Hurriyat*, and *Jasarat* stopped coming in. *Hurriyat* was banned for printing the headline: 'Khanpur Inundated, Larkana Saved.' It was restored after a one-day strike by journalists. *Jasarat*, *Jamhoor*, *Chattan*, *Frontier Guardian*, and *Outlook* were punished by being denied the newsprint quota.

Official advertisements for *Al Fatah* also stopped. At one point, its newsprint quota was cancelled for not obtaining certification from Audit Bureau of Circulation although it had submitted all the required documentation and proofs a year earlier.

Some periodicals and major newspapers turned into official mouthpieces of Mr Bhutto the moment PPP came to power. Therefore, he did not need any of those publications who supported him on the basis of principles. Ironically, he started considering the party publication, *Musawat*, an unnecessary burden. When twelve journalists from *Musawat* (Lahore) were fired, the PFUJ announced to launch a movement and court arrests. Mr Bhutto invited Barna to Islamabad for talks. He refused to accept the demands made and said that he had the support of all major publications—*Nawa-e-Waqt*, Jang Group, and *Dawn*—therefore, he did not need *Musawat*. To this, Barna replied:

'These newspapers are supporting you today. Tomorrow, *Musawat* will be on your side when you would be no longer in power.' Barna's words proved ominous. *Musawat* played a fundamental role in keeping the PPP united when Bhutto was arrested after the imposition of martial law on 5 July 1977.

Barna was arrested under the Safety of Pakistan Act a day

before the launch of the movement in support of the suspended employees of *Musawat* (Lahore). Nevertheless, the movement began on the decided date. During this movement, 120 journalists courted arrests. Federal and provincial PPP ministers launched a vicious propaganda campaign claiming that this movement was being instigated by National Awami Party (NAP). These ministers claimed that the protesting journalists were friends of Wali Khan.

Such accusations were frequently leveled at the PFUJ. When it organized protest rallies against brick-batting on *Mashriq* (Peshawar), Wali Khan labeled the PFUJ as a subsidiary organization of the PPP and said that the purpose of the protests was to topple the coalition government of NAP and JI.

It is interesting to note that Barna filed a petition against his arrest in Lahore High Court. He was brought in handcuffs to the hearing. When an opposition member moved a postponement resolution in Punjab Assembly, the Finance Minister Hanif Ramay responded by saying:

'Handcuffs do not insult Mr Barna because they are the symbol of manhood in Punjab.' However, later when Ramay had to put on the same 'symbol of manhood' around his hands, he fainted.

Bhutto's rule was bad for journalism and press freedom in Pakistan. However, what the journalist community was made to go through in Zia's time broke all records. The press in Pakistan had never suffered the way it did during Zia's rule. I speak from personal experience as I was the editor of *Al Fatah*. *Al Fatah* was banned in April 1978 after I published the news of the killing of workers associated with Colony Textile Mills, Multan. I was imprisoned in Camp Jail, Lahore. The owner and publisher of *Al Fatah*, Irshad Rao, arranged declarations for twelve publications: *Riyasat*, *Rahi*, *Parbhaat*, *Inqilab* etc. However, Zia's government shut down all of them within fifteen months.

The weekly *Al Fatah* was restored in February 1980 on the orders of Sindh High Court but those were the times of pre-publication censorship. Initially, an officer of Sindh Information Department used to censor the contents of *Al Fatah*.

On 1 January 1981, an army major led a police raid on the office of *Al Fatah* and at Irshad Rao's home. Rao, assistant editor, Wahid Basheer, Naeem Arvi, Sharaf Ali, Zamin Ali Shah, Abdul Saleem, Murtaza, my younger brother, Nizam Siddiqui, and I were arrested. Naeem Arvi, Sharaf Ali, Murtaza, and Nizam were released in a few days but I remained in Civil Lines lockup till 14 March 1981. I was one of the 54 political prisoners released in exchange for passengers on a PIA plane hijacked by Al-Zulfikar and was sent to Syria. I received asylum in Holland after spending thirteen months in Syria.

Irshad Rao, Wahid Basheer, Zamin Ali, and Abdul Saleem were sentenced to rigorous imprisonment by summary military courts. They were released after two and a half years. *Al Fatah* resumed publication during Benazir Bhutto's first term. However, I do not know why Rao stopped publishing it.

Journalism had drastically changed in Pakistan when I returned from Holland in May 2003. The Press and Publication Ordinance had been cancelled because of the long struggle of the PFUJ and APNEC and private television channels had been established. On the other hand, media houses had become slave drivers. People were employed on an ad-hoc basis. Some media houses would issue appointment letters by a printing press, cable company, or some other company but employ the incumbents in a newspaper or television channel. The owners refused to pay all seven Wage Board Awards. Print media and especially the electronic media would retrench employees en masse without being reported in any newspaper or television broadcast. The PFUJ and APNEC would protest and hold rallies for the rights of workers and Wage Board Awards but the news was blacked out. The extent to which the newspaper owners were allergic to PFUJ and APNEC leadership can be gauged by the following incident.

The launching ceremony of Council of Pakistan Newspaper Editors' website was being held at Beach Luxury Hotel, Karachi. The secretary of the organization and a friend of mine, Jabbar Khattak, also invited Ahfaz ur Rehman, then president of the PFUJ, as one of the speakers. Ahfaz severely criticized the government and newspaper owners for the economic massacre of workers. Despite repeated interruptions, Ahfaz continued his speech defiantly.

The irony was that the huge banner put up at the launch of the CPNE website had Faiz Ahmed Faiz's verse '*bol ke lab azad hain tere*' (speak, for your lips are liberated), inscribed on it.

It is a matter of serious grief that even some people in the journalist community wanted to transform the PFUJ and APNEC into NGO-like bodies instead of running them as trade unions. International Federation of Journalists and South Asian Free Media Association are NGOs. Besides, according to a report, there are about seventy journalists running NGOs. Actually, these people do not even qualify as 'working journalists', as defined by the document that serves as the basis for the PFUJ's formation. The basic source of livelihood for such individuals is not journalism but the wealth generated by their NGOs. Some journalists also wanted to be merged with the 'Dastoori' group created by General Zia. In my personal opinion, it was because of such conditions that Ahfaz refused to contest the elections as PFUJ president for the second term.

This book is divided into two parts. The first part consists of four chapters where Ahfaz has narrated the events of the December 1977 movement, the April 1978 movement, and the July 1978 movement. The second part is a compilation of prison diaries, letters written from jail, and stories of torture.

Generally, there are three fundamental sources of writing a historical account: events, factual evidence, and personal accounts. Sometimes, events are invented, therefore, it is necessary to present them with evidence. Narration and analyses are as important as the events; however, the historian is at a liberty to interpret according to his views. Ahfaz has very responsibly narrated the events of the movements and gathered proof from newspapers and magazines of the day. During the movements, he was secretary general of KUJ and general secretary of the Joint Federal Action Committee of the PFUJ and APNEC. He is an eyewitness to many events. The analytical articles of the second part reflect his thinking as he believes in class struggle. In the war between haves and have-nots, he sides with the have-nots and stands opposed to the haves.

Ahfaz ur Rehman is an experienced journalist, writer, and poet. It is due to this that even his newspaper articles have a literary flavour. He pays close attention to language and diction. He deserves our gratitude for writing this book and preserving the history of the PFUJ and APNEC in terms of their contribution to the most important national and democratic movements of Pakistan. I can only ask Ahfaz to remain steadfast until the war between the oppressors and the oppressed culminates in the victory of the latter.

Foreword II

by Iqbal Khursheed

This book is the tale of a great war fought on the grounds of hope and righteousness. It is an epic in prose and a complete treasure trove of happiness linked to joyful moments. It covers the kind of events that fortify my determination while dealing with the hardships of life.

I was overjoyed when my esteemed teacher, Ahfaz ur Rehman, expressed his intention to compile the memories of the momentous 1977–8 journalists' movement in the form of a book. The wish of my colleagues that a veteran journalist, who emerged from the kiln of struggle, would narrate his story and that of his tribe of dawn worshippers (a rapidly diminishing breed) was granted. Undoubtedly, the decision was perfectly timed because what could be a better moment to pen the history of the movement of 1977–8 than today when the fourth pillar of the state is trembling with the blows of opportunists and their vested interests?

During those long hours when Rehman shaped his memories into words, whatever he said was preserved by a voice recorder and my pen would be constantly moving. I no longer remained a mere listener. Powerful words took me to the middle of those daring press workers who were battling against repression and for human rights, and whose number was small but they possessed mountain-high resolve. The mention of various valiant journalists—Nisar Usmani,

Hafeez Raqeeb, Wahab Siddiqui, Shabbar Azmi, Khawar Naeem Hashmi, Nasir Zaidi, Iqbal Jafri, and Minhaj Barna—added weight to the account. Barna was the central figure in the movement for freedom of the press. He is a real character who appears mythical at times.

Rummaging through old issues of *Al Fatah* and identifying heroic events from their decaying pages was a satisfying experience. At least to a certain measure, I had the opportunity to live those glorious days.

Rehman's experiences, observations, and feelings are a legacy which is being passed on to the next generation in the form of a book. This book is a wonderful compilation of memories from an endless struggle for those who were a part of that movement. For the new generation, it will serve as the foundation on which they will build their future in journalism.

Part One

1

Beginning of the Affair

The distinguished South American author, Gabriel García Márquez, did not exaggerate when he said, 'I give great importance to the first line of a novel. Sometimes, writing the first line consumes more time than writing the entire novel.'

It is because of this that I wonder how to begin writing about the magnificent 1977–8 movement for freedom of the press, and how to portray a compelling picture of this great phenomenon. There is a whole treasure trove of memories. Years have gone by but those memories keep flashing. This story is about exceptional men whose hearts brimmed with the radiance of love. The season of coming out on to the streets with their fetters was beckoning them and they yielded, dancing madly to confront their tormentors who had blood in their eyes.

The *Times of India* mentioned this unparalleled event in these words: 'Had there been an organization like the Pakistan Federal Union of Journalists in India, Indira Gandhi wouldn't have dared to impose emergency rule.'

So where do I begin writing this unforgettable story? From Kalapul or Korangi Road, or from that village tent where I opened my eyes, or Krishan Chander's short story *'Kaloo Bhangi'*, which touched my soul? Should I start writing this story with Sahir's poem *'Chaklay'*, which exposes the hypocrisy of our society from several angles, or from Faiz's poem *'Kuttay'* which speaks about the humiliation the destitute are subjected to? Since our struggle was against a dictator (Zia ul-Haq), I thought it was better to begin writing its account with Pakistan's first military ruler, Ayub Khan. Ayub raided the corridors of power and snatched people's rights to freedom of speech and thought. He coerced all those newspapers that wrote truth into submission and implemented the infamous Press and Publications Ordinance, pushing this country into a dark abyss. This was the point where the first organized struggle against military dictatorship by our journalist community began.

AYUB'S PERIOD: THE FIRST ERA OF OPPRESSION AND BRUTALITY

The civilian government was undoubtedly weak but nothing can ever justify the ousting of a sitting government by military dictators. Perhaps, those who gained power and pelf from dictators and bartered their principles for privileges would think otherwise. Even today, such elements continue to assert that Western democratic systems cannot work here. Hasn't the same system been working in our neighbouring country for years? Has there ever been a military takeover in India? Has an elected prime minister ever been hanged there? The reply to these questions by such people is always an outrageous one. They argue that the ground realities of this 'god-gifted' country are different and even the use of proxies is justified to save this ideological state.

There is ample factual evidence hinting at Pakistan's use of proxies. Those opportunists who legitimized cruelty have kept this country shackled to lowliness and disgrace, where gasping patients have no access to medicine, thousands of children have no books, and millions have no bread. The supporters of ruling, oppressing classes can well be questioned about those considerations of 'national interest' that have fed the monster of dictatorship, encouraged the crucifixion of democratic rights, enabled the creation of new iron chains against freedom of speech and thought, and have instigated sectarianism and terrorism.

The month of October in 1958 was chilly. The military establishment in Pakistan was shrewd as well as powerful. Its assault was successful. Commander-in-chief, Ayub Khan, strangled the weak democracy, deposed Iskander Mirza, and took over the country's reins. There is no doubt that the ground was already prepared for this tragedy. This shameful opportunism was initiated during Prime Minister Mohammad Ali Bogra's tenure when Ayub Khan was assigned the office of Defence Minister. It was probably the most novel event, among hundreds of other strange historical incidences in this country, when the army chief held the portfolio of a defence minister. On 17 October 1958, Iskander Mirza imposed martial law and appointed Ayub Khan as the Martial Law Administrator. Ayub cherished the taste of power to the extent that he toppled his benefactor after only twenty days. Those who came to power later on followed suit.

Similar to other dictators in the world, Ayub Khan struck the deadliest blow to freedom of the press. He turned all his guns towards press workers. It is understandable because no matter how powerful a dictator is, he does not possess the strength to face criticism.

Mian Iftikharuddin's Progressive Papers Limited (PPL) was his special target. The English and Urdu newspapers published under its banner were extremely popular. The new government was scared of their popularity. Within a few days of the so-called revolution, the editor of the weekly *Lail-o-Nahaar*, Sibte Hassan, was arrested under the Safety Act. Four days later, the editor of *Imroz*, Ahmed Nadeem Qasmi, was also taken into custody. When the chief editor of *Pakistan Times*, Faiz Ahmed Faiz, returned from a literary conference in Tashkent, all preparations for his arrest were also complete. Praise goes to Justice M. R. Kiyani, who ordered the release of the arrested editors in 1959. However, there was going to be no peace for journalists.

By 18 April 1959, all PPL papers were confiscated and many of its workers were declared communists and fired. Subsequently, more terrifying steps were taken. The infamous Press and Publications Ordinance was promulgated in 1962, which strangulated all freedoms of the journalist community. Then in 1964, a new official institution, National Press Trust (NPT), was formed. All PPL publications mentioned above, in addition to eleven Urdu, Bengali, and English papers from East and West Pakistan were brought under the Trust. Along with this, the largest private news agency of the country, Associated Press of Pakistan (APP), was also taken over by the government. In other words, all arrangements to bury freedom of expression were complete.

After coming under the control of NPT, all newspapers became de facto mouthpieces of the government because their purpose was reduced to propaganda in favour of the military regime. As expected, this seriously damaged their reputation. The readers became weary of one-sided news coverage. The circulation of newspapers started to decrease with time. Another negative effect which seeped among the press workers was that they were all now government employees and consequently prone to catching the bureaucratic culture of lethargy and incompetence. Besides NPT publications, other private papers were also intimidated by tactics like press advice, newspaper quotas, official advertisements, and the constant threat of cancellation of the printing-press declaration. All of this resulted in shrinking the criticism of government policies.

The first Wage Board Award was established in 1960 on the demand of journalists. Justice Ahad Jan was its head. In December of that year, the first Wage Award was announced. It had been decided that the Wage Award would be announced every five years in view of the increasing costs of living. However, with the connivance of newspaper owners and government, the next Wage

Board was not formed in time and the subsequent ones were delayed continuously. This is further endorsed by the fact that only seven Wage Awards have been announced in fifty-four long years. The implementation of the seventh award is still hanging in the air. Several different governments have been formed in Pakistan but the characteristics of the ruling elite have remained the same.

The darkest law of 1963, The Press and Publications Amendment Ordinance, became a symbol of tyranny. Even the British government had not introduced such legislation during its rule. Pakistan Federal Union of Journalists (PFUJ), the representative organization of journalists all across the country, practically opposed every government's cruel measures through processions, protests, and resolutions. The PFUJ had its branches in all newspaper hubs in East and West Pakistan. It raised its courageous voice against every dictatorial measure right from its inception. Therefore, a twenty-four hour countrywide strike took place on 6 September 1963. On the appeal of PFUJ, protests were held and newspapers did not come out the following day.

The PFUJ continued its brave exercises in subsequent years. This struggle was carried on irrespective of the political leanings of the ruling government or the ideology of the targeted journalist. The guiding principle was that in a democratic society, every individual adhering to any school of thought should have the right to express his point of view. The PFUJ did not give any concessions even to the democratic government of Zulfikar Ali Bhutto and kept raising its voice for the rights of journalists during his rule. Countrywide strikes were launched when *The Sun* was shut down in 1972, and *Hurriyat*, *Jasarat*, and *Mehran* in 1973. Protests were launched against restrictions on *Urdu Digest*, *Zindagi*, and *Punjab Punch*. Again, in 1974, an exemplary movement was initiated against the forced dismissal of employees of the daily *Musawat*.

During Ayub's rule, protesting journalists belonging to the PFUJ and its affiliates were arrested. Journalists were declared troublemakers and cases of treason were registered against them but nobody stepped back from their principled stance. Civil society, especially students, extended overwhelming support to the journalists. Massive support came from all progressive student organizations and their members struggled alongside us against the oppressive government. In fact, when Ayub Khan usurped power, the first victim to bear the brunt of the military government was the popular student organization, the National Students Federation (NSF). All of its core leadership was arrested. Their cases were heard in summary courts, and they were sentenced and exiled from Karachi but they did not bow. Habib Jalib's famous poem *Shehr Badar* was inspired by this episode.

I was a member of the NSF at that time. Sahir Ludhianvi's poetry, Krishan Chander's short stories, and the company of enlightened friends nourished my mind with humanistic ideologies and pushed me towards active struggle. The 1962–3 student movements are still fresh in my mind when we braced ourselves on the streets of Karachi to resist all kinds of tyrannical avalanches. After I became a journalist, this training proved to be very useful in keeping the fire of struggle burning from the platforms of Karachi Union of Journalists and the PFUJ.

The black tenure of General Yahya also continued with suppressive measures to crush freedom of the press. With the help of some politicians and newspaper owners, his minister of information, General Sher Ali, ran a malicious and hateful campaign against the PFUJ. The conspiracy revolved around a single agenda: to expel all 'Communists' and 'enemies of Islam' from the newspaper industry. One might ask who these 'Communists' and 'enemies of Islam' were? These were people who refused to bow down in the face of tyranny.

Three of the numerous movements that the PFUJ gave birth to possess historical importance due to their size, span, and effectiveness. These are the pride of the PFUJ. The first one is famous as the 1970 movement, the second as the 1974 movement, and the third as 1977–8 movement.

The first one was launched during Yahya Khan's rule. Its background was the long-standing demand of the PFUJ's for Wage Board formation in view of the rising costs of living. When this demand was not met through peaceful means, the PFUJ decided to hold a countrywide referendum for a pen-drop strike. Majority of the East and West Pakistani journalists voted in favour. The PFUJ participated with full force in this event. For ten days, no newspaper appeared except for a couple of those which were run by opportunists. As a result of this strike, newspaper owners terminated the services of 250 journalists. Z. A. Bhutto's movement against dictatorship was at its peak at that time. He promised the reinstatement of the sacked journalists if he came to power. He kept his word and helped in restoring most of the terminated journalists when he succeeded. However, it is another issue that after coming into power, Bhutto could not cultivate the habit of tolerating criticism and started restricting the press in his own way.

As far as the 1977–8 movement is concerned, it became the biggest struggle for freedom of the press because of its size, scope, duration, number of arrests, severity of torture, and exemplary steadfastness of the journalist community. This was the environment in which we acquired political awareness, participated in student politics, and began the journey of journalism. This journey became our raison d'être. The following pages will vouch for the veracity of this claim.

TOWARDS CHINA

I was deprived of taking part in the 1970 movement even though I had been in the field of journalism for three years by that time. I was a member of the founding team of the weekly *Akhbar-e-Jahan*.

Journalists' protest against the Ayub government was ongoing, although it was later on sabotaged by force and constant intrigues. All measures were employed to clamp down on journalists and attempts were made to buy them. On the other hand, the rightist fanatics were set to punish them with full force. The aspiration to bring positive change in society and being seen as 'anti-religion' for wishing so, continued in a loathsome manner. Since such elements could not gain a majority in the PFUJ, therefore, their machinations failed. Journalists stood by each other firmly on the PFUJ platform all across the country. The opportunistic journalists failed to break it from inside.

In 1968, owners of the weekly *Akhbar-e-Jahan* terminated the services of four journalists at the stroke of a pen. I resigned the same day in protest against this cruel act and remained jobless for the following few months which was part and parcel of being associated with journalism in those days. Then, through Jamiluddin Aali, a possibility emerged for me to go to China. He was a member of the advisory board of *Akhbar-e-Jahan* along with Mir Khalil-ur-Rehman and Pir Ali Mohammad Rashdi, and was saddened by my resignation.

The Writers' Guild of Pakistan in those days was affiliated with the Afro-Asian Writers Association. Most of the Asian and African countries, including China, were its members. Aali was the founder and secretary general of the Writers' Guild. The Chinese Foreign Languages Press required an Urdu translator/editor for which they approached Aali, who in turn recommended me. This was a great honour for me because my predecessors had been giants like Tufail Ahmed Jamali, Dr Aalia Imam, and Zahid Chaudhary. The terms of employment were agreed; however, this journey was not a simple one. It took six months for the passport to be issued.

Actually, in those days a passport was stamped with the remarks that it was valid for all countries except Israel and Communist states. China was a Communist country. Therefore, I needed special permission as well. Although the Sino-Pak friendship was passionately celebrated, the period was worrisome nevertheless. We were young and had no idea who to approach. As it was my only hope of getting a job, I did not pursue other work. When the passport was issued after a long delay, I applied for the visa. The Chinese Embassy took a long time too. In desperation, I narrated the whole episode to Aali. He sent me to the head of Anjuman-e-Taraqi-e-Urdu, Shabbir Kazmi, to talk to him about a job. However, the very next day, during a programme at the Arts Council, someone tapped on my shoulder. It was Aali's son, Raju Jamil, whom I knew but was never formally introduced to.

'Are you Ahfaz ur Rehman?' Raju Jamil asked.

I nodded in the affirmative. 'Congratulations! Your visa has been issued,' he said.

Consequently, I did not have to work at the Anjuman.

I reached China on 1 January 1969. It was a new and beautiful world to me. Warm enthusiasm demonstrated by the Chinese neutralized the effects of the cold weather. The inhabitants were hospitable and sincere. They seemed familiar despite being strangers. I started working at Foreign Languages Press, Beijing, where my predecessor, Rasheed Butt, was serving. He returned to Pakistan a couple of months after my arrival in China. Our job was mostly translation/editing but we were called 'language experts' over there.

It was quite a busy period. Due to the Cultural Revolution, preference in the press was given to ideological books. Initially I translated such books in Urdu, along with translating books on other subjects for adults and children. I was also associated with Beijing University and assisted my Chinese colleagues in preparing the syllabus for the Urdu department of the university. The senior East Pakistani journalist, Jameel Akhtar, who later became news editor in *Khaleej Times* and *Dawn*, was associated with the Urdu service of Radio China. Aleem-ul-Zafar was associated with Radio

Beijing's Hindi service and the Hindi section of the monthly *China*. Later, Hamid Hashmi joined the monthly *China's* Urdu section. The House of Foreign Languages, Radio Beijing, and China in Pictures worked on all major languages of the world and were staffed by prominent litterateurs and intellectuals from Africa, Asia, South America, Europe, and North America, with whom commoners like me also ventured. I returned to Pakistan after almost four years upon the expiry of my contract in 1972.

After my return, my companionship with Irshad Rao and Wahab Siddiqui of the weekly *Al Fatah* started developing. They had appointed me as a correspondent of their magazine in China and had published my contributions regularly. This was when I had my first detailed meeting with a person who was going to leave an indelible impression on me. My generation saw this person as an upright journalist and a teacher. He was a symbol of journalistic struggle. His name was Minhaj Barna.

The connection established with Minhaj Barna lasted for life. Although he is no longer with us, his teachings, and above all, the rousing memories of his incomparable struggle still fill my heart and mind.

BEGINNING OF A NEW JOURNEY

The weekly *Al Fatah* was the most popular weekly newspaper of Pakistan. It was owned by Irshad Rao and Wahab Siddiqui was its editor. Both were skilled, courageous, and highly sensitive to the agonies of workers and the destitute. They were willing to sacrifice their life to uphold democratic values. They had a small office which also served as their residence. They worked late into the night and when tired, slept on the floor or a broken wicker cot. Both of them and their weekly were destined to play an important role in the 1977–8 movement.

I became associated with *Al Fatah* after returning from China. It turned out to be a pleasant experience. Naeem Arvi, who had been a colleague earlier at *Akhbar-e-Jahan*, also became a team member. At *Al Fatah*, I met political activists, students, and leaders of labourers and farmers from every corner of Pakistan, who used to dream about the supremacy of the rule of law in this country. These and other brave and sympathetic comrades played an unforgettable role in the movement for freedom of the press.

I remained associated with *Al Fatah* for about five or six months. During the same period, *Musawat* was launched in Karachi. It was already being published in Lahore and Faisalabad by the Pakistan People's Party (PPP). Famous novelist and journalist, Shaukat Siddiqui, was nominated as its editor. Its office was located opposite the Sindh Madressatul Islam in Karachi. Siddiqui was secretary of the Writers' Guild and used to interview candidates at the guild's office. He always addressed me as 'beta' (Urdu for son). One day he called me at the office of *Al Fatah* and offered me the position of magazine editor in *Musawat*. Irshad Rao came to know about the job offer. Although Siddiqui was a respected elder, Rao spoke to him in his typical frank manner.

'Baba, I will not let Ahfaz go. Find someone else; there are a lot of people in the city.'

I kept quiet during this conversation between the two editors. Ultimately, the ball was in my court. I paused for a few moments. *Al Fatah* was undoubtedly a popular paper with significant circulation; however, its resources were limited. Further, I could not disregard Siddiqui's opinion who had explained that joining *Musawat* was the path to mainstream journalism. Consequently, I opted for it. Rao did not mind my decision too much. The matter was resolved amicably and in 1973, I took over the responsibilities of magazine editor in *Musawat*. Four years later, the great struggle for freedom of the press began and all of us dedicated ourselves to its success.

After my experiences in NSF and due to my complete faith in our ideological struggle, being associated with the dignified organization of journalists, PFUJ, was very natural. Right from the beginning, I also started taking an active part in the activities of the Karachi Union of Journalists (KUJ).

The KUJ elections were held in 1973–4. I was not interested in holding any office but in a group meeting headed by Barna, it was decided that I should take part in the elections. Although newcomers were nominated for the executive committee, I was ordered to contest directly for the position of joint secretary. Not only did I win with a clear majority but also bagged more votes than all of the candidates contesting for other positions. Back then, the member base of KUJ was five hundred. This was also the case with Karachi Press Club. In the next elections, my colleagues showed complete faith in me and I was elected joint secretary for the second term. In the 1976 elections, I had to contest for the general secretary's position on the directives of my group. I also won this election with a huge margin. I had no idea at that time that the PFUJ members were headed towards severe travails.

It would not be out of place to mention that the right-wingers, with the support of other opportunists, had been working against the Barna group for years. They never gained significant success in the PFUJ or Karachi Press Club elections and lost by heavy margins. Barna had already founded All Pakistan Newspapers Employees Confederation (APNEC) after the 1970 Movement, where our supporters were in a majority. It should be noted that there was only one PFUJ at that time and the right-wing journalists were also its members. The Rasheed Siddiqui and *Dastori* group did not exist. They were born out of conspiracies later on. They weaved a web of conspiracies all around and raised a counterfeit PFUJ which was redundant and could not perform any role in improving the economic conditions of the working journalists, or contribute in any way to the movement for freedom of the press. It had only been content with issuing occasional press statements.

The coming days were hectic. We were broke but our dreams were big. We were committed not to bow in the face of any injustice. Together, we laid the foundation of the employees union in *Musawat* and the most popular Sindhi newspaper, *Hilal-e-Pakistan*. I acquired experience of organizing large-scale congregations and other forms of protests in the capacity of general secretary of KUJ. I learnt a great deal from participating in the executive committee meetings of the PFUJ conducted under the leadership of Minhaj Barna and Nisar Usmani.

Soon, the country was enveloped in chaos. The 1977 elections gave birth to another movement. The PPP was accused of rigging the elections. The opposition parties were already united on the platform of Pakistan National Alliance (PNA). A series of rallies and sit-ins unfolded. When the conflict reached its peak, the members of PNA held talks with Zulfikar Ali Bhutto and his advisors. Although slowly, the talks reached the threshold of success and just before the signing of the conciliatory agreement, 5 July dawned. The infamous military dictator, Zia ul-Haq, toppled the democratic government and a black era began.

THE ERA OF CRAFTINESS

Zia ul-Haq was notorious for reneging on his promises. One needs a great deal of courage to make a promise and then forget it. In the holy city of Mecca, he promised to hold national elections within three months and then went back on his word only to cling to power for the next ten years. The irony is that such a person was a so-called champion of Islam.

He made numerous appealing promises to the nation in his very first public address, including the promise that the press will be completely free under his rule. He declared that the Press and Publications Ordinance would be scraped and all kinds of restrictions on newspapers would be removed.

It would have been gullible to trust him especially after witnessing anti-journalism measures of democratic governments and having been victims of the animosity of Ayub Khan before that. To attach hopes with a new usurper would have been nonsensical. Nevertheless, wisdom demanded that we welcome his statement. Therefore, the president of the PFUJ and the chairman of APNEC, Minhaj Barna, sent a memorandum to Zia ul-Haq narrating the unfair restrictions on journalists and the legitimate demands of newspaper workers. A request for a meeting was also included to offer concrete recommendations for a pleasant relationship between the press and the government. As expected, Zia ul-Haq paid no attention to the memorandum.

The response was understandable and no different than what was expected. The press could become the biggest obstacle in fulfilling the plan for which he grabbed power. To extend further liberties to the press was a different question altogether as the military dictator was set to stifle the freedom that already existed.

However, there were some simpleton journalists who took his bait. They thought that the government had already promised to hold elections in three months and it does not have any political aspirations; therefore, it would not restrict the press. Then there were those opportunists within the journalistic circles whose only objective was to please the government. Such people could only consider criticizing the ousted government of Bhutto as freedom of the press. When reminded that freedom of the press entailed much more than criticizing the ousted government of Bhutto, these people responded by playing deaf. They didn't understand that a free press ought to hold the ruling government accountable, communicate facts to the public, hint at oppressive measures of the state, and represent the masses.

Such naïve or opportunistic journalists exist in overwhelming numbers even today. In 2014, some self-proclaimed journalists and 'public intellectuals' were seen apologetically harping on television screens for the need of a code of conduct for journalists. Most of them purport to be journalists without going through the hardships required to become one in the true sense of the word and are increasingly bringing a bad name to our community. They are absolutely ignorant of the fact that even if a written code of conduct does not exist, their conscience should determine what is right and what is wrong. Does the United Kingdom have a codified constitution? Through mere adherence to convention, this state has become an example of democracy. Nevertheless, to keep the record straight, the PFUJ has had a written code of conduct right from the start. However, our 'popular' journalists, who consider themselves to represent public opinion and are seen ranting on different channels, have never bothered to read it. That should be sufficient to assess their intellectual level.

In the PFUJ's Code of Conduct, which comprises of thirteen points, the first two are of key importance:

1. A member should do nothing that will bring disgrace to himself, his union, the newspaper, or his profession. He should study the rules of the union and should not, by commission or omission, act against the interest of the union.

2. Whether for publication or suppression, the acceptance of a bribe by a journalist is one of the gravest professional offences.

Notice another three points:

11. A journalist should fully realize his personal responsibility for everything that he sends to his newspaper or agency. He should not disclose professional secrets and should respect all necessary confidences regarding source of information and private documents. He should not falsify information or documents, or distort or misrepresent facts.

12. In obtaining news or pictures, reporters and press photographers

should do nothing that will cause pain or humiliation to innocent, bereaved, or otherwise distressed persons.

13. Every journalist should keep in mind the danger in the laws of libel, contempt of court, or copyright. In reports of courtroom proceedings, it is necessary to observe and practice the rule of fair play to parties.

These clauses have always been a part of the constitution of the PFUJ and cover all kinds of possible scenarios. It proves that unbridled freedom is against our constitution. If someone amongst us is flagrantly violating professional principles, it is not because that 'poor' fellow is ignorant. It is no secret that such 'poor fellows' not only insult their sacred profession but they also don't refrain from financial irregularities and conspiracies on the union level.

In short, the points mentioned above provide a solid foundation in the light of which we can protect the dignity of our profession. In fact, our test begins when we step outside our home. We should know that people keep an eye on all our moves, expressions, personal traits, acts, and utterances. It is akin to walking on a tight rope every day. A minor slip can bury us in deep infamy. Our pen and lips should narrate the event and not reflect our personal whims. The damaging effects of slight variance in facts will not only envelop the concerned individuals but the entire society. Deliberately hiding facts, killing a story, or implying vagueness, sensationalism, and obscenity to malign someone is a serious crime under journalistic rules. The public is bound to condemn us if our hands are dirty. Don't we have amongst us those who receive favours, donations, and gifts? Do you expose them or do you strive to defend and please them? What is the purpose of ranting that 'we must have a code of ethics,' or 'we should be taught the code of ethics?' It is really simple: expose the black sheep amongst you and quit the habit of mixing with them.

I have strayed away from my main stream of thought, perhaps because this is my favourite subject and I have always desired that my colleagues learn to live with dignity. Today, everybody seems to be pointing fingers at the integrity of journalists. In such circumstances, we need to be more alert, cautious, and concerned.

Coming back to where we were, General Zia ul-Haq did not feel the need to meet the PFUJ's or APNEC's leadership. As expected, the promise to hold general elections in three months was also not fulfilled. Those individuals, who never got tired of demanding the commencement of transparent elections during Bhutto's rule, sat in the lap of the Zia government. A group of journalists with vested interests also joined them.

An ardent follower of Ayub Khan, Zia ul-Haq did not take long to initiate anti-press measures. In September 1977, Barna was removed from *Pakistan Times*, a National Press Trust (NPT) newspaper. The ridiculous reason given for the dismissal was that Barna also contributed articles in *Al Fatah* whose policies conflicted with those of NPT. It was also said that *Al Fatah* preached ethno-nationalism. Before that, the chief editor of *Musawat*, Badruddin, was arrested under Martial Law Regulations. Afterwards, the editor of the weekly *Mayar*, Mahmood Sham, was arrested on the ridiculous charge of publishing an interior ministry directive sent to the State Bank of Pakistan.

This was the first organized attack on freedom of the press. The newspaper workers were not oblivious of this fact. Due to their courage and principles, the PFUJ and APNEC were troubling the rulers. The assault on Barna was actually aimed at weakening these organizations. On 23 September 1977, it was decided in the Joint Action Committee meeting of the PFUJ and APNEC that if Barna's dismissal was not reversed, a countrywide movement would be started against it. After our announcement, different organizations and distinguished individuals protested against this decision which forced the government to retreat.

The dailies *Hilal-e-Pakistan* and *Musawat*, and weekly *Nusrat* were the Bhutto family's publications. Their circulation was initially not high but after Bhutto's arrest and his judicial murder, these papers came to be read far and wide. The government's attitude towards the opposition, particularly the PPP, was extremely contemptuous. Zia was haunted by the fear of reprisal against Bhutto's killing. Therefore, the martial law government began a series of maddening disciplinary actions against these publications. Then they found a 'secret weapon' to strike a crippling blow to *Musawat* (Karachi). Thus began an incredible struggle by the newspaper workers.

ATTACK ON MUSAWAT

Winter had begun. Every dawn was mildly foggy. Night would set in soon. The streets were deserted earlier than usual.

Although Barna's dismissal was reversed under pressure from the journalists, the very next month the government made another shameful move.

The daily *Musawat* was printed at Sheikh Sultan bin Al Nahyan Trust Press, Karachi. Before that, it was called Peoples' Foundation Trust and the Bhutto family owned it. Fearful of the Bhuttos and the PPP, the government had confiscated their assets and renamed the press. The Trust refused to print *Musawat* in October. The government planned to create a crisis and take control of the newspaper as well. This cruel decision pushed about 200 journalists and workers into the dark abyss of unemployment. The existence of the largest Sindhi newspaper *Hilal-e-Pakistan* and the Urdu weekly, *Nusrat*, was also endangered.

This was the era of martial law where censorship prevailed. An innocuous press release was issued by the Inter Services Public Relations (ISPR) for newspapers, radio, television, and news agencies. It stated that the government had nothing to do with the shutting down of *Musawat*. The publication owed PKR 1,80,000 to Sheikh Sultan Al Nahyan Trust Press and since the dues were not cleared despite notices, the Trust refused to print *Musawat*. This action was cleverly executed. If the license of *Musawat* had been cancelled straight away, the public opinion would have gone against the government, accusing it of causing damage to Bhutto family and providing ready justification to the journalist organizations for protests. By declaring it a debtor, the government could easily claim its legal right in closing down *Musawat*.

Some colleagues at *Musawat* suggested approaching another printing press. This idea was not workable since a lot of courage was required to confront the government. Why would any press invite trouble from the military government by agreeing to print it?

Restlessness was growing at the *Musawat* office on Sarai Road close to Sindh Madressatul Islam. The workers arrived in the morning, sat idly throughout the day, and returned frustrated to their homes in the evening. The disappointment soon turned into agitation. We had the forums of Musawat Employees Union, the Karachi Union of Journalists, and APNEC (Karachi). When the agitation escalated, the advisor to Zia ul-Haq, Lt. General Mujeeb-ur-Rehman, gave this foolish statement to the press: 'We did not stop the publication of *Musawat*. The Trust has refused to print it because *Musawat* has not paid its dues. It will start printing as soon as the dues are cleared.' This carefully crafted statement could not obstruct our agitation.

During that period, the distinguished author and journalist, Ibrahim Jalees, was *Musawat's* editor. He made great efforts by calling the information department and knocking on the doors of several officials but nothing bore fruit. One day, while sitting in his office, he clenched his chest, became breathless, and dazed. He was taken to the hospital where the following day this remarkable writer left the world. His death was a great shock not only for *Musawat's* employees but also for the whole writers' community. The death of a respected colleague in those oppressive days further intensified our agony.

'IS THIS AN OFFICE OR A WAREHOUSE?'—ARRIVAL OF BEGUM BHUTTO

The old building of *Musawat's* office was dilapidated and dark. Damaged wooden floor, broken furniture, and the leaking wooden ceiling showed the extent to which the building was in shambles. During rains, we would struggle to protect the copies of the newspaper. In short, it was an ugly structure. The office was established during the PPP rule but the officials paid no attention to its upkeep.

Jalees suffered a heart attack in the same crumbling building. In his memory, KUJ, of which I was the general secretary, held a large congregation at Karachi Press Club. All literary, social, and political personalities of Karachi attended that gathering. It is inevitable that I mention the memoriam which the Musawat Employees Union held because that is where our protests shaped into a larger movement. This congregation was held in our rundown office.

Shabbar Azmi was the president and I participated in the event as an employee of *Musawat* and as KUJ's general secretary. Speeches were being delivered when we heard footsteps ascending the rickety wooden staircase. The sound struck us as portent.

It emerged that Begum Nusrat and Benazir Bhutto had come. We were very surprised because none of the 'important' leaders of the PPP had come for condolence; so what made its head to come over?

The proceedings were paused momentarily upon their arrival. Benazir Bhutto was very young at that time. Both the mother and daughter were deeply shocked due to the vicious acts of Zia ul-Haq. They were flabbergasted when they saw the pathetic office of *Musawat*. All the chairs were broken; a few in better condition were offered to the ladies. The event resumed and Shabbar invited me to address the gathering after his speech. I was sitting among the audience and said, 'I will speak from here.' They were all surprised.

An angry young man, I made a harsh speech against Zia ul-Haq and strongly criticized the PPP leaders who had not cared to console us. I also drew their attention towards the dismal condition of the office premises and pointed out the overdue payments to the printing press.

'Look at it! Is this an office or a warehouse? The wooden ceiling leaks during rain; the furniture is broken.' I said this to Begum Bhutto, who listened to me silently. Benazir was looking down; I am not sure if she could understand Urdu then. Finally, Begum Bhutto expressed her views and apologized. Both the ladies left dejected and the gathering dispersed.

Monotony and weariness engulfed all. Nothing changed. People walked into the office casually. Some laid down the chessboard; others took to playing cards or reading novels. There was no work to be done. Rallies had begun to take place outside Karachi Press Club against the cruel martial law acts. Our spirits were undoubtedly high but the unemployment and idleness had exhausted us.

The next morning around ten o'clock, *Musawat's* chief photographer, Altaf Rana, who had been in Bahrain for the last twenty years entered the office alarmed and nervous. He was a famous photographer in Karachi and closely followed Bhutto during his movement. Like our photographer, Zahid Hussain, he was very close to the Bhutto family. Altaf Rana used to address me as 'chief'.

'Chief, Begum Bhutto wants you at 70 Clifton.' He announced.

It was a routine morning and I was not expecting this sort of news which sounded like a joke so I laughed.

'Me? She doesn't even know my name. In any case, it is too difficult for her to pronounce,' I replied.

Hussain then said, 'You are right. She said that "send the young man who spoke in a harsh tone and uttered a lot of things against us."'

I had thought it was a joke, but his last sentence made me think. Perhaps, somebody told her that I was also the general secretary of KUJ.

It was 10 a.m. in the morning. I took out my bike and drove towards 70 Clifton. It was a usual morning. There were thin clouds. Although the weather was pleasant, there was sadness in my heart. I was constantly thinking what would happen to my jobless colleagues and when we would get rid of Zia? I also wondered why Begum Bhutto had summoned me.

A HEFTY CHEQUE AT 70 CLIFTON

Silence prevailed in the Bhuttos' residence. The windows were heavily draped. Servants moved around noiselessly on thick carpets. Even a minor sound startled them. Obviously, the ambiance was mournful. The head of the family and a beloved leader of millions of Pakistanis had been thrown into prison by a barbaric dictator who didn't want to see him alive.

I was called into the drawing room. Chief editor of *Musawat*, Badruddin, manager Noor Mohammad, and the accountant Hashmi were with Begum Bhutto. They had probably fixed a meeting beforehand.

Begum Bhutto was very kind to me. She inquired about my well-being, ordered tea and biscuits for me, and insisted on my having lunch. I was sad and thought that relishing biscuits and tea in the presence of a grieving wife and daughter would be rude. Finding me quiet, she said, 'You spoke a great deal against us.'

I thought her complaint would go further but she was perceptive and changed the subject.

'Now tell us, what should we do? Zia ul-Haq is not going to spare us.'

'Ask your party leaders what should be done,' I replied.

To this, Begum Bhutto said, 'I am asking you. I will ask them when needed.'

I was not mentally ready for this. After a pause, I said, 'Begum Sahiba, the government's excuse for not letting the paper come out is the amount overdue to the printing press but it has nothing to do with the matter. Pay them off and we will see what happens next.'

She gave a bitter smile and said, 'I will put it in a straight forward manner. You say that if we paid them the dues, they will allow us to publish. Your colleagues here, the editor and the manager, believe that this is only an excuse. They will pocket the money but will not let us publish. Now what do you say?'

Her apprehensions were not misplaced. I had no way to guarantee that the paper would be published after we had paid. However, I insisted on a principled stance.

'At the moment, the government has a justification which is causing misunderstandings and we are forced to give it the benefit of doubt. Even some of our KUJ colleagues believe this is not an attack on freedom of the press but an issue of outstanding bills. This misunderstanding should be removed. If they don't let us publish even after making the payment, we will gain moral superiority over them.'

It is a fact that there were several bona fide names in the PFUJ and APNEC who were certain that to initiate a movement in the prevailing situation would be adventurism. *Musawat* was a PPP publication. There were opponents of the PPP in the PFUJ, and some colleagues were hesitant and afraid. During martial law, even a minor protest was termed as a challenge to the state. Summary courts were brutal in their decisions and an unsuccessful agitation could become a misadventure.

She remained quiet for a while, then called her secretary and whispered something to him and then turned towards me. 'Have some biscuits,' she said.

'Nothing tastes good anymore.' I replied.

She very kindly said, 'You are a brave young man. Time will change. We must have faith.'

Meanwhile, the secretary returned with a cheque in his hand. I had a feeling that the cheque had been prepared beforehand.

Begum Bhutto signed the cheque and handed it to me. It was a cheque of PKR 1,80,000.

'These gentlemen do not agree. Take it and do what you like,' she said.

I was surprised over this unexpected response. To be honest, I panicked and held the cheque towards her.

'Madam, I am just an ordinary employee of *Musawat*. Our officials present here should be the ones to carry it.'

She refused and so did I. We debated for a while and eventually she said, 'Alright, if you want them to take the cheque then I want you to accompany them.'

This was the voice of a wife and a mother who was in agony. A shiver ran through my body as I looked in her eyes.

'As you wish, ma'am,' I said gently.

We all stood up. She extended her hand to shake mine.

I proceeded towards Sheikh Al Nahyan Trust office with Hashmi, the chief accountant of *Musawat*. It was no longer an ordinary day; it had transformed. My heart said that we would defeat Zia ul-Haq.

EXPOSURE OF DUPLICITY AND OUR RESPONSE

The apprehensions of the destitute and oppressed tend to win over their hopes. Although I did not expect it but that is what happened. Begum Bhutto's doubts proved to be correct.

When I parked my bike outside the Trust building, the sun had slipped behind the clouds signalling a downpour.

'What will happen?' I asked Hashmi. He didn't say anything. My heart started beating faster.

Masoom Ali was the general manager of the Trust. He was appointed during the PPP's rule and had held the same position in *Musawat*, which means that he had been a colleague. When the Trust was taken over by the government, he became a civil servant.

'Please come. Sit down,' he said in a mechanical tone. Evidently, he knew that our visit was due to something unusual.

Tea was ordered and we started talking. When the restlessness among *Musawat* employees was mentioned, he expressed concern about the lurking threat of joblessness.

'Masoom Sahib, thank you for your concern but who is responsible for this situation? Besides the government, the Trust had also issued a statement that *Musawat* owes it PKR 1,80,000. Here is the cheque. The outstanding dues have been paid. Please start printing the newspaper from today,' I said.

He saw the cheque and turned it around in his hands. While attempting to smile and play with the paperweight on his desk, he said, 'Ahfaz ur Rehman, do you really believe this matter is so simple?' Hashmi kept quiet.

'What do you mean? We have paid your dues, haven't we?' I asked.

'This is just one instalment of the dues. There are several other outstanding payments. We cannot start printing *Musawat* like this.'

I lost my cool and said, 'This is dishonesty. You never said this before. General Mujeeb-ur-Rehman also stated only this figure.'

He took a deep breath and said, 'Actually, you have no idea. The government does not want *Musawat* to appear. Making this payment or not is the same. I suggest you take this cheque back.'

This was a worrisome situation and I had to make a quick decision. Hashmi did not seem as if he wanted to say anything.

'The government stopped us on the pretext of non-payment of dues. We are making the payment, so please receive it,' I said in a rough tone. He shrugged his shoulders and took the cheque.

It was drizzling when we came out. I was dripping wet by the time I reached my office. All of my colleagues were filled with excitement and joy on hearing the news of the payment of outstanding dues. We started working on the paper. However, by evening time, our spirits took a dive; the Trust had refused to print the newspaper despite having received the cheque.

Shabbar and I were smoking on the balcony.

'The weather is changing,' Shabbar said on hearing a thunder while looking up at the sky. Then he asked, 'What do you think will happen?'

I laughed and said, 'If the weather doesn't change, then we will have to do something about it. Be ready.'

Indeed, the weather had changed. Paying the dues proved to be the right decision. The mala fide intent of the military government was exposed which strengthened our case. It was easier to explain to our comrades that this was not an issue of outstanding dues but a direct attack on the freedom of press. Public opinion was turning in our favour.

As president of the PFUJ and chairman of APNEC, Barna took notice of the incident. Initially, meetings were held on the local level by APNEC and KUJ units. Debates were held and a unanimous policy was agreed upon. Then it was discussed on the federal level. The federal organizations adopted a peaceful way of protest. It was demanded of the government that the publication of *Musawat* be allowed with immediate effect. The rulers had donned the mantle of stubbornness and arrogance. Our demand went unheard and unheeded. A federal action committee of the PFUJ and APNEC was formed under the leadership of Barna and I was assigned the responsibilities of secretary general.

On 17 November 1977, the Federal Action Committee decided that if *Musawat* was not allowed to be printed at the Trust, a hunger strike would begin on 3 November at Karachi Press Club which would continue until the acceptance of our demands.

The newspaper workers of the whole country announced their support for us. Journalists from various cities started arriving in Karachi. We had a long list of volunteers.

This announcement shook government circles. This was not an ordinary hunger strike. In the presence of martial law regulations, hunger strike meant only one thing: courting arrest. Government officials began deliberating. The government disregarded the journalists' movement as a political one launched at the behest of the Bhutto family. Though the entire Right wing in Pakistan supported Zia and opposed Bhutto, in this instance, Jamaat-e-Islami's (JI) role was extremely negative. The JI journalists overwhelmingly opposed this movement.

The secretary information, Lt. General Mujeeb-ur-Rehman, was perceived as a 'strategic expert'. A vicious propaganda against the journalist bodies was initiated from his office. Old accusations were dug-up and polished to label individuals associated with the press as 'terrorists', 'enemies of state', 'traitors', and 'communists'. The JI took the lead in this campaign but what could such crafty moves do to us? The decision was made and we had begun gathering against the forces of darkness. We were fearless and armed with determination. 3 November was approaching and a great movement was about to commence.

However, a small incident occurred before the movement began. That vibrant scene is still fresh in my mind with all its details. It was the defining moment for the movement of 1977–8. Even today, I feel very enthusiastic whenever I recall it.

The central character of that incident was Minhaj Barna, who earned this rhythmic slogan by the newspaper workers of Lahore: '*tere saath jeena, tere saath marna, Minhaj Barna, Minhaj Barna*' (We live with you and we die with you, Minhaj Barna).

'OUR PRESS RELEASE IS READY TOO.'—A STRONG MAN'S BROKEN TYPEWRITER

Afridi Pathan, a son of Teerah tribe and the elder brother of an upright leader, Meraj Mohammad Khan, was a teacher. To yield under pressure was not in his blood. He had been struggling against the oppressive class system since his youth. A few years after Independence, he was arrested under the Security of Pakistan Act. Now he was active in journalism. Thousands of supporters rallied behind him on a single call to fight injustice and repression.

Barna had learnt the trait of speaking the truth in the face of tyranny from his father, Maulvi Taj Mohammad, who was also a brave man. His story is also quite interesting.

The British rulers needed human fodder for the First World War. Orders were issued in London to lure the Indians into joining the military. In a gathering held at Khaliq Dina Hall, Karachi, a few so-called scholars accompanied the British Governor. They glorified WWI as 'jihad' through their rhetoric. At that point, Maulvi Taj Mohammad Khan went up to the stage and declared, 'The British are our worst enemies. This war is in no way a jihad.' His words created a commotion and he was exiled from the district for 48 hours for speaking the truth. Being a Pathan, he chose not to return to Karachi and went back to Qaem Ganj in Uttar Pradesh.

Barna was born to his second wife in 1928 in Ahmedabad. He did his matriculation in Nagpur and taught Urdu and Farsi in Anjuman-e-Islam School, Bombay. Initially, he worked as sub-editor for the daily *Iqbal*. He graduated from Jamia Millia, Delhi, in 1949. Later, he earned his Master's degree in Urdu from University of Karachi. In Delhi, he had been an office bearer of the All India Student's Federation. Trade union activities began to attract him from that period. He arrived in Quetta in 1950 and established the Progressive Writers Association's branch there. In addition to this, he also formed a union for sweepers in Quetta. After coming to

Karachi, he took a clerical job at an organization from where he was fired for being too progressive.

After Pakistan signed the SEATO agreement with the US in 1954, the Communist Party of Pakistan was banned. Consequently, labour leaders and progressives were victimized. Barna was also arrested. It was his first incarceration but not his last.

After his release in 1956, he joined the daily *Imroz* and remained active as a KUJ member. When the Writers' Guild was established in 1959, he was elected as a member of the executive committee of its Sindh branch. When the government took over *Imroz* and *Pakistan Times* after the imposition of martial law, the employment of Barna and his colleagues was terminated. This official decision caused so much agitation that the military government had to reluctantly withdraw it and restore the services of Barna and his associates. In 1963, he was elected as general secretary of KUJ and as its president in 1965. He remained at the forefront of all the movements against the dictatorial measures of Ayub's government. When workers of the daily *Anjam* went on a strike for their rights, Barna extended his full support to them. This violation resulted in him being despatched to Dacca.

He remained in Dacca from 1966 to 1969. East Pakistani journalists also became his fans. They nominated him for the office of secretary general of the PFUJ and he was elected unopposed.

He played a key role in the pen-down strike of 1970. At that time, he was also the secretary of the Action Committee. This time when 250 'trouble-maker' journalists from West Pakistan were terminated, Barna was among them too.

In 1973, he was elected as the president of the PFUJ. The founding of All Pakistan Newspaper Employees Confederation (APNEC) was also one of his significant accomplishments. Barna was elected the chairman of this organization. He raised his voice for all classes of workers and not only for his own industry.

It was due to his efforts that the Labourers Coordination

Committee was formed in 1977, which played an important role in our movement. The truth is that without mentioning him, the narrative of the movements for a free press in Pakistan is incomplete. A small incident is still glowing in my recollections which occurred just before the start of our movement.

It was a pleasant day. Fifteen jobless *Musawat* colleagues were quietly gathered in the office of *Pakistan Times*. Anxiety as well as hopefulness filled our minds. The hunger strike had already been announced from the following day.

Barna sat quietly in front of his rickety typewriter hitting the keys with one finger when the phone rang. A. T. Chaudhary was on the other end. He was a distinguished and respected journalist and was the editor of *Pakistan Times* at that time. It was rumoured that he was a close friend of Lt. General Mujeeb-ur-Rehman. The General had sent a message through Chaudhary for Barna.

'If the strike takes place, severe action will follow,' warned Chaudhary.

'Yes, alright,' Barna calmly replied and returned to his typewriter.

Chaudhary called again a few minutes later and said, 'Have you thought about it? Mujeeb says that if you go ahead, an example will be made of the entire journalist community. You still have time to rethink.'

Barna looked unaffected and replied, 'Alright. Do what you want; use cannons and swords, crush us. We are not going to change our decision.' With this, he disconnected the phone without waiting for a reply.

I am sure that Mujeeb must have gone into a rage after the message had reached him. Five minutes later, Chaudhary was calling again.

'Barna, Mujeeb says that if you don't listen, our press release is ready. We are telling everyone that PFUJ members are miscreants and conspiring against the country.'

It was a very interesting moment. Our eyes were fixed on Barna. The enemy was relentlessly threatening him but his face was radiating defiance. Barna turned the typewriter scroll, looked at the wall, and while pulling out typed sheets of paper, told Chaudhary, 'Tell him our press release is also ready.'

To be honest, on that December afternoon after hearing Barna's conversation, the strength of my conviction only grew. I knew that victory was our destiny. This caravan under the leadership of Barna was going to reach its destination and my estimation proved to be right.

2

Preparations for the Struggle

Karachi Press Club, once called Pakistan's Hyde Park, had become the headquarters of journalists engaged in the struggle for press freedom. Agitation was at its peak and the faces of workers brimmed with fervour. Their life was acquiring a purpose. Rallies were held, slogans were chanted, resolutions were passed, pamphlets were distributed, and democracy-loving people from different walks of life came to the press club to express their support.

The Action Committee had held numerous meetings where KUJ units and newspaper unions were informed about the government's plans. This activity was not restricted to Karachi. It went on in other cities as well where PFUJ and newspaper workers of affiliated unions of APNEC were told that the atrocities of martial law had to be resisted. Passion ran high in other cities and people came to Karachi to voluntarily court arrests. The lists of volunteers who were to arrive in Karachi were made. Everyone knew that this was going to be a long-drawn battle and the preparations would also be for a longer term. The message was clear and we knew that the time to render sacrifices for a free press had arrived. The government had attacked the press' freedom. At that time, the sword of unemployment hung over the heads of *Musawat* employees. We knew that if the government was allowed to have its way, other publications would soon be taken on as well.

Everybody knew that in the preceding two or three months, several appeals were made to the government for resuming the publication of *Musawat*. In turn, the government slapped the newspaper with more outstanding bills after initially receiving a payment of PKR 1,80,000. General Zia ul-Haq's dishonesty was revealed. Consequently, the PFUJ and APNEC decided to protest against the government from 3 December at Karachi Press Club. It was decided that on the first day, nine press workers including Minhaj Barna would go on a 48-hour long hunger strike. We decided to violate martial law and court arrests.

THIRD DECEMBER ARRIVES

A day earlier, on 2 December, the press release prepared by Barna was issued to the newspapers. As expected, the news did not receive adequate coverage, whereas the interior ministry's misleading press release was widely published. This press release absolved the government of all responsibility and portrayed the PFUJ as the main troublemaker. That day was different than the preceding days and seems conducive for future events of the movement in retrospect.

The hearts of PFUJ members brimmed with faith while marching towards Karachi Press Club. Their heads were raised and their eyes shone with the desire for freedom.

The struggle was on the verge of taking off. The clock was about to strike five. The ambiance at the press club resembled that of a carnival site. Banners and placards hung all around. Slogans were being chanted. There were some turncoats as well who had come to witness our beating. These were the same people who had formed a second PFUJ during the Lahore movement.

Eleven journalists, including two brave women, went on a 48-hour long hunger strike on 3 December.

These journalists included Minhaj Barna (president of the PFUJ, then associated with *Pakistan Times*), Hafeez Raqeeb (secretary general of APNEC and president of Musawat Workers Union Lahore), Wali Mohammad Wajid (assistant secretary general of

APNEC and president of Daily Imroz Employees Union), Majeed Gill (president, Bahawalpur Union of Journalists), G. N. Parvez (general secretary of Faisalabad Union of Journalists), Ghulam Nabi Mughal (treasurer of Daily Hilal-e-Pakistan Karachi Workers Union), Amir Mohammad Khan of APNEC (Karachi), Hassan Sangrami, Gulzar Sanam, Shehnaz Ahad, and Nuzhat Sadiq.

The addition of two women to the nine hunger strikers was encouraging. We absolutely rejected the idea of women being inferior to men. The participation of these two women in our hunger strike against the rule of Zia ul-Haq was both symbolic and daring. Women regularly visited the press club but Shehnaz and Nuzhat were the only ones willing to stay overnight. We created a makeshift section for their privacy and asked my wife Mehnaz to stay along and look after them.

An enthusiastic and determined crowd gathered around the camp. Such determination had toppled down dictators in the past as well and we were sure that Zia ul-Haq would ultimately see a similar end. At five in the evening, Barna presided over a meeting of newspaper workers where he clarified the meaning of freedom of the press in his speech.

Barna said that the press was the voice of society—a right which could not be snatched from it under any circumstances. He demanded the immediate restoration of *Musawat*, along with the resolution of all the problems that confronted the weekly *Nusrat* and daily *Hilal-e-Pakistan*. He made it very clear that journalists would never be intimidated by guns and swords and that they were prepared to go through every trial.

The secretary general of the PFUJ, Nisar Usmani, was also present there and said, 'From Karachi to Khyber, all journalists and newspaper workers are united and this is their strength. The repressive measures taken by the government are not only a severe blow to freedom of the press but they have also rendered our colleagues jobless. This situation is not acceptable to us in any way.'

The secretary general of APNEC, Hafeez Raqeeb, termed the government's attitude as vengeful and unjust. He said that journalists would always fight against those who snatched the labourers' right to have a dignified living. As secretary general of the Federal Action Committee, I termed the government's actions of blocking the publication of *Musawat* and creating hardships for *Hilal-e-Pakistan* and the weekly *Nusrat* tantamount to murdering freedom of the press. I further reiterated that newspaper workers were not weak; they were in fact united and conscientious. On behalf of my comrades, I vowed to continue the struggle until the fulfilment of our demands.

During this time, there was an overwhelming presence of representatives from different labourers' and farmer unions, including students, writers, poets, doctors, teachers, lawyers, and political and social workers. We had placed a register in order to enlist their names and they could also jot down their comments in it. We received fervent support for our struggle from all over. People queued at the press club and expressed their regard for us. It was dangerous to challenge the military regime but these seemingly weak citizens stood by us nevertheless.

Police contingents were stationed outside the press club. The secret police (CID) was also active back then. They kept an eye on our every move. In every gathering of journalists, farmers, labourers, students, and littérateurs, they would bring their notebooks and used to record what the banners displayed, the slogans that were chanted, and the speeches that were made. At times, they also made audio recordings. Since they were performing their duties, we did not intervene.

Although we had always noted the presence of these spies, they became more active after martial law was declared. Separate cells pursued the journalists, students, and political workers. No segment of society was free from surveillance.

The government hurled several accusations at us. In its press releases, we were called miscreants, the enemies of state, and traitors. Unfortunately, this has been the prevalent manner of dealing with dissent in our country. Although these tactics have been used by all governments against journalists, the martial law regimes were more arrogant and atrocious due to the unrestrained power they could wield. In some of our published press releases, we asserted that we were not miscreants and had resorted to protests after the government denied fulfilling our peaceful demands.

AN UNEXPECTED PHONE CALL

A cool breeze was blowing in the city when at about nine in the evening, an active PFUJ member, Sabihuddin Ghosi (who had been talking on the phone), nervously called for Barna. Barna walked towards Ghosi and I followed him. It emerged that his call had been abruptly interrupted by someone who said, 'General Mujeeb wants to speak to Minhaj Barna.'

Barna held the telephone receiver while I stood next to him. On the other end was the man who had sent threatening messages to Barna a few hours earlier. We didn't know why he had come on the line himself.

'We do not want any kind of clash because our demands are legitimate. We will be free to implement our decision if you are not ready to accept them,' Barna said.

In response to something he heard from the other side, Barna replied, 'We are neither threatening anyone nor would we allow anyone to threaten us. All that we want is the amicable resolution of this crisis by the consensus of both parties. Nothing can be achieved by dragging this matter any further. We are not retreating an inch from our stance.'

Harsh and threatening words must have been delivered from the other end, to which Barna responded, 'Yes, so be it.'

Barna came inside the protest camp and informed everyone about what had happened. Nobody was intimidated by the threat. We all kept our cool.

I had prepared a list of participants for the following days' hunger strike. The number of volunteers was swiftly increasing. We decided that a new batch of four volunteers would sit in a hunger strike daily. In other words, it meant that four of our comrades would be arrested every day. 120 volunteers registered their names on the first day. None of us were prepared to bow down. Our first batch of hungry protesters had to be replaced on 5 December but the martial law authorities had other plans.

CALL FROM THE PRISON

The people gathered in droves and remained energetic throughout the day. They started to quiet down as evening approached. Makeshift beds were set up and everyone began to recline and relax. One of us sought solace in folk songs. This was the melodious voice of late Wali Mohammad Wajid of Multan. Others either recited the poetry of Faiz, Sahir, and Jalib, or exchanged jokes with each other.

Barna was not feeling well and Shehnaz, who was troubled by her blood pressure issues, went to the ladies section where Nuzhat and Mehnaz accompanied her. I had grown weary of advising the hunger strikers to rest and save their energies for the following day but they wouldn't listen. I was very tired too as we had been on our toes for a month and a half now. Eventually, all went to sleep.

The sun was unusually bright on 4 December. The night shift newspaper workers were the first to arrive at Karachi Press Club in the morning. As time passed, representatives of farmer and student organizations, followed by members of democratic groups, social workers, doctors, lawyers, and teachers also began to pour in. They brought garlands to greet us and assured us of their warm support.

Political parties had also formed a beeline with the exception of Jamaat-e-Islami. They would sit with us, write their comments in the register, and then leave.

Police patrols outside Karachi Press Club had increased. Secret agents began to hover around the premises as evening approached. By the time the meeting began in the evening, a huge crowd had already assembled.

We all delivered speeches, chanted slogans, and recited poetry. Barna was the centre of everyone's attention. He was smiling despite being physically weak. Doctors from Pakistan Medical Association were present for the medical examination of the hunger strikers. The day quickly passed, making way for a cold but pleasant evening.

This was the night between 4 and 5 December. We wondered if the rulers would launch their assault or not. Would they ignore our actions like the day before, or were they going to give us a taste of the action?

The situation that night was effectively described in *Al Fatah's* issue of 9–16 December. It did not have a by-line but we knew that Naeem Arvi penned it. He wrote:

It is early morning of 5 December. The time is 4 a.m.

The building of Karachi Press Club is cloaked in silence. The grass is covered with mist and trees stretch over the hunger strikers in anticipation of what is to come. The eleven strikers are not fully awake yet. Some of them have just closed their eyes while others are still awake. Some are turning in their beds. Minhaj Barna is violently coughing because he has a cold and Wali Mohammad Wajid is fast asleep. Ghulam Nabi Mughal's face shows his fatigue while Hassan Sangrami chants slogans in [his] sleep. Shehnaz Ahad is perturbed by her blood pressure issues while Nuzhat Sadiq is lying beside her. These two brave girls are among the first group of hunger strikers. When the second group will takeover by 5 p.m. today, these two will have completed forty-eight hours of their hunger strike.

I remember it was the break of dawn and we were sleeping on mats under the tent erected on the terrace of Karachi Press Club when suddenly, there was noise and commotion. Before I could open my eyes, a loud and husky voice fell on my ears.

'Don't go there! That section is for females. Don't go there!'

I thought I was in a dream. I quickly gathered my senses and rubbed my eyes but before I could make sense of anything, I heard the thud of heavy boots. All arrangements to shatter the peace of Karachi Press Club had been made. Our energetic colleague, Achhi Memon, was standing behind a Venetian blind on the first floor. He was a *Musawat* reporter from Larkana and had a loud voice.

'Don't go there!' He repeated.

He was trying to prevent the police from going to the women's section where Shehnaz, Nuzhat, and Mehnaz were reclining.

Everybody woke up because of the noise. The police vehicles parked outside added to the noise. Six or seven senior police officers entered the press club accompanied by dozens of other policemen.

'What is the matter?' I asked them.

'We have orders to arrest the hunger strikers,' replied one of the officers.

Barna was called outside from the TV room where he was sleeping.

The weekly *Al Fatah*, dated 9–16 December, described this incident as follows:

A police officer entered and shouted, 'Where is Minhaj Barna?'

'I am here!' Barna responded with a determined voice.

'You are under arrest,' said the police officer.

'Show me the warrants,' replied Barna.

The police officer then showed him arrest warrants for seven individuals: Minhaj Barna, Hafeez Raqeeb, Wali Mohammad Wajid, G. N. Parvez, Amir Mohammad Khan, Ghulam Nabi Mughal, and Majeed Gill. Oddly, the two female hunger strikers were spared. The arrest warrants were issued under Section 309, Martial Law Order 13 and 24. As they were being escorted out, Barna spoke to me, at which the officer ordered for my arrest as well.

'Where is the warrant for his arrest?' Barna sternly asked. The police denied having it.

Barna then asked the police to leave me.

While sitting in the police van, Barna chanted a slogan and the people who had come out in our support responded to it.

The members present in the Press Club became restive. Post-arrests, the police was surprised to see that the demonstrators were energized instead of being scared.

In those days, as you entered Karachi Press Club, there was a telephone set placed on the left. I reached for the phone to inform Usmani that the protesters were being arrested but a policeman stopped me from doing so.

Nine of our colleagues were arrested which was not surprising. What was surprising—and something that I still find amusing—was Hassan Sangrami's facial expressions at that moment.

Police had exited from the main gate along with the arrested volunteers. There was complete silence all around. The prisoners were boarding the police vehicles one by one when suddenly Sangrami started chanting slogans in Bangla. He was a very enthusiastic man, an honest and upright worker, and belonged to Dacca. Sangrami literally means 'war'. Now, he has been settled in Canada for a long time.

At pre-dawn, Sangrami's piercing slogans, 'Rule of Generals and Colonels Will Not Prevail!' and 'Accept Workers' Demands!' broke out. The police contingent returned within a few seconds and the personnel seemed worried.

'What have you people done!' A senior police officer exclaimed.

We came to know that it wasn't just the police present outside but martial law officers also accompanied them. They ordered the police to round up all of us when they heard our slogans.

Nine of us had already been rounded up while fifteen others were left including Shehnaz Ahad, Nuzhat Sadiq, and Mehnaz. The orders were for the arrest of men only. Barna was president of the Action Committee and was already in custody which increased my responsibilities. My arrest was imminent. Our colleague, Mushtaq Memon, told me to slip away somehow. Shehnaz Ahad concurred and requested me to flee.

I told them that running away does not look right. Even if I had escaped for the sake of the movement, the police were everywhere and they wouldn't have let me go.

Twenty-two people were arrested that morning, including me and the nine hunger strikers. They were:

- Minhaj Barna, president of the PFUJ
- Hafeez Raqeeb, secretary general of APNEC
- Wali Mohammad Wajid, assistant secretary general of APNEC
- Majeed Gill, president of Bahawalpur Union of Journalists
- G. N. Parvez, general secretary of Faisalabad Union of Journalists
- Ghulam Nabi Mughal, treasurer of Hilal-e-Pakistan Workers Union
- Amir Mohammad Khan, general secretary of APNEC, Karachi
- Hassan Sangrami, photographer of *Musawat*, Karachi
- Gulzar Sanam from the daily *Nusrat*, Karachi
- Habibur Rehman of *Mashriq*, Peshawar
- Shabbar Azmi, president of Musawat Employees Union
- Nasr Malik, reporter of *Mashriq*, Karachi
- Mushtaq Memon, a reporter from PPI
- Yaqub Ali Soz, head calligrapher of *Musawat*, Karachi
- Achhi Memon of *Musawat*, Larkana
- Rasheed Chaudhry of *Dawn*, Karachi

- Faqeer Mohammad of *Musawat*, Karachi
- Urs Mallah, general secretary of Hilal-e-Pakistan Workers Union
- Moosa Taer, president of Hilal-e-Pakistan Workers Union
- Ahfaz ur Rehman, General Secretary of Karachi Union of Journalists

Minhaj Barna and a few others were locked up at Clifton Police Station. The rest were taken to Artillery Maidan Police Station. When Barna was served breakfast by the police, he told them that he was on hunger strike and thus wouldn't eat. However, he asked for a glass of water which was refused. Others were also refused water by the so-called well-mannered staff who was offering them breakfast.

After the arrests, Colonel Tariq called the secretary of Karachi Press Club and said, 'You have turned the press club into a protest venue. Why did you allow the hunger strike to happen within the club's premises? Shut down the strikers' camp!'

HOW FAR TYRANNY GOES

After two hours of being arrested, all of us prisoners boarded the special bus for detainees and headed towards Landhi Prison on the outskirts of Karachi. After the paperwork was finished, we were allocated a barrack with just one floor mat. We were brimming with energy and sang revolutionary songs. None of us was worried or gloomy; instead, we joked with each other and laughed. The colleague from Multan sang his native folk songs. Sindhis recited Shah Latif's Sufi verses. Although we were in a Class-C prison, we didn't find the barrack too bad. In any case, nobody really cared about such things in a struggle of that nature.

The news of our arrest spread like wildfire. The BBC broadcasted a detailed report. My wife, Mehnaz, and the distinguished labour leader, Shamim Asghar (who later joined the legal profession), were the first to visit us. They were followed by other supporters, all of whom brought food and drinks for us. They told us that our arrest had strengthened the resolve of journalists all over the country. They were ready to render sacrifices. Messages of vehement support poured in from all over the country. Political, social, and labour organizations were fiercely condemning the crackdown of the state. The public was also extremely agitated.

Interestingly, a leader of the Jamaat-e-Islami, which was against us and hand-in-glove with the government, condemned the arrest of these journalists and supported our movement for freedom of the press in a statement issued by Professor Ghafoor Ahmed, the general secretary of Pakistan National Alliance. This statement was published in *Hilal-e-Pakistan*.

We also came to know that Shehnaz was hospitalized due to hypertension. Nisar Usmani, the general secretary of the PFUJ, was leading the movement after Barna's arrest. On the day of our arrest, a meeting was held at Karachi Press Club. Our release was demanded in strong words along with a warning to the government to desist from using devious methods against the journalists. One of the accusations by our detractors was that we were helping Pakistan's People's Party under the garb of demanding to restore *Musawat*. This was entirely ridiculous. Had it been so, why would journalists from other publications be a part of the movement? The truth was that the government's measures struck a deadly blow to freedom of expression and to not resist it would have been akin to accepting a death sentence.

Usmani refuted these allegations in strong words in a meeting at Karachi Press Club. He said that the objectives of journalists' struggle were not political and that we had been pursuing such goals in the past and would continue to do so in future as well. Representatives of journalists from all across the country expressed similar sentiments.

Meanwhile, the second batch of hunger strikers had taken their place. It included Ahmed Ali Alvi (president of Jang Employees Union), Johar Mir (former president of Khyber Union of Journalists), Agha Masood Hussain of Nusrat Employees Union, Lyallpur Union of Journalists and Federal Action Committee's member, Javed Siddiqui, and female sub-editors of the dailies *Musawat* and *Nusrat*, Naheed Sultan and Shamim Akhter. December was heady and signalled that the movement for freedom of the press would continue to move forward with full force. No gun or sword could stop it.

Supporters from other organizations of farmers and labourers, and workers from different political parties continued to gather at the press club as they had in the preceding days. In fact, their enthusiasm had escalated further and volunteers were arriving from all over the country. I had already prepared the lists of those who were to court arrest for the following month. The government could see that its efforts were in vain. It failed to defeat the resolve of journalists because our movement was disciplined. Hand in hand, we had formed a human chain that resisted the suppressive state machinery. We had decided that we would never let ourselves be intimidated by martial law.

This unity forced the authorities to come to their knees and they started to devise face-saving measures. They staggered under criticism and had to come out of the whirlpool, so they sought the intervention of the editors' organisation, CPNE, as their arrogance did not allow them to address the journalists directly.

An official handout was issued which said that in view of the appeal by CPNE, the Martial Law Administrator Zone-C, Lt. General Jahanzeb Arbab, has ordered the release of all detained journalists on 6 December.

This order was proof of their defeat. The role of the editors' appeal was only influential in the sense that the CPNE was holding a meeting in Quetta where the supporters of the government

Shabbar Azmi

Zafar Qureshi

Masood Qamar

Farhad Zaidi

Aurangzeb

Aslam Shaikh

Ali Ahmed Khan

'Let him die; he is a traitor', reads the headline of a news story quoting the response of a
sitting bureaucrat when he was informed of Minhaj Barna's deteriorating health.

Hunger strike till death.

Courting arrests with our heads held high.

Khawar Naeem Hashmi arrested from Mazar-i-Quaid, Karachi.

An example of police brutality.

'No mercy. You deserve rigorous punishment.'
The gist of several newspaper headlines reporting the brutality of martial
law regime against protesting journalists.

Nasreen Zehra, Asifa Rizvi, and Tamkinat Ara with Mrs Minhaj Barna after their release from police custody.

Hameeda Ghangro and Lalarukh Hussain arrested and tortured.

PFUJ activists courting arrests at Regal Chowk, Karachi.

Qaisar Mahmood Butt, Rahim Bux Jatoi, Minhaj Barna, Zahid Sammoon, and
Ahmad Khalid ready to court arrest at Karachi Press Club.

Minhaj Barna addressing a rally in Faisalabad. Hafeez Raqeeb is also seen.

Khawar Naeem Hashmi and Iqbal Jafery after receiving the punishment of
five whiplashes each, pledging not to bow down.

A participant of Movement for Freedom of the Press, who came all the way
from Gujranwala to court arrest.

Participants of the movement making victory signs while heading towards Landhi Jail in a police truck. Their faces radiate with wide smiles.

'Use all your might, but you cannot suppress our voice.'

Summary military court sent these individuals to jail.

A glimpse of the high-handedness and suppression unleashed by martial law regime.

Brutally attacking peaceful journalists was a norm back then.

Leading office bearers of the Joint Federal Action Committee of PFUJ and APNEC. From L-R: Nisar Usmani, Minhaj Barna, Ahfaz ur Rehman, and Hafeez Raqeeb.

Protest meeting organized by Karachi Union of Journalists at Karachi Press Club. The speakers include Aslam Shaikh, Ahfaz ur Rehman, and Minhaj Barna.

Fareeda Hafeez, Nisar Usmani, and Mahmood Ali Asad addressing a rally
at Karachi Press Club.

From L-R: Shahnaz Ahad, Nuzhat Sadiq, Shameem Akhtar, and Naheed
Sultan on hunger strike.

Akram Qaimkhani and Habib-ur-Rehman leading the hunger strike at Karachi Press Club.

Minhaj Barna, Nisar Usmani, and Ahfaz ur Rehman addressing a
huge rally at Karachi Press Club.

Detainees at Landhi Jail return to Karachi Press Club.

Minhaj Barna offering biscuits to the lady hunger-strikers after the end of hunger strike.

First batch of hunger-strikers sitting in the compound of the daily *Musawat*, Lahore. From L-R: Urs Mallah, Ghani Dars, Zahid Sammoon, Johar Mir, Rahim Bux Jatoi, Wahab Siddiqui, Ahmad Khalid, and Tahir Najmi.

Minhaj Barna speaking at a huge rally in Karachi.

The weekly *Al Fatah*'s editor, Wahab Siddiqui, courting arrest at Regal Chowk with three other colleagues.

Our immortal heroes (from L-R), Khawar Naeem Hashmi, Masoodullah Khan, Iqbal Jafery, and Nasir Zaidi, who were punished with flogging on the orders of the summary military court in Lahore.

From L-R: Nisar Usmani, Minhaj Barna, Wali Mohammad Wajid, Shahnaz Ahad, Gulzar Sanam, Nuzhat Sadiq, Hassan Sangrami, Hafeez Raqeeb, Ghulam Nabi Mughal, Majeed Gill, Amir Mohammad Khan, and G.N Pervaiz, participating in a protest rally at Karachi Press Club.

Celebrations at Karachi Press Club after the release of 30 detained journalists from Landhi Jail, Karachi. Pictured above are Majeed Gill, G.N. Pervaiz, Ahfaz ur Rehman, Hassan Sangrami, Urs Mallah, Ghulam Nabi Mughal, Moosa Tair, Minhaj Barna, and Habib Ghauri.

persuaded them to file a request which became an excuse to order the release of journalists.

We received this news from the jailer of Landhi Prison. He told us that according to a radio announcement, all detainees would be released. Their number had reached thirty by that time. The jail barrack vibrated with our slogans. We hugged and congratulated each other and as usual, Barna only smiled. We congratulated him while Wali Mohammad Wajid kissed his hand in his typical manner. All of us then returned to the press club. We were sure that along with our release, the decision to restore *Musawat* must have been made and we could not have been more correct.

On 7 December, the chief editor of *Musawat*, Mir Jameel-ur-Rehman, received the letter of restoration which allowed for the resumption of the newspaper's publication from 9 December. The Action Committee of the PFUJ and APNEC declared the ending of the hunger strike.

THE DAY OF VICTORY

This was a great victory. Freedom-seeking journalists converged at the press club dancing and singing, and the released workers were showered with rose petals. It was a festive atmosphere.

Everyone was brimming with joy because they had earned their freedom. Karachi Press Club in those days was the centre of democracy-loving journalists and activists. Foreign correspondents were present in the press club in large numbers as they now had a major story to report. Cameras flashed to record a significant event in the journalistic history of Pakistan: the defeat of martial law.

The occasion was described in the following words by Ashraf Shad in weekly *Mayar*.

Behind the iron gate are locked leaders and workers with iron will. The release orders for arrested journalists have been received. At the other side of the gate, Nisar Usmani, Aslam Shaikh, and local representatives of the press are waiting to welcome them but it appears that no one is in a hurry to come out. Barna alone comes up to the gate and informs his colleagues of the journalists' decision to come out only if the release orders are unconditional. Usmani assures Barna that the release is unconditional. Barna and the rest of the colleagues come out to a warm reception under the shower of rose petals. The procession moves on towards the press club in a convoy. Wali Mohammad Wajid is complaining because when the vehicle drove them to jail, the distance was covered in a flash and now it is taking ages on the way back. A huge crowd is waiting at the press club to welcome the released. They are received with loud slogans of 'Long Live the Unity of Journalists!', 'Long Live Barna!' The last group of hunger strikers is overjoyed when they see Barna, who held a dish of cookies and offered it to them, thus marking the end of hunger strike.

Afterwards, Barna thanked all those who supported the protests and demanded immediate restoration of the editors of *Hilal-e-Pakistan* and *Nusrat*. He strongly refuted the propaganda that his movement had anything to do with the PPP or any other political party. He categorically stated that the movement was mobilized on the basis of principles. Its objectives were to safeguard the employment of journalists and to fight for freedom of expression. He also stated that the journalist community will not shy away from rendering sacrifices if ever a similar situation confronts them in future. He also demanded the withdrawal of the Press and Publications Ordinance. Nisar Usmani thanked the comrades and said that no society could survive without freedom of the press; then he called me to issue concluding remarks. I thanked each individual and organization by name for their support in a principled battle. I also warned the government that we would not remain silent over the so-called disciplinary measures underway against *Musawat*, Lahore. I was actually hinting to launch a similar movement in Lahore if the government did not relent. Strangely, my fear proved ominous.

The first phase of the movement concluded and *Musawat* hit the news stands on 9 December. However, there was more to come.

3

The Government's Stubbornness

The military dictatorship was apparently strong but in actuality scared. *Musawat* was a PPP publication; therefore, it was like a thorn in the government's side. The military regime could not stand even minor criticism and craved the silence of graveyard. Ideally, the military regime should have learnt a lesson from the 1977 movement, desisted the urge to confiscate the right of expression, and withdrawn authoritarian laws but nothing like that happened. It continued to pressurize the press and intensified restrictions. In order to repress the publications of the opposition, it instituted a system of cash bonds. The government could demand cash bonds for any objectionable news item. The objective was to create financial pressure on the opposition publications so that they would give up criticizing the military regime for its excesses. They had been deprived of government advertisements and private advertisers were too afraid of the martial law authorities to release ads in these publications. Soon after the restoration of *Musawat*, an assault on the employees of the daily *Imroz*, Multan, was launched. Its editor, Masood Ashar, was terminated. Consequently, the employees of *Imroz* were forced to protest at a roadside camp in the extreme cold weather for the acceptance of their demands. When the PFUJ and the Federal Action Committee announced the start of a movement, the officers of the Information Department adopted a conciliatory attitude in Islamabad and negotiated a settlement with the protesters.

Similarly, PPP's weekly *Nusrat* was going through rough

conditions. Its editor and officiating editors had to resign due
to threats and restrictions. The editor and printer of the daily
Sadaqat, Basheer Rana and Iftikhar Hussain, had been arrested
under Martial Law Regulation 33. Dailies *Aman* and *Tameer*, and
the weeklies *Mayar* and *Al-Fatah* were served notices for cash bonds.
In the next phase, the publication of *Al-Fatah* and *Mayar* was
stopped. Minhaj Barna's employment as editor of *Pakistan Times*
was terminated. The publications, which expressed a difference
of opinion, were constantly harassed and their printing presses
faced threats of being confiscated. By collaborating with the
Jamaat-e-Islami journalists, a list of 'enlightened' press workers
was prepared to set an example for others. The press industry's
condition was deteriorating by the day. Another critical incident
occurred in this context.

On 22 March 1978, the printing press of the daily *Musawat*
(Lahore) was sealed due to which the newspaper's Lahore and
Faisalabad editions could not be published. The next day, the door
of the press was dismantled and replaced with a brick wall. Before
this act was carried out, the chief editor, Mir Jameel-ur-Rehman;
editor, Badruddin; and assistant editor, Zaheer Kaashmiri (a
distinguished poet), were summarily tried and sentenced to one-year
rigorous imprisonment. The charges were the same old ones and the
pretext for confiscating the printing press was that *Musawat*, Lahore,
had published the oath statement of Zulfikar Ali Bhutto made in
Lahore High Court. In other words, a statement given in a court
of law rang alarm bells for the nervous and scared military rulers.
One could ask, was this oath statement a secret? Did India gain
military superiority by its publication? The statement was made in
the High Court, so then what was there to be afraid of? What was
the rationale for keeping it hidden? Zia ul-Haq's government was
made jittery by a free press and was determined to suppress it by
the force of bayonet because it considered the outspoken, truthful
journalists as the biggest danger.

The PFUJ was already protesting against the arrest of *Musawat* editors because after the latest restrictions, the unemployment of journalists had become a serious issue. During the same period, the president of Lahore Press Club, Abbas Athar, and editor of *Payam-e-Quaid*, Muzzaffar Abbas were arrested under various martial law sections. The charge against these two was that they had published the Urdu translation of Bhutto's book, *If I Am Assassinated*. The brave reporter, Khalid Chaudhry, was also among those arrested. He was charged with a concocted case of bomb-making and was atrociously tortured in Shahi Qila. The bomb-making charge was common in those days. The government would always slap the charge of bomb-making whenever it wanted to arrest someone. The situation was grave.

Under these circumstances, emergency meetings of the executive committees of the PFUJ and APNEC were held in Lahore under Barna on 3 and 4 April. It was decided that members of both organizations will go on hunger strikes and court arrests if the restriction on *Musawat*, Lahore was not lifted by 23 April, followed by the release of all editors from detention.

Everyone knew that the government wanted to crush the press, particularly the newspapers and magazines of the opposition. Direct attack on *Musawat* (Lahore) had rendered 250 journalists and workers jobless. Altogether, more than 600 employees had become unemployed due to forced closure. Under those circumstances, remaining silent and indifferent would have proved deadly as the government would have been emboldened. Once again, the government had imposed a warlike situation on the APNEC and PFUJ, leaving no option but to launch a movement. Apart from our opponents who had labelled us traitors and enemies, there were even some senior and cautious members in the APNEC and PFUJ who were not in favour of taking direct action. Barna presided over night-long debates in Basheer Bakhtiar Labourers Hall, Lahore. I also took part in these debates. Finally, it was decided that if we yielded to the government's pressure, an unending wave of damage will ensue, hence resulting in the death of journalism in Pakistan.

Agitating without reason had never been a practice for the APNEC and PFUJ. We were being pushed against a wall. Banning of *Musawat* (Lahore) was a plan to further prolong the night of oppression. The perpetrators of martial law planned to settle scores in Lahore for the humiliation they had suffered in Karachi. Meanwhile, Zia ul-Haq openly stated in a press conference to 'forget *Musawat*'. He also made derogatory remarks about journalists in that press conference. In other words, the powerful CMLA was challenging the unarmed journalists.

On 14 April, the secretary general APNEC and president of Musawat Employees Union (Lahore), Hafeez Raqeeb, was arrested in a mysterious manner. Instead of being locked up in a police station, he was presented to military officers who not only verbally threatened him but also ordered for him to be tortured. Tensions rose with each passing day as the accusations against us were intensifying. The coterie that wanted to seal our lips became vigorously active but we were prepared for the worst. Threats could not scare us.

We were not seeking confrontation with the government and desired to resolve the matter through talks. Minhaj Barna and Nisar Usmani held several meetings with government functionaries, but the government's short-sightedness turned it into an ego issue. The talks remained inconclusive. Numerous meetings of the Central Action Committee were held by 14 April. I participated in all of those meetings as the general secretary of the committee. It was unanimously agreed that we would resist, fight, and not bow before a dictator.

The movement was to start from 30 April. The next day was May Day which reminds us of the martyrs who demanded better conditions for workers and put their lives on the line for it. On Zia ul-Haq's nudging, the discussions about banning the May Day rallies started. Signals were given to the workers that they should consider themselves under arrest if they took out processions on that day. There was only one objective for such steps: to scare the journalist community from starting their hunger strike against the unjust banning of *Musawat*. And in case they persisted, arrests would commence, although the regime did not require an excuse for this.

I was staying in Lahore with Barna. Our Action Committee with Barna, Usmani, and other members went around visiting different newspaper offices and met leaders of journalist and student organizations. Meanwhile, volunteers for the hunger strike started arriving from Karachi, interior of Sindh, and other cities of Punjab. It was decided that if needed, student and labourers would also join the movement.

BARNA'S EXILE FROM THE PROVINCE

The military regime had power and abundant resources, and the entire state machinery was in its pocket, yet it was afraid of an unarmed civilian.

Minhaj Barna got on their nerves. They were flabbergasted about how a defenceless individual could gather such a strong force. All press workers of Pakistan stood behind this man. His co-voyagers were as determined as he was. This is precisely why the regime was scared of him.

The tyrants may display bloody eyes to their victims but their hearts quiver like dry leaves. Minhaj Barna was like the captain of a ship trapped in a storm; a captain who knew that the shore was near. It was understandable that the authorities were afraid of this confident man.

I, and a few other colleagues who were bracing for arrests, stayed at the home of a senior journalist, Khushtar Amrohvi. Barna stayed at the distinguished journalist, Aziz Siddiqui's place. Government spies followed him and he was under constant surveillance. A jeep would follow him whenever he ventured out. If he walked, the jeep rolled behind him stealthily. The reports of his whereabouts and meetings were sent to the martial law authorities continuously.

The government was still licking its wounds after what had happened in Karachi. It could not bear another defeat. Barna and I were on our way to Usmani's office on the afternoon of 28 April when he stopped at a roadside kiosk to buy a packet of cigarettes. As he took out one to smoke, a hand with a burning lighter reached out to him.

'Thank you. I am afraid I haven't recognized you?' Barna said.

'Can I tell you something, sir? You are a very daring man.' He uttered this in Punjabi and walked away quickly. Incidentally, he was a member of the CID.

Barna's presence in Lahore was increasing the government's nervousness by the minute. His name was among the first batch that went on hunger strike on 30 April. Under the circumstances, the only option for the short-sighted decision makers was to exile Barna from the province.

However, before that they played another trick. The Punjab martial law administrator, General Sawar Khan, invited the leaders of the PFUJ and APNEC for talks on 29 April. Although we could see through their ruse to gain time, we went along to give peace a chance despite the failure of the long dialogue in the past. Nevertheless, we were firm about not compromising on principles.

Minhaj Barna and Nisar Usmani met the Martial Law Administrator. No concrete proposal was presented by the government which demonstrated that it was not interested in resolving the dispute. They only emphasized that the press workers and journalists should give the government more time for consideration and the hunger strike of 30 April should be postponed.

Both the leaders took the stance that the government had already been given enough time and could not be given more. Accepting the invitation for talks by the press unions was to prove that they did not want unnecessary confrontation and desired a peaceful solution. The gesture had been made. After returning from the failed talks, Barna announced that the hunger strike would start from 30 April no matter what. As planned, the government issued orders to exile Barna from the province and he was taken into custody at Aziz Siddiqui's home. Barna refused to accept the decision but he was forcefully taken to the Civil Lines police station and from there to the airport and put on an 11 p.m. flight to Karachi.

This action might have cheered up the martial law authorities and helped them sleep better that night. However, the next day they were struck by dejection.

WHEN WE WERE ARRESTED

Our responsibilities increased after Barna's exile. We were aware that the authorities would do their utmost to sabotage our movement but we were not worried because we were fully prepared. Volunteers for the hunger strike had arrived in Lahore from different regions of the country and were put up in secret locations. They were not kept together but divided in various places as a safeguard against police raids.

Passions ran high. The prospect of fighting a big and powerful force is exhilarating, especially when you are right, and you believe that the opponent is strong as well as a tyrant. Challenging a tyrant fills your heart with elation.

Those were tyrannical times. The doors of the brutal inferno were thrown wide open for the democracy-loving political workers, particularly those from the PPP. They were arrested and ruthlessly tortured in the streets, police stations, and jails. They were accused of being enemies of the state, terrorists, and traitors, and charged with bomb-making. The 'honourable' military judges of summary courts swiftly sentenced them to terms ranging from a minimum of six months to a maximum of ten years of rigorous imprisonment. The more condemnable were sent to the dreaded forts of Lahore and Attock. Our three brave colleagues, Hussain Naqi, Khushtar Amrohvi, and Khalid Chaudhry were also put through the cruelties of the forts. Then the way our four great associates were flogged set a horrible and shameful example of barbarity.

Therefore, what would you call those elements in our ranks that sat in the lap of the dictator and stabbed us in the back? They raised a parallel organization and received power and pelf from the 'pious' man. What would you call those who embraced, went soft on, and sided with such elements?

Our organization decided to erect the hunger strikers' camp in the compound of *Musawat*. The hustle and bustle had started before 30 April. Congregations were held every evening where journalists and newspaper workers from organizations besides *Musawat* participated. Labourers and student representatives also came to express solidarity. Many social and political personalities paid visits. We chanted slogans fearlessly, not only for freedom of the press but also for the restoration of democracy. The secret police used to hover around while the police vehicles used to be parked outside.

Around 4 p.m. on 30 April, the first batch went on hunger strike amidst thunderous clapping and fanfare. The volunteers were garlanded by friends and their faces glowed with resolve. Crowds of supporters from other publications also poured in to participate.

The office-bearers were on the first floor of the building. A meeting headed by Usmani was ongoing when we heard running footsteps. Suddenly a young *Musawat* journalist barged in. Breathing heavily, he addressed Usmani.

'Sir, the Judicial Magistrate has arrived. The police have locked the entrance and a large number of supporters are locked out. They are not being allowed to enter. They say no one can go inside now.'

Usmani, Hafeez Raqeeb, Ehsanullah Khan, and I rushed downstairs. The gate was closed and the magistrate was standing outside surrounded by senior police officials who knew Usmani. They let us out.

A large crowd of press workers was trying to push their way in the Musawat building compound. Usmani asked the magistrate what the problem was and why he was not letting those people in.

'We are not allowed to let them in,' replied the magistrate.

'For what reason? They want to meet the hunger strikers so you better open the gates and let them in,' Usmani said.

The magistrate refused. I was young then and sternly said, 'This is bullying.'

The magistrate got angry and yelled at us. He said, 'Now the four of you are also not going back in.'

Tensions were escalating. 'End this strike or get in the police van,' the magistrate said while addressing Usmani.

Usmani took us aside for consultation. He said that we should end the strike and begin courting arrests at Regal Square from the following day. I did not agree with him. I believed that if we ended the strike, it would be taken as a sign of weakness and that we were intimidated. I thought it would be extremely damaging for the movement. My apprehension proved to be right later as the government had decided to crush our movement by force. I told Usmani that this particular course of action would fizzle out our movement. Our followers had attached high hopes with us and they looked up to us. If we retreated now, it would dash their hopes and the authorities would be encouraged as they seemed to be set on violent means to end the movement. Would they allow us to court arrests the next day? If they were determined to sabotage our action in a close compound then carrying out action against us in the open area of Regal Square would be even easier with a larger force.

Usmani looked inquiringly towards Raqeeb who endorsed my stance. Ehsanullah, who was not a member of the Action Committee, stood quietly. Meanwhile, the magistrate kept interrupting us to hurry up and decide. He kept talking and I could feel my anger rising. I was not prepared to concede and kept responding to him angrily. Usmani remained silent for a few moments to reflect and then broke his silence.

'Okay, then. Let us get in the police van.'

I felt relieved and glad that the magistrate who had been staring at me would not have the satisfaction of calling us cowards or weak. All four of us boarded the van. Our colleagues inside were watching the entire scene through the gate and over the walls.

It was the evening of 30 April and we had been arrested. The police action had begun. That is how the second phase of the movement for freedom of the press began.

SLOGAN-CHANTING MISCREANTS

Our destination was Civil Lines police station where the prison bars awaited us. My apprehensions proved to be correct. After our arrests, the police entered the compound of *Musawat* and baton-charged the workers inside. They tortured those on hunger strike and arrested 22 protesters, including all hunger strikers. Soon after, they joined us in the Civil Lines police station.

It was a small lockup barely enough for 10–15 people. We were literally piled on each other through the night. The next morning dawned with the message of Labour Day. On my suggestion, we decided to commemorate the martyrs of First May inside the detention room. Twenty-six is not a small group, so all of us managed to energize the place. Usmani, Raqeeb, and I delivered speeches and the listeners chanted slogans. The police in-charge came running.

'Please have mercy and don't make noise. I will be in trouble!'

Actually, the whole episode was being handled by the military and the police was afraid of them too.

They transported us to Camp Jail in the afternoon. While completing the paperwork and formalities for the inmates, I emptied my pockets but the supervisor wanted my wristwatch which I refused to surrender. The commotion brought Usmani closer who put his hand on my shoulder.

'Give them the watch; that's the rule since the British Raj.'

We were warmly welcomed inside by the workers and journalists already in custody at Camp Jail. Abbas Athar and Khalid Chaudhry were also there who had been charged with different offences. They had prepared potato curry with bread for us.

A majority of the political detainees comprised PPP workers. They included 15-year-old boys who were 'dangerous criminals', who were mostly charged with the offence of bomb-making. Whoever they wanted to arrest was slapped with the bomb-making charge.

After we had finished eating, those already incarcerated enquired about the events happening outside and expressed their hopes and apprehensions. After sunset, the jail authorities divided us into groups of four and locked us in separate cells for the night.

I was accompanied by Usmani, Raqeeb, and Riaz Ahmed of Jang Press Karachi in my 8 by 10 cell. All of us were in the habit of smoking and our cell was tiny and damp. It stank because there was no fresh air. A can was placed inside to serve as toilet. Usmani was diabetic and had to make frequent use of the can with embarrassment. We either looked the other way or would change the subject.

We managed to spend the night somehow. We breathed deeply to ward off fatigue when we ventured into the open space the next morning. There was a tap outside where we washed under the open sky. The jail authorities had not considered it necessary to build a wall around it.

Summons were received in the meantime to meet the warden. The procedure was to bundle up our belongings outside the cell, remove our shoes, and sit on the unpaved floor outside our respective cells. The 'boss' (jail warden) would sit on a chair. It was mandatory for the prisoners to sit with their heads down. Raising one's head was equated with defiance and was punishable. We did not tolerate that.

'That is the practice,' Usmani reproached but complied.

Anyway, the warden was a reasonable man and did not make an issue out of it but lectured us on jail culture and discipline.

Though we were in a prison, somehow, it wouldn't be wrong if I call the ambiance recreational. Divided into small groups, we would play chess and cards, or sing songs. Some would even climb trees and sit there. Along with the telling of jokes, others narrated stories of their favourite movies animatedly.

We were isolated from the outside world. Barna was in Karachi and Usmani, Raqeeb and I, along with the rest of the Action Committee members, were in prison. Although we were worried about the direction our movement would take, nevertheless, we had faith in our comrades as each one of them was a general in his own right.

The recent successful experience of organizing the movement in Karachi was still fresh. Everyone knew how groups of volunteers would be secretly gathering for hunger strikes and how communication would be established across the country for that purpose. Our associates from Lahore were more experienced. Earlier, in 1974, when the editor of *Musawat* (Lahore), Abbas Athar, had fired 12 journalists, they had mobilized a similar movement.

We had complete faith in the support of our active and fervent colleagues from Lahore. The three of us had discussed the matter several times and had apprised our colleagues about it. The local leaders and senior colleagues had taken charge in Lahore. It was this unity which enabled us to redeploy ourselves against the oppressive regime of Zia ul-Haq within only three months. One can also attribute it to the government's stubbornness and its arrogance over possessing unbridled powers and force.

The government exercised force and first demolished our camp for hunger strikers in the *Musawat* compound but the resolve of the volunteers remained high. Our brave colleagues from Lahore and the members of the executive committees of both the organizations were in touch with Barna who was exiled to Karachi. He was constantly providing guidance.

Every day, people would receive our colleagues with overwhelming enthusiasm when four of them would suddenly appear on the streets chanting slogans and carrying placards. The crop was ready for harvest against a military usurper. Everyone was anxious and more than willing to join hands.

Beginning on May Day, the shadow of agitation roared and flashed on the horizon of Lahore with mounting intensity. The procedure for courting arrest was that a batch of four volunteers from different cities would covertly reach a rendezvous point. The location of Montgomery Road near *Musawat* office was the most appropriate. Other supporters with volunteers used to be present there. Loud slogans were chanted and backed by the crowds of men and women. Garlands were put around the necks of the volunteers which would make them stand out. Banners would also appear and in the meantime, someone would start distributing flyers. Cameras flashed. The volunteers would smile and laugh energetically and move forward.

As I said earlier, the whole affair was being monitored by the military officers. The civilian departments were merely obeying their orders and were on high alert. Police in uniform and civvies were scattered around the whole city. Due to the heavy security, our colleagues would suddenly appear on the road so that they could attract as large a crowd as possible. Police would run in the direction of the slogans and would dash as if worried that the protestors might escape. They did not seem to realize that if escape had been an option, the hunger strikers would never have shown up in the first place!

After arrest, the police would lift the protesters and throw them in their vans. The arrested volunteers would face the crowd with a smile and make victory signs while the vans sped away.

The detention centre for the arrested was Camp Jail where we were also kept. The following day, we received our four colleagues warmly. They informed us about the happenings outside. It was reassuring to know that our colleagues outside were fully prepared to launch a strong movement. On the first day, 22 volunteers were arrested, who came from various cities. In the days that followed, their number increased rapidly. The arrested included Wahab Siddiqui, Johar Mir, Urs Mallah, Zahid Sammoon, Rahim Bux Jatoi, Ahmed Khalid, Sikandar Malik, Parvez Iqbal, Abdul Ghani Dars, Riaz Ahmed Khan, Saleem Shahid, Mushtaq Ahmed, Mohammad Ilyas, Mohammad Sharif, Mohammad Akram, and two Saleem Akhters. The arrests continued for the entire month. The warrior journalists courted arrests with heightened resolve until 30 May and by this time, their number had reached 165.

A team of journalists from Lahore were assigned the job of covertly receiving and settling those journalists who had come from other cities. The team performed its responsibilities with courage. They not only received those coming from other towns but also arranged for safely taking them to court arrest at predetermined locations.

We took courage from the good company and ambience. The martial law authorities were stunned as they could not understand how the 'miscreants' could be infused with unlimited reserves of valour and fortitude. A handful of singing and slogan-chanting lunatics had humiliated and unnerved them. They were conniving devious moves to end the movement.

A NOVEL ACTION AGAINST 'DANGEROUS' CRIMINALS

The third day of our detention was warm. Usmani, Raqeeb, Riaz, and I were lying down on the floor when I heard someone whispering outside. It seemed as if two men were debating the pronunciation of my name. A short while later, the bailiff's face appeared on the other side of the prison bars. He looked at each one of us one by one.

'Ajaz ... is summoned by the boss.'

As I accompanied him through the corridor, I saw our stylish colleague from Peshawar, Johar Mir. Then I caught a glimpse of Urs Mallah, who was a press worker of *Hilal-e-Pakistan* (Karachi). Meanwhile, the young journalist from Hyderabad, Zahid Sammoon, also joined us. It emerged that the four of us were being summoned together which raised our apprehensions. What was common among the four of us was that none of us was from Punjab.

As we passed the adjacent barrack, we came across Abbas Athar and Khalid Chaudhry. They were curious about our unscheduled stroll. When we told them that we had been summoned, they said, 'It must be summons from the military court. Today is the day for awarding sentences.'

We had thought the same and were fully ready for punishment, however, what happened next was so strange that it could only be attributed to the bewilderment of the government. The SHO of Qila Gujjar Singh police station was waiting for us inside the jailer's office. He stood up and said:

'Sir, you will have to come with me.'

'Okay, but where?' I asked, assuming that he would take us to a military court.

'We have received orders that you have been exiled from the province of Punjab for six months.'

'Do you have the orders in your possession?' I asked.

He pulled a piece of paper from his pocket and extended it towards me. I took the paper and showed it to my colleagues. It said, 'There is threat to law and order from your person, therefore, you are being exiled from the province for six months.' I read the order and strongly said:

'We will remain in the jail and will not go anywhere else.'

'Please sir, don't put me through a test. Please bring your belongings from the barrack.' In other words, he had been ordered to take us by force.

I went back to the barrack and informed Usmani about this. All of them were surprised and wondered what the secret behind the exile orders was. Usmani appeared worried.

Anyway, we bade farewell to our prison mates and left with a heavy heart. We were made to sit in a jeep but without handcuffs. The inspector sat next to the driver and we sped away.

We had no idea what procedures would be adopted to exile us from the province. It was possible that they would drop us at a deserted road across the provincial boundary of Punjab province. Mir suspected the exile was a mere excuse. In his disarming smile, he said:

'Ahfaz, remember, our destination is Shahi Qila where torture cells await us.'

We speculated the future development with anxiety. Nevertheless, our morale was high. There was an earthen smell in the air. The jeep had come on a main road and slowed down. It was equipped with a wireless set which buzzed every now and then, and the SHO would obediently report. It was not difficult to figure out that on the other end was a uniformed person of pedigree who was afraid that the 'dangerous' criminals might dodge them.

The jeep made a turn and entered through a huge gate. We could see a sprawling building and realized that we had reached the airport. The service entrance reserved for big officers and security personnel was used.

The jeep was speeding on the runway where a PIA aircraft was parked in front of us. Stairs were attached to the rear section of the aircraft where two airline staffers were positioned. The jeep stopped next to them and we stepped out. The SHO pulled out four tickets from his pocket and handed one to each of us.

Other passengers were looking at us through the windows and seemed puzzled. Later, we learnt that the flight had been waiting for twenty minutes for us to arrive and that had made the passengers uneasy. After settling down, the passengers told us that they had been gossiping about the flight delay suspecting a VIP or a senior military official was the cause. They were startled to see four perfectly ordinary persons, who were sleep deprived, and looked unwashed and bewildered. We boarded the plane while the SHO remained on the tarmac until the plane started taxiing.

THE DREAM OF ABDUL HAMEED CHHAPRA

We were welcomed by the sea breeze of Karachi. The city spread its arms to welcome us. It was dusk and there was a nip in the air.

We hired a taxi and went straight to the press club where everyone was astonished to see us. We were surrounded by a puzzled crowd who wondered why we were in Karachi when we were supposed to be in Camp Jail, Lahore.

When we told our story to the crowd gathered at the press club, our narrative reflected the confusion of the scared martial law rulers. It renewed the motivation of our audience. Abdul Hameed

Chhapra's sudden emotional outburst was also quite interesting for the entire crowd.

'Shabbar, write down my name. I am going to Lahore tomorrow to court arrest. My party (Tehreek-e-Istiqlal) is meeting in Karachi in three days.'

Shabbar Azmi was chairman of the Karachi Action Committee. He despatched volunteers from Karachi and the interior of Sindh to Lahore.

Probably, Chhapra thought that all the detainees would be released gradually and there could be a reason for that.

Despite two or three agreements, the editor of *Musawat*, Abbas Athar, did not relent. Eventually the movement was launched. Journalists from various cities reached Lahore. The police would arrest and put them in prison cells. Later, they adopted a different method; they would transport them far away at deserted places outside the city and tell them to walk back. This 'facility' was withdrawn soon.

Banking on this context, Chhapra thought that the Zia government would also follow the Bhutto government's tactics of arresting the agitators and then letting them go.

This assumption proved to be wrong. Chhapra was sent to Lahore, as he desired, and there he was arrested. Soon, from 7 May, military courts began their trials and he was sentenced to a jail term which he spent in Sahiwal Jail with the notorious dacoit Mohammad Khan as his next-door prisoner.

TWELVE MONTHS, TEN LASHES

Lenin said, 'There are decades where nothing happens and there are weeks where decades happen.'

Those days were like that. The freedom seekers were in the

streets, busy writing a new history. They were at loggerheads with
the usurpers of the right to freedom of expression.

There was no shortage of volunteers. They were enlisting in
large numbers at various cities to go to Lahore. The government's
failure, on the other hand, bewildered it. Baton charge and arrests
proved futile. When the agitation continued, the military courts
were assigned with unleashing oppression on the protesters. Just in
a month, 156 colleagues were sentenced to rigorous imprisonment
and sent to jails in Lahore, Multan, Sahiwal, Mianwali, Faisalabad,
and Bahawalpur. There were many senior and well-known
journalists among them. *Musawat* editors, Badruddin, Zaheer
Kaashmiri, and Jameel-ur-Rehman were also arrested during
the movement while three journalists of National Press Trust
were fired.

The rigorous jail sentences by the military courts began from
7 May. That day, 14 of our leaders and active members were
awarded six-month to one-year imprisonment plus PKR 1,000
to PKR 10,000 in penalties. They included the PFUJ's secretary
general, Nisar Usmani; APNEC secretary general, Hafeez Raqeeb;
Ehsanullah Khan, Mushtaq Ahmed, Sharif Shaivi, Saleem Akhter,
Rahim Bakhsh Jatoi, Yaqoob Chaudhry, Mohammad Younus Butt,
Saleem Shah, Mohammad Ilyas, Sikandar Malik, Ahmed Khalid,
and Parvez Iqbal.

The first three decided to boycott the proceedings of the military
courts when they were not allowed to defend themselves. They
clearly declared that these punishments would not hold them back,
and that they had fought against tyranny before and would continue
to do so.

Meanwhile, the sun of 13 May ascended. While 13 May is
termed as a shameful and dark day of Pakistani journalism, it was,
at the same time, a day of victory for our four worthy colleagues.
That day three of our brave colleagues, Khawar Naeem Hashmi,
Nasir Zaidi, and Iqbal Jafri received whiplashes on the orders of

the military court. The popular senior journalist, Masoodullah Khan, was also awarded the same punishment but due to his age and medical condition, and upon the doctors' intervention, he was spared. The punishments were implemented within 70 minutes of their announcement. Those three colleagues of ours who received whiplashes were very young at that time.

Nasir Zaidi was from the city of Sufis, Multan. Khawar was from the city of the gracious, Lahore, and Iqbal Jafri was from Karachi. The whole world protested against this incident. Littérateurs in Pakistan also raised their voice in our favour; however, a displeasing incident occurred in Karachi.

Ten days later, an event called 'Jashn-e-Majnoon' was held in Intercontinental Hotel, Karachi, in which not even a resolution was passed against the public lashings of journalists in Lahore despite a reminder. A section of intelligentsia had always upheld the idea that writers have nothing to do with politics. In other words it declared that writers lived in heaven. It is another story that their 'higher creations' were not read even in their own literary circles and were destined to diminishing readership. This agonizing news came as a deep shock. I remember that Barna and I were sadly sitting in the press club and then I went to the backyard to shed some tears. Barna probably did the same but pride overtook grief soon because we were very proud of our colleagues. Barna's elegy, 'Twelve months, ten lashes' marked the distress.

If the government had any idea about the consequences of this terrible act and how it would internationally damage Pakistan's reputation, it would have reconsidered its decision ten times before executing it. However, the tragedy of a dictator is his tunnel vision and that he lives in constant fear. Every constitution violator gets a haunted throne which compels him to commit foolish acts. The 13 May incident was flagrant proof of the 'pious' man's lack of thought and his barbarity.

Time has proved who gained notoriety and who earned honours.

Gagging the domestic press had been planned but silencing foreign media institutions was not possible. The BBC, Voice of America, and others exposed the tyrannical government of Pakistan which was followed by a strong worldwide condemnation of this action by the international journalist community. Severe notice was taken of this despotic decision. A communiqué by a renowned international organization of journalists condemning the public lashings of journalists was handed to Pakistani foreign minister, Agha Shahi, in the General Assembly of the UNO. Shahi had to admit that, 'Wherever I go, I am besieged by people who call us beasts for whipping journalists.' I heard rumours that he had threatened to resign.

GANG OF TRAITORS

The entire world condemned the military government while the dictator was busy weaving another repulsive conspiracy with his coterie. In the corridors of power, a plan was being hatched to co-opt some journalists. A plan had been put in place to raise a parallel block within the PFUJ. The government was aware that black sheep exist where upright individuals work, who can be used to disrupt their formations.

A group of individuals with a contentious attitude existed from the beginning in the PFUJ and APNEC. These were mostly fundamentalists of the Right, led by the JI supporters. They always dreamt of controlling the PFUJ but never won the elections. They had opposed us on every front in the past but remained helpless before the majority; however, they grabbed the opportunity of playing their games in mid-July while we were in a state of war against the military government.

After the end of the movement, some journalists who had stabbed us in the back suddenly appeared during the first meeting of the

Federal Executive Committees of the PFUJ and APNEC at the Basheer Bakhtiar Hall in Lahore. Barna was chairing the meeting and asked them what they were doing there after conniving with the government. They were completely indifferent to the fact that it was only five days after our brave colleagues had suffered lashes and their wounds were still fresh. Their only concern was their own interests; therefore, they had gone to Islamabad on the invitation of the ministry of information on 18 May. Senior officials of the information ministry welcomed them at the Islamabad airport. Television and radio announced the arrival of these 'leaders of PFUJ and APNEC', whereas, both the central leaders, Minhaj Barna and Nisar Usmani, along with their supporters from various cities languished in jails under the oppression inflicted by Zia ul-Haq. The very same day, General Zia's information secretary, Lt. General Mujib-ur-Rehman, met some journalists and planned the formation of PFUJ's Rasheed Siddiqui Group. It's the same phony organization which later acquired the new name of *'Dastoori'* (Constitutional) Group. Later, these four individuals also organized a parallel APNEC of which Naseem-ul-Haq was appointed the chairman.

Anyhow, after the 18 May meeting, this opportunist group announced that it would press the government to meet a committee of leading personalities of the PFUJ and APNEC in order to bring back normalcy. This way the self-styled 'leaders' not only feigned a dialogue with the government but also signed an already prepared agreement and declared that an agreement has been reached between the journalists and the government. They also announced that the restrictions on *Musawat* (Lahore) would be lifted and all arrested journalists would be released.

There was no mention of the 30 employees of the different newspapers affiliated to National Press Trust, whose services had been terminated earlier, nor of the economic demands of newspaper workers. The eight-point demands of the APNEC and PFUJ also did not feature in this so-called agreement. Their source of satisfaction rested in the perception that they had succeeded in creating a split in the journalist community. Although later events proved to be quite contrary to their negative beliefs, in those conditions the executive committees of the PFUJ and APNEC declared temporary suspension of their movement.

The Lahore movement continued for a whole month. During that period, the government stooped to the lowest level in order to carry poisonous propaganda against us through television, radio, and the publications it controlled. It poured all its strength into this campaign and used all possible means to glorify the group of traitors. Their accommodation was arranged in air-conditioned hotels at government's expense in various cities so that they could break the influence of our movement and gather the handful of opportunists to form more parallel unions. For all that trouble, the government only gained notoriety and these four individuals could never go beyond issuing press statements.

LIST OF INDIVIDUALS ARRESTED DURING THE LAHORE MOVEMENT

These statistics were taken from the 13–20 May 1978 issue of the weekly *Mayar*, Karachi. The factual details present in this issue are incomplete. Despite all our efforts, we have not been able to gather the complete list of volunteers who courted arrests during the movement because most newspapers and magazines were heavily censored back then. There were only a handful of newspapers and magazines that managed to avoid censorship and honestly wrote whatever was happening. Sadly, due to the tyranny unleashed by Zia's military government, these publications did not appear uninterruptedly as they were repeatedly banned. Naeem-ul-Hassan of Punjab University wrote his thesis on the movement for freedom of the press which did not carry the list under question due to the same reason; however, an incomplete list of those arrested later in Karachi was included. I contacted some very senior journalists in Lahore regarding this but they were also unable to help. This shows that the complete list was not published in any of the Lahore-based publications also. In comparison to other newspapers and magazines, the Karachi-based *Al Fatah* and *Mayar* did cover the movement and published lists of arrested volunteers. Unfortunately, the task of acquiring these lists from the aforementioned magazines is still incomplete. If any student of journalism can find that source in future, it would be a great service towards compiling the history of the movement. Anyhow, until then we must do with what we have. It is important to remember that in Karachi and Lahore, at least four individuals voluntarily courted arrests every day in addition to those carried out by police by means of rounding up protesters. The series of arrests continued for a month in Lahore and for eighty-four days in Karachi. Considering this, I believe that a more accurate estimate of those arrested could be worked out.

1. Nisar Usmani, secretary general of the PFUJ.
2. Hafeez Raqeeb, secretary general of APNEC.
3. Ehsanullah Khan of *Hayat*, Lahore.
4. Mushtaq Ahmed of *Musawat*, Lahore.
5. Sharif Shewa of *Musawat*, Lahore.
6. Saleem Akhtar of *Musawat*, Lahore.
7. Rahim Bux Jatoi of *Imroz*, Multan.
8. Pervez Iqbal of *Hayat*, Lahore.
9. Yaqoob Chaudhry of *Musawat*, Lahore.
10. Younas Butt of *Musawat*, Lahore.
11. Saleem Shah of *Musawat*, Lahore.
12. Muhammad Ilyas of *Musawat*, Lahore.
13. Sikander Malik of *Musawat*, Lahore.
14. Ahmed Khalid of *Musawat*, Lahore.
15. Aslam Shaikh of *Pakistan Times*, Lahore.

16. Shafqat Tanweer Mirza of *Imroz*, Lahore.
17. Muhammad Afzal Khan of APP, Multan.
18. Ali Muhammad Khan of *Sun*, Karachi.
19. Hashmat Wafa of *Imroz*, Multan.
20. Sabihuddin Ghosi of PPI, Karachi.
21. Zia-ur-Rehman of *Pakistan Times*, Rawalpindi.
22. Atif Shaikh of *Musawat*, Karachi.
23. Naseem Anwar of *Pakistan Times*, Rawalpindi.
24. Tahera Sabih of *Musawat*, Lahore.
25. Sher Afgan of *Musawat*, Lahore.
26. Abdul Hafeez Khan of *Millat*, Karachi.
27. Muhammad Iqbal of *Hayat*, Lahore.
28. Habib-ur-Rehman of *Pakistan Times*, Rawalpindi.
29. Khalid Saeed of *Mashriq*, Karachi.
30. Muhammad Sadiq of *Musawat*, Lahore.
31. Ejaz Mahmood of *Musawat*, Lahore.
32. Muhammad Arshad of *Musawat*, Lahore.
33. Muhammad Ashraf of *Musawat*, Lahore.
34. Acchi Memon of Larkana Union of Journalists.
35. Muhammad Ilyas of *Pakistan Times*.
36. Abdul Hameed Chhapra of *Jang*, Karachi.
37. Raja Nisar of *Jang*, Karachi.
38. Syed Muhammad Sufi of *Musawat*, Karachi.
39. Fateh Muhammad Memon of *Dawn*, Karachi.
40. Rana Nayyar Iqbal of *Musawat*, Lahore.
41. Muhammad Ashraf Ali of *Sadaqat*, Karachi.
42. Muhammad Khan of *Sun*, Karachi.
43. Saleem Shahid of *Imroz*, Multan.
44. Saleem Asmi of *Pakistan Times*, Rawalpindi.
45. Aziz Siddiqui of *Pakistan Times*, Lahore.
46. Syed Shaukat Hussain of *Musawat*, Lahore.
47. Muhammad Hasan of *Hilal-e-Pakistan*, Karachi.
48. Mukhtar Hussain of *Imroz*, Multan.

49. Salahuddin of *Musawat*, Lahore.
50. Ghulam Haider of *Musawat*, Lahore.
51. Muhammad Ayub of *Azad*, Lahore.
52. Habib-ur-Rehman of *Musawat*, Karachi.
53. Jameel Ashraf Malik of *Musawat*, Karachi.
54. Liaquat Ali of *Aman*, Karachi.
55. Shabih Khan of *Sun*, Karachi.
56. Muhammad Ayaz of *Imroz*, Multan.
57. Khalid Jawaid of *Mashriq*, Lahore.
58. Ustad Mukhtar Hussain from Multan.
59. Dost Muhammad of *Pakistan Times*, Rawalpindi,
60. Muhammad Hasan Mureed of *Hilal-e-Pakistan*, Karachi.
61. Shaukat Hussain of *Musawat*, Lahore.
62. Ghulam Muhammad, former president of Musawat Workers' Union, Lahore.
63. Salahuddin Butt, secretary of Musawat Workers' Union, Lahore.
64. Muhammad Yaqoob of *Azad*, Lahore.
65. Waheed Baghi of *Hayat*, Lahore.
66. Habib-ur-Rehman of *Musawat*, Lahore.
67. Aftab Ahmed Malik of *Pakistan Times*, Rawalpindi.
68. Riaz Ahmed Bhatti of *Musawat*, Lahore.
69. Muhammad Fahim of *Musawat*, Karachi.
70. Muhammad Usman of *Azad*, Lahore.
71. Mrs Elizabeth Khalid
72. Durdana Yasmin of Punjab University
73. Rosy Majeed of Punjab University
74. Anwar Sultana of *Sadaqat*, Lahore.
75. Nasir Malik of *Sun*, Lahore.
76. Azizullah Khan of *Musawat*, Karachi.
77. Irshad Ahmed of *Musawat*, Lahore.
78. Munir Hussain of *Sun*, Lahore.
79. Ashiq Ali Shirazi of *Aftab*, Hyderabad.
80. Dwyer Dino of *Aftab*, Hyderabad.

81. Rehmat Ali Razi of *Azadi*, Hyderabad.
82. Ibadat Shah of *Musawat*, Lahore.
83. Riaz Malik, president of Punjab Union of Journalists.
84. Asif Ali Shah, president of PPL Workers' Union, Lahore.
85. I.H. Rashid, former president of PUJ.
86. Hamraz Ahsan, vice-president of PUJ.
87. Ali Akhter Mirza, former president of PPL Workers' Union, Lahore.
88. Badar-ul-Islam Butt, former secretary of PPL Workers' Union, Lahore.
89. Zafar Qureshi of *Hurriyat*, Karachi.
90. Rauf Bhatti of *Musawat*, Makran.
91. Muhammad Yousuf Soomro of *Aftab*, Hyderabad.
92. Fateh Muhammad Bhatti of *Hidayat*, Hyderabad.
93. Saghirudeen of *Pakistan Times*, Lahore.
94. Ahsan-ul-Haq of *Musawat*, Lahore.
95. Ahmed Khalid of *Musawat*, Lahore.
96. Abdul Hameed of *Musawat*, Lahore.

4

The Final Front

Nothing has changed. The arrogance of tyranny and power never ceases to be destructive; oppression continues to reign.

Although *Musawat* (Lahore) was permitted to operate, the fundamental issues remained unaddressed because any form of empathy from those in power for the many unemployed journalists would have threatened the very foundations of the legitimacy of the ruling class. The former continued to remain comfortably cocooned in their lavish homes and only journalists, press employees, and common men were visible on the streets. Freedom of expression was completely crushed. Newspapers and magazines were shut down and editors were arrested on one ridiculous charge or another. A regime was ushered in of press and publications ordinances, a spate of government advertisements, newsprint quotas, censorship, pre-censorship, and press-injunction. Journalists and press employees were sacked, imprisoned, and tortured. That notwithstanding, our colleagues, with an exception of a few, remained steadfast and adamantly refused to be cowed.

During the Lahore movement, some demands of protesting journalists were met as an attempt at face-saving but the five key economic demands of the press workers were not met, nor were those press employees who had been sacked reinstated. Cash deposits were still being demanded from the publications owned by the opposition. The Press and Publication Ordinance was blatantly misused. Some publications were banned while the rest were heavily censored and could be shut down at a minute's notice leaving their employees on the streets.

Our eight demands were:

1. The Press and Publications Ordinance and other black laws should be withdrawn and action taken against newspaper employees under these laws be revoked. There should be a uniformity in the application of law which should be adjudicated by the civil courts.

2. The bans imposed on the publication of the weeklies *Al Fatah* (Karachi) and *Mayar* (Karachi), and other newspapers be lifted. The notices issued to weeklies and dailies relating to cash deposits should be withdrawn.

3. The release of all the editors, printers, and press employees who had been arrested.

4. A 10 per cent cost of living allowance with arrears should be paid to all newspaper employees with effect from June 1974.

5. An additional 50 per cent dearness allowance be paid to newspaper employees in view of the spiralling costs of living.

6. House rent allowance should be raised from 15 to 50 per cent of the basic salary.

7. Given the rising cost of living, increments should be made according to the rate of inflation which should be decided by the Tribunal for Implementation of the Wage Board Award.

18. The Tribunal should function more effectively to implement the Wage Board Award and swiftly dispose of cases.

The reason for the postponement of our movement in Lahore was to make it apparent to the government and its allies that the government itself was at the root of the conflict rather than the APNEC and PFUJ. We gave the government some time to demonstrate their seriousness and hold talks with the genuine journalists' representatives. However, the former kept patronising those who had betrayed the cause and once again banned *Musawat*

(Karachi). The only reason for this was that *Musawat* was an organ of the PPP and the military dictatorship was frightened of Bhutto and wanted him hanged at all costs.

After the joint meeting of the executive committees of the PFUJ and APNEC on 27 June 1978, it was decided that if *Musawat* was not reinstated by 18 July, the ban on *Al Fatah*, *Mayar*, and other publications was not lifted, and the economic demands of journalists were not met, the suspended hunger strike would be resumed. In other words, the movement to court arrests would be resumed.

The government demonstrated stubbornness and paid no heed to our demands. The Karachi movement was also unique in terms of the active participation of democracy-loving farmers and students. They voluntarily courted arrest alongside press employees which lent greater strength to the movement that encompassed as many as 350 volunteers

Our communiqué issued following the 27 June meeting gave the government a jolt. It had assumed that we would not resume our movement so soon after the Lahore episode. They, therefore, began devising plans to sabotage our movement. Some journalists who supported the martial law regime were again hand-picked to undertake the task of fomenting differences within the journalist community. To this day, I recall those times with great joy. All the conspiracies hatched failed miserably and we were, more than ever before, prepared for a much longer struggle. This was an example of the courage and steadfastness of Pakistani journalists of which we should be very proud.

On 18 July, Minhaj Barna led the first batch of hunger-strikers, an event which was described as follows by *Al Fatah*: 'There was great hustle and bustle in Karachi Press Club. Black and red banners declaring, "Scrap the Black Laws", "Don't Spread Darkness of Tyranny by Caging the Sun of Journalism", and "The Struggle Will Continue" adorned the terrace [of the press club] from all four sides.' The fervour of the charged crowd was spectacular. A large number of protestors had reached the press club much before the appointed hour. The lawns of the club were literally taken over by the protesting journalists and the action began at 4 p.m. Amidst thunderous applause and sloganeering, Amir Mohammad Khan of the daily *Sun* and the general secretary of APNEC, Lahore, announced that a hunger strike would be launched. He read out the names of *jeeala*s (participants) in the first batch. Nisar Usmani garlanded all the volunteers: Minhaj Barna, Kaiser Mahmood Butt (reporter of the daily *Aitemad*, Quetta), Rahim Bux Jatoi (sub-editor of the daily *Imroz*, Multan), Zahid Sammoon of the daily *Aftab*, Hyderabad, and Ahmed Khalid (sub-editor of the daily *Musawat*, Lahore).

We were aware that the government was prepared to crack down severely on the movement, and were therefore prepared for a long-drawn confrontation. Barna's arrest was inevitable. We had received information that the government was not going to restrict itself to arresting only those on hunger strike because that strategy had not worked on the past two occasions but was preparing a widespread crackdown calculated to destroy the movement.

The names of Nisar Usmani, Hafeez Raqeeb, and mine were on the top of their list. In meetings preceding the strike we had prepared our strategy to counter the government's possible moves. Barna had specifically instructed me during an Action Committee meeting that when the movement began I should go underground, organize our supporters, and evade arrest to the best degree possible. He had said that as I was from Karachi, I should shoulder greater responsibility.

The government adopted the same methods that it had during our movement in December of the previous year on the morning of 20 July. The police arrived at the press club in trucks accompanied by screeching police cars. There was a thumping of boots echoing everywhere. When they entered, our companions were awaiting them. Our hunger-striking colleagues began chanting slogans when they saw the perpetrators of oppression and were joined by everyone else. The press club was electrified. The police advanced but those leading this 'great expedition' were pulverized by fear.

Barna, Jatoi, Khalid, Butt, and Sammoon were taken into custody. The slogans did not stop until the police were out of sight. The news of the arrests spread throughout the city and across the country like wildfire.

The final battle had begun.

THE DIRECTION OF STRUGGLE

We were in a state of war. The opponent was strong and well-equipped with financial and human resources; however, this was no physical combat but a psychological battle. The secretary of information, General Mujeeb, was well-versed in psychological warfare but we had to succeed.

A network of spies spread throughout the city. The leaders of the journalists were placed under surveillance. Traitors amongst us provided them with minute to minute information about our movements. Following Barna's instructions, Usmani, Raqeeb, Nasir Malik of the daily *Mashriq*, and I went underground. We remained alert, continually changing our location, spending a day in one safe house and the night in another to evade informers. We were kept updated about their round the clock monitoring of the press club.

Shamim Alam and Altaf Siddiqui of *Musawat* (Karachi) were constantly in touch with us. They relayed our instructions to colleagues and brought back their replies. They shouldered a greater responsibility than us. They evaded their watchers to reach us and if apprehended, revealed nothing to their captors. However, Altaf Siddiqui did falter once. He slipped out around midnight to see his family and was apprehended and severely beaten up. In a letter that he wrote from jail, he said they were particularly interested in apprehending me and questioned other prisoners too about me. He warned that I must be cautious and remain hidden because there have been 'simpleton' couriers who had led the police to other comrades in hiding and justified such betrayal by remarking, 'We thought they must have moved out of that safe house by then!'

Shamim Alam later became director of Arts Council, Karachi and joint secretary of Karachi Press Club for 25 years. He is still active from the Arts Council platform. Altaf Siddiqui was an active student leader and office-bearer of National Students' Federation before becoming a journalist. Later, he became secretary of Karachi Press Club. Both of them played important roles in the third phase of the movement.

We spent the first two days at the home of the PFUJ's active member, Aleem-ud-Din Pathan (*Sun*, Karachi), where, besides the four of us, volunteers from other cities were also in hiding. We were altogether about 13 or 14 persons. Aleem was a very dedicated member but his family was very anxious about his safety given the large number of uninvited guests who had gathered. When his father, a religious individual, inquired about us, he laughingly said, 'They are travellers. They will board a vessel for Dubai in a couple of days. They are going to work there.' In any event, we could not stay there for long so we moved after two days but as the rest had to court arrest in smaller groups, Aleem had to feed and house them until then.

After the arrest of the first batch of hunger-strikers, Amir Mohammad Khan, general secretary of APNEC in Karachi; Achhi Memon, president of the Larkana Union of Journalists; Zafar Alam, secretary, Rawalpindi Union of Journalists; and Agha Baqir from *Tameer* (Peshawar), occupied the camp. They were also arrested and sent to Central Jail, Hyderabad, where Barna was also incarcerated for a month. In his message to the public from jail, he said, 'Even if we are kept imprisoned for a century on charges of disrupting public order or whatever, we will remain steadfast.'

Our morale was high, indeed. We were providing additional testimony to Zia's authoritarianism. The third batch of those courting arrests comprised Hashmat Ali Wafa *(Imroz,* Multan); Ali Rizwan (Faisalabad); Wahid Baghi (*Hayat,* Lahore); and Shabbir Hussain (*Musawat,* Karachi). On 24 July, Shabbar Azmi (president, Musawat Employees Union, Karachi) courted arrest along with his three companions. *Al Fatah* (which was then published under the name of *Parbhaat)* narrated the course of events in the following words:

Seven days have passed since the peaceful protests were launched by journalists. During these seven days, 30 journalists and press workers have been imprisoned. They include Ali Asad, president of APNEC in Karachi, who was arrested in a raid on his home on the night of 20 July.

[*Asad heard a familiar voice calling him as he reached home after a struggle and prepared to go to sleep. The caller was his college mate, Tajamul Hussain, who was a police inspector and had come to arrest him, so they hugged with an embarrassed laughter first.—Ahfaz ur Rehman.*]

The arrest warrants for Nisar Usmani, Hafeez Raqeeb, Ahfaz ur Rehman, Ashfaq Bukhari and Habib Ghori have been issued. The tyrant government is set to push us against the wall. On the other hand, the gang of traitors is being lavished. The arrest warrants were prepared with the help of lists provided by Naseem-ul-Haq Usmani, Rasheed Chaudhry, Khalid Butt, Iqbal Mirza, and Mahmood Jafri. The traitors advised the government to 'use force to suppress the movement; we are with you. There won't remain an effective workers' organization, nor demands and neither any danger of protests and hunger strikes.' The flattery loving government generously rewarded the sycophants. It is also rumoured that the gang of traitors are being allocated four rooms for a new press club near the old AGPR building which will be inaugurated soon.

The police action was not limited to arresting those who were on hunger strike. They would barge into Karachi Press Club without a warrant, search the rooms, and ransack files and documents there. In this context, a detailed statement was published by the president of the Karachi Press Club, Ashfaq Bukhari. But who could provide security to the club in the face of martial law? All civil laws and democratic rights were surrendered to martial law regulations. In the following few days, the raids on the homes of activists accelerated. The home of secretary Karachi Press Club, Habib Ghori, was raided at midnight and his frail and ailing mother was harassed. Nonetheless, Ghori was cautious and gave himself up the following day after Friday prayers in front of Saddar Jam'a Mosque. This process continued intermittently. The homes of the Karachi Action Committee secretary, Shabbar Azmi and Shamim Alam, were similarly raided and their elderly occupants mistreated.

If anyone wishes to corroborate the above-mentioned *Al Fatah* report about the conspiracies and opposition from within the journalist community, one can refer to the *Jasarat, Zindagi, Urdu Digest, Islami Jamhooria*, and *Nawa-e-Waqt* issues of that period for revelations that testify to the journalists' devotion to democracy and principles.

According to the *Al Fatah* report:

A few rooms above the Labourers Court in Sindh Secretariat have been converted to operation rooms. Both the entrances of the press club are swarming with plainclothes police who stare at each person entering and leaving as a hunter zeroing in on his prey. Any vehicle that leaves the press club is followed and harassed to obtain information. In the beginning they only had few bicycles but now they possess fleets of motorbikes, small cars, and jeeps. They have established a permanent CIA centre opposite the main entrance.

What threat could a peaceful struggle for eight-point demands by journalists pose for the state? In any event, these journalists were volunteering to be arrested. Nonetheless, the government's reaction made it appear that a civil war was in the offing.

HEFTY BRIBES

The reminiscences of those days are more vivid than all the other memories etched in my mind during my 49-year career in journalism.

We kept on changing our locations. I was assigned the responsibility of mobilizing volunteers in various cities. We wrote letters, made telephone calls, and sent messengers. Usually, I performed these tasks during the night. I covertly met Altaf Siddiqui and Shamim Alam every now and again; they constituted the major communication channel. Making calls to other cities was tedious as we did not have telephone connections at every place in which we stayed; this made it necessary to venture out. In any case, making inter-city calls was not as simple as it is today. Venturing out was perilous but there was no other alternative. I established contact with imprisoned colleagues, including Barna, principally by letters received through jail visitors. Some letters were brought by Irshad Rao and Wahab Siddiqui, others by Shamim Alam. Barna did not remain idle and sent us detailed instructions which we tried our utmost to implement. It was a taxing task to remain in hiding and evade arrest.

I remember an interesting and amusing incident. While Usmani and I stayed in Lyari in the early days of the movement and were doing our utmost to remain incognito, one day the former suggested: 'My wife's sister lives nearby, let's go and see her'.

I was reluctant and tried to dissuade him but he was adamant and insisted on my coming along. I eventually agreed with great reluctance. I had a motorbike which I had bought on instalments. There is an interesting story concerning it which I will narrate later.

Wearing a safety helmet was not mandatory then; but I had one and arranged another for Usmani. I convinced him to put on the helmet as it would impede recognition. We left Lyari as the sun was setting. Our host had explained how we could follow narrow streets to arrive at Mereweather Tower, a major road intersection. As soon as I reached Bandar Road, I became apprehensive as a policeman waved to stop me. There was no space for rapid escape, an option that I might have adopted. Certain that I would be arrested, I took a deep breath and stopped. More than fear, I felt a sense of frustration about the fact that I was about to fall into the hands of the authorities due to a reckless adventure and that too right at the outset of our movement.

'Yes, sir?' I asked the officer.

He gestured to indicate that I should stop and wait while he spoke to another man standing beside him. I availed that opportunity to whisper to Usmani: 'It would be a great loss if we were both to be apprehended. Why don't you get off the bike and wait on the opposite side of the road. If I am caught, you can take a taxi to Nursery.'

Usmani was aware of the situation and quietly went over and sat on the pavement. Whether out of caution or nervousness, he did not take off the helmet. I stood by the bike waiting for the policeman to talk to me when a man in civvies approached me.

'What happened? What is the problem?' He asked.

'I don't know. He stopped me but seems to be avoiding me now,' I responded.

He smiled and said, 'Actually, it is a one-way street you came along,' he said smiling.

'I am sorry, I didn't realize that. We are law abiding citizens and are even wearing helmets, as you can see,' I said.

He smiled broadly again and said, 'Just pay something and end the matter.'

These days, you can get away with breaking the law in return for a bribe of PKR 20 or 30; in those days you could do it for PKR 5 which was a large sum then. Since we were in a fix and had to get away as soon as possible, not to mention the ignominy of arrest, I pulled out the first currency note I was able to find in my pocket. It was a PKR 50 note. The policeman grabbed it, while I crossed the road, picked Usmani, and headed towards Nursery. We returned without any further mishaps but laughed long and hard about the incident.

I am sure the policeman must have laughed too and treated his colleagues to sweets boasting a big catch. But the truth is I was extremely upset that I had lost a significant sum of money.

A MESSAGE FROM BENAZIR

It was probably the eighth day of the movement when an important event occurred. Usmani, Raqeeb, and I were staying with the famous writer Shaukat Siddiqui in North Nazimabad. Our fourth companion, Nasr Malik, had left two days earlier to sort out a family matter and then courted arrest, and was jailed. Shaukat Siddiqui had been our editor at *Musawat* and treated me like a son. He spent most of his time in his room during our stay with him. Our meals were sent to our room and he never spoke about the movement when our paths crossed.

That day however, when he came to our room, he was wearing a serious expression on his face. He ushered me into another room.

'Look son, the thing is that Benazir wants to meet you.'

I was stunned. 'But why? Why does she want to meet only me?'

'I don't know. That is the message I have received.' He replied. (I discovered later that he had received the message through Irshad Rao.)

I paused. It was a difficult decision to make. I was very young but having been in the company of elders, I had developed a certain maturity.

'Shaukat sahib, we are running a movement for freedom of the press. *Musawat* of course is owned by the Bhutto family and Mr Bhutto is in jail. Nevertheless, our movement purely concerns journalism and therefore, meeting Benazir will not be appropriate.' I replied.

As it was, our opponents had been levelling accusations that the journalists' movement basically concerned political objectives and was backed by the PPP. My meeting with Benazir would provide the traitors more fuel. Then there was another issue which I pointed out to Shaukat, 'I am being hunted by the police. Reaching 70 Clifton would be difficult. If, God forbid, I get caught over there, our detractors will have a field day and our people will be disappointed if I am arrested at 70 Clifton!'

The debate continued for a while. I continually declined to go which irritated Shaukat but he did not exercise his right to scold me as a respected elder. Instead, he said nothing at all.

Benazir was very young at that time. The PPP was being run by Nusrat Bhutto, whom I met in September 1977 at the *Musawat* office and 70 Clifton before the movement began. I have no idea what impression she formed of me to want to meet me rather than my seniors.

The following day, Shaukat came again and took me to another room. 'Alright, if you don't want to go to 70 Clifton, don't. An alternate arrangement has been made. Khanum Gohar Ijaz lives in my vicinity. Benazir will come to her place. After sunset, a car will take you there and then bring you back after meeting her.'

Khanum Gohar Ijaz was one of Benazir's closest companions. I had to concoct another excuse after the one I had made earlier.

'It is fine if she comes here but I cannot understand why she wants to meet me?' He then boiled over.

'First you objected because it was dangerous for you to go to 70

Clifton. Now that an alternate arrangement has been made you make a new excuse.'

'But Shaukat sahib, at least the purpose of the meeting should be clear. Granted that they own *Musawat* but the movement is being run on the basis of a decision made by our organization. We have had no contact with the PPP at any stage. If she wants to express solidarity with the journalists, she can go to Karachi Press Club where we are camping,' I replied hesitantly.

'Lots of journalists are in jail and many of them have come from other cities to court arrest. Perhaps she may offer some logistical help in this regard,' he responded.

I was incensed as financial assistance directly clashed with our ideology and principles.

'Shaukat sahib, our colleagues declare in their speeches and chant slogans about having our heads cut off to defend our principles rather than bow them. If they don't get facilities, it's okay; they get what other prisoners receive. If she wants to offer financial assistance, then I refuse to meet her.'

We had a lengthy debate and he tried hard to persuade me but in vain. Some years after the movement came to an end, we learnt about the entire background of that episode. Everyone knows that Barna's younger brother, Meraj Mohammad Khan, was at one time the most important pillar of the PPP. Zulfikar Bhutto had once nominated him as his successor, although differences had arisen, but now when the Bhutto family was facing a crisis, Meraj's sympathies were with the Bhuttos. Apparently, he met Benazir during our Karachi movement. She asked him who was running the journalists' movement and Meraj gave her my name. At her request, Meraj contacted Irshad Rao. When Benazir learnt that I was at Shaukat Siddiqui's home, she got directly in touch with Siddiqui.

Anyhow, I did not agree to the meeting. You may call it my harsh attitude but I believe that the decision was correct. I feel frustrated today when I see my colleagues, including office-bearers of unions,

appearing eager to meet politicians and civil servants and who are
never tired of uttering, 'Sir, Sir…'. It seems like they are even willing
to prostrate before them.

REUNION OF REBELS

It was the eleventh day of the movement. Suddenly, one morning
Usmani declared that he was leaving for Lahore. Raqeeb and I
opposed this as it was most likely that he would be arrested as soon
as he resurfaced in Karachi. There was intense surveillance outside
but he did not agree. Actually, Usmani was a gregarious man and
having to go underground had dampened his spirits. He justified
his decision on the basis of the argument that he would organize
supporters in Lahore to join us in Karachi. Well, that certainly was
an important task.

He left and reached Lahore safely. Now Raqeeb and I were
left alone. We continued our activities but engaged in no form
of adventurism. We received regular information from our jailed
colleagues. Most of them, especially those from Karachi, were asked
during interrogations, 'Where is Ahfaz ur Rehman? If you tell us
his whereabouts, we will release you.' That necessitated my being
more cautious although I had to take risks when it became essential.

Altaf Siddiqui, who was arrested from his home, sent me a
message through Shamim Alam: 'Tell Ahfaz to be very careful.
Whoever is captured is severely tortured and asked to reveal Ahfaz's
address to save himself.'

Later, close friends like Shamim Asghar and Hassan Zaheer
were severely tortured to reveal my whereabouts but they remained
resolute and, in any event, were not aware of my whereabouts. I
was aware of the danger and that is why we did not stay for more
than two or three days at one location. After the conclusion of the
movement, I calculated that in 80 days we had moved 30 times.

By 27 July, 36 journalists had been arrested. Because of the daily arrests, no batch could complete its 48-hour hunger strike. However, for reasons unknown, the police somewhat changed its strategy. They stopped arresting people from within Karachi Press Club. Two friends completed their 48-hour hunger strike but the police did not act. When their attention was drawn to this and they were invited to arrest the strikers, the police and intelligence personnel smiled and looked away.

Towards the end of 1977, a horrible tragedy occurred at Colony Textile Mills, Multan. According to labour representatives, the management had ordered 25 protesting workers to be shot.

The owner of Colony Textile Mills was considered a close friend of Zia ul-Haq. It was rumoured that they became close when Zia was posted as a brigadier in Multan. It must have been assumed that no one would dare to confront the mill owners but the reaction was totally the opposite. The entire country protested against this shameful act. All labour organizations took to the streets and journalists came out in their support. After the incident, Barna met the secretary-general of the Pakistan Workers Federation, S. P. Lodhi, and toured Multan, visited the mills, and expressed solidarity with the labourers and their leaders. Then Barna gathered all concerned and formed a Labourers Coordination Committee, which included a number of labourers' unions. Barna was elected as the president, Lodhi its general secretary, and Habib-ud-Din Junaidi its vice-president. As secretary of the KUJ, I too was a member and participated in its meetings.

On the formation of this committee, some of the 'pure' journalists amongst us expressed displeasure but subsequently, this decision had far-reaching effects. Such journalists had also objected to the formation of APNEC and criticized Barna. They boasted their support for human rights and civil rights but fell back when it came to uniting with others. What did they have to lose by such unity? It continues to remain an open question. If the PFUJ subsequently witnessed a decline, it was for an entirely different reason. Some of its important leaders were lured by fame, wealth, and power. They fought amongst one another, casting professionalism and organizational principles to the side with catastrophic results.

Before the third phase of the movement was launched in Karachi, the idea of joining hands with labourers, students, and farmers was discussed at executive committees of the PFUJ and APNEC in order to further strengthen the movement. It was decided that if necessary, other sympathizers would also be included. The same decision had earlier been taken by the Lahore movement.

Barna had been arrested, Usmani had left for Lahore, and therefore the burden of responsibility came to rest on Raqeeb and me. We approached the labour leaders who responded positively. Student and farmer unions had already announced their support. Hence, we proceeded with a new policy.

A new chapter was added to the struggle on 29 July when, among the tenth batch of hunger strikers there was one volunteer each representing farmers and students, Manzoor Hussain and Ansar Beg respectively. The inclusion of other workers in the journalists' struggle was testimony of the support we enjoyed amongst farmers, labourers, and students across Pakistan. The movement had acquired a unique status. The workers' organizing committee's president, Mohammad Jaffar, said, 'Today is a historic day. The union of journalists and labourers established today will live forever. The exploiter classes are afraid of this and are doing their utmost to break it but they will never succeed.'

The participation of labourers and students in the press workers' struggle was a cause for concern for the government and their movement outside the press club on the evening of 29 July suddenly accelerated. Police trucks and other vehicles began to converge there. Perhaps they had received fresh orders. Around 2:30 a.m. on 30 July, police arrested the six-member, tenth batch of hunger-strikers. This comprised of Wali Mohammad Wajid, chief reporter of *Imroz* (Multan) and the assistant secretary general of APNEC; Rashid Abbasi, president of APNEC (Peshawar); Sardar Qureshi, sub-editor, *Hilal-e-Pakistan*; Ghulam Rabbani of *Musawat* (Lahore); Manzoor Hussain of the public coordination committee; and, Ansar Beg, student of Government College, Nazimabad. This marked a new high for the movement.

Although every volunteer from amongst journalists, labourers, and students deserves credit, I would like to specially mention Nasir Zaidi of *Nawa-e-Multan* and *Al Fatah* from the twelfth batch. Like Khawar Naeem, Zaidi too was an emaciated youngster. He already had fever and the hunger strike inevitably worsened his condition. He was unable to swallow and had to be hospitalized. In Lahore, he had been subjected to the punishment of five lashes. Colleagues pleaded that he end the hunger strike but he stoutly refused: 'I will not end the hunger strike even if I die.'

When the police arrested the twelfth batch from the press club, they found one 'miscreant' missing because he had been hospitalized. A search was conducted and when the police found him in the hospital, they shackled him to the bed. The doctors protested against this inhuman treatment but the police paid no heed.

WHO WILL SAVE PAKISTAN? STUDENTS, LABOURERS, AND FARMERS!

'Do not worry about robbers ... thieves are harmless ... don't bother yourself over such trivial issues like which politician is corrupt, which civil servant is crooked ... focus on the real miscreants ... yes, yes you guessed it ... the scoundrels sitting at the press club ... your enemies, sir. They are all communists, trouble-makers, agents of the PPP... just control them; the entire journalist community endorses this.' So whispered the traitors of the community into the ears of the emperor, Zia ul-Haq.

For about three weeks, groups of volunteers began a hunger-strike and were arrested and transferred to two Karachi prisons, as well as, to prisons in Hyderabad, Khairpur, Nawabshah, and Sukkur. Then we took the decision to stop courting arrest in the press club and to move to the streets. (All protests were banned under martial law, and therefore, taking to the streets was a guarantee of arrest).

The third batch of hunger-strikers took over on 14 August. This group consisted of Jabbar Khattak of the National Students Federation (later chief editor of *Awami Awaz*, a Sindhi daily, and secretary general of the CPNE, an association of chief editors); Mohammad Sulaiman Lund of Sindhi Hari Committee; and four journalists, Mohammad Riaz Bhatti (Lahore), Masood Qamar (Faisalabad), Ghulam Rasul (Hyderabad), and Ghulam Nabi Rumani (Sukkur). This was the last batch of hunger strikers in the Karachi Press Club. From 15 August, we planned to continue the struggle in different areas of the city.

On the evening of 14 August, addressing a congregation in the press club consisting of members from the newspaper industry, labourers, farmers, and students, the president of Jang Employees Union, Karachi, Ahmed Ali Alvi, said:

> We conducted a peaceful movement from within a boundary wall but because of the stubbornness of the government, adequate results have not been achieved. Therefore, this is our last get-together in these premises. Tomorrow this movement is going to be taken to the streets. Today, the blood of labourers, farmers, and students is infused in the journalists' struggle. I appeal to them to come forward and lead.

The decision to move beyond the walls of Karachi Press Club enthused our supporters but terrified the government. The spies were there as usual and became more alert with the news of this new turn of events. They conferred amongst themselves and left immediately to inform their paymasters that the following day we would assemble at Regal Chowk.

On the evening of 5 August, all normal activities at Regal Chowk were suddenly disrupted. A few protesters began to chant moving slogans. Apparently, unconnected supporters in the crowds that had gathered, garlanded those going on hunger strike. They pulled out banners concealed within their clothing while one individual began distributing pamphlets. This batch consisted of four journalists, one student, and one farmer; all were passionately chanting slogans.

The celebrated poet, the late Johar Mir's voice dominated the chorus. He was a member of the Peshawar Action Committee. Melody blended with resolve and hope for a better tomorrow. The late Shabih-ul-Hassan, better known by his nom de plume, Naeem Arvi, effectively captured the scene in *Parbhat* (*Al Fatah* publications), in its August 1978 issue:

Regal Chowk was choked with plainclothesmen. Traffic was on the move. There was the habitual hustle and bustle with busy shoppers in a festive mood. One could spot several familiar faces. We pause in front of Cafe George: two CID agents stand shoulder to shoulder and then move on.

We have no idea where the press workers, labourers, students, and farmers will court arrest. A large police van is parked in front of Odeon Cinema. A large contingent with an SP and DSP is stationed near the bookshops looking out for prey. A rightist crime reporter stood nearby; he is known to collect a separate fee as an informant. We were surprised to see him there; how did he know the time and place to be at when we had no clue about it.

At precisely 5:15 p.m., a bus coming from the direction of Frere Road started offloading press workers, labourers, farmers, and student representatives. They carried banners, which displayed: 'Reduce Prices!'; 'Accept Eight-point Demands of Press Workers!';

'Free the Press!'; 'Stop Retrenchment from Factories!'; 'Resolve Students' Issues!'; 'Stop Uprooting Farmers!'.

The police immediately ran towards the protesters like maniacs. The lunatics stood still on the rock of their principles. They did not intend to escape but wished to irritate the police. They slipped out of their grasp chanting loud slogans and displaying victory signs. The crowds endorsed them. Johar Mir and Kaleem Durrani would repeatedly stand up in the open police truck shouting slogans. The crowds responded with, 'Long Live the Unity of Journalists, Students, Labourers, and Farmers!'

The truck sped away but the slogans trailed behind. Energy infused Regal Chowk and there was a momentary pause in oppression. In Shabih-ul-Hassan's words, 'People were astonished by these crazy individuals, who were openly raising their voice against oppression and injustice. They are journalists and press workers, labourers and students. They are the nation's heart and mind, bloodstream, body, and backbone. Who will save Pakistan? Students, labourers and farmers!'

THE ARREST OF WAHAB SIDDIQUI

The editor of *Al Fatah*, Wahab Siddiqui, was among those arrested the following day. Siddiqui related the incident to me but the late Naeem Arvi's description in his article *'Who will save Pakistan?'* is so vivid that you feel directly involved in the action.

I met Wahab Siddiqui on the morning of 6 August. Both of us worked at *Al Fatah*. He was uppish and beaming. His characteristic smile that had been drowned by overwork, returned. Wearing a blue shalwar kameez, he tapped the Red & White cigarette packet in his pocket as he exhaled fumes of smoke.

'I am well-stocked!'

'So you are set for some good work. Great, we will have a couple of leisurely days. Let Wahid bhai [Wahid Basheer, senior journalist and trade unionist] hold down the fort.'

Following this exchange in the office, Naeem depicts the scene at Regal Chowk:

Regal Chowk was crowded in the evening. After the previous day's incident, the news had spread that press workers, students, labourers, and farmers were going to court arrest on a daily basis in support of their demands. There were a large number of women too. The police looked more organized with a network spread throughout the area. There was a plainclothesman on every step in their trademark shalwar kameez and a duster-like scarf slung over shoulder. Both the public and police awaited the arrival of the journalists. The police rushed towards every approaching bus and would board it to search for journalists, but in vain. Senior police officials stumbled around in bewilderment. Their informants had probably failed to inform them of the direction from which the protesters would emerge. Suddenly, Wahab appeared heading a group of colleagues consisting of Hut Laghari of *Ibrat*; Ghulam Mohammad Jatoi of *Hilal-e-Pakistan*; Mohammad Azeem of *Musawat*, Lahore; Malak Haq Nawaz of the Labourers Organizing Committee; and Yaqub Khoro of Sindhi Hari Committee. The police were taken by surprise and could not figure out where these people were coming from. Whistles began trilling and vehicles turned around sharply. At this time, two large vehicles were brought for the 'culprits'. One was stationed opposite the old location, Odeon Cinema, and the other at Frere Road. The protesting workers were decked in wreathes of flowers and carried placards displaying their demands: *Fulfil the Eight Demands of Journalists! Reduce Prices! Stop Retrenchment of Journalists! Solve Students' Problems!*

The first assault of the police was on the banners and placards; after snatching them, they turned to the protesters, arresting and herding them into the vehicles. Meanwhile, a huge mob gathered there who passionately responded to the slogans being chanted by those arrested. All traffic came to a standstill. Passengers disembarked from the buses and joined the mob.

Wahab Siddiqui, who is a go-getter and a workaholic, turned his attention to a very important task. Earlier, during the Lahore movement, he was a volunteer for the first batch of hunger-strikers, but to his chagrin, he was bundled into an aeroplane and exiled from the province. This time he was not going to be disappointed. He was arrested in the midst of a marketplace like a brave man. I was however apprehensive about how this irrepressible individual would cope with the idle days and nights in jail; how would he walk around exhaling cigarette smoke; what publication would he edit? There is no dearth of such dashing youths in the ranks of the PFUJ and APNEC. They cannot not be bought with a bag of PKR 70,000. They are very clear about the goal of their struggle; so much so that they are able to visualize the distant fruits of their success.

After the publication of the narrative of the journalists' movement, another attempt was made to gag the outspoken *Al Fatah*. Now the government was intent on banning the publication of *Parbhaat* too. Irshad Rao however strongly resisted. He went on to publish one magazine after another, setting a new record in Pakistani journalism of bringing out twelve magazines one after another with different names within a brief period of time. Sadly, I have not seen any suitable commendation of Rao's and Wahab's unique feat in any book, magazine, or report.

In a similar vein, Mahmood Sham and Ashraf Shad of *Mayar* published *Shah Jahan, Kehkashan, Awaz,* and *Sach'ai,* one after the other in the face of the dictatorial press restrictions. Most newspapers and magazines played it safe and only a few, besides these two, resisted the undemocratic diktats prevalent at the time. These were *Musawat, Amn, Ailan,* and *Sadaqat* from Karachi; *Viewpoint, Punjab*

Punch, Musawat, and *Hayat* from Lahore; and, *Tameer* and *Hayat* from Rawalpindi.

NEW SERIES OF ARRESTS

Jalib had said: I am rising; you are about to set. Oppression is their weapon, resolve is our shield. They carry the spear of ignorance; we bear the torch of knowledge. The month of August which witnessed the freedom movement a few decades earlier was nurturing another story of struggle.

The arrests continued. Regal Chowk had been our hub. Within a few days the area became the preserve of the law enforcement agencies. They camped there and the police spies were everywhere. Before you were decked with a wreath, you found yourself in the police van.

As mentioned earlier, Shamim Alam and Altaf Siddiqui were the link between us and our other colleagues. They played an important role in the selection of our hideouts too. Occasionally, we would also suggest a location along with Irshad Rao, who was proactive in this context. Our other colleagues worried about us getting caught so they too made suggestions. Shaukat Siddiqui, Chaudhry Rafiq, journalists Ghazi Salahuddin and Mohammad Ali Siddiqui, politicians Taj Haider, Seth Ibrahim, Khadim Ali Shah, intellectual Arif Hassan, and friends such as Ahmed Shamsi and Musa Raza, and others I cannot immediately recall, acted as gracious hosts. We were never short of safe-houses because of the loving generosity of individuals like them.

Once the arrests began at Regal Chowk, the government issued a strongly-worded press-release warning the protesters and their sympathizers that if the 'agitation' continued, all their resources would be mobilized to severely deal with the trouble-makers. One could have asked, hadn't they already done so?

Notwithstanding this warning, our sympathizers did not shrink and we found a new hideout every couple of days given the innumerable supporters of the pen. Even those who did not belong to the literary community offered us shelter because they realized that freedom of the press was the soul of democracy and fighting a dictatorship was a noble cause.

The protest at Regal Chowk on the day following the press release was a strong response to the government's threat. That day protesters were severely baton-charged before being arrested. Besides our activists, many non-participating bystanders found themselves herded into police vans.

A number of people were exiled from the city or the province on 6 August. On the tenth of the same month, summary courts sentenced 14 journalists to seven months of rigorous imprisonment but the official figure announced was only 6. Those sentenced included Kaleem Durrani of the Youth Front; distinguished poet and journalist, Johar Mir of *Musawat*; Wahab Siddiqui, editor of the weekly *Al Fatah*; and, Ali Ahmed Khan of the BBC. The last three were also arrested during the 30 April 1978 Lahore movement and were sentenced to rigorous imprisonment. The interesting accounts of their time in prison are included in this book.

The traitors had already submitted a list of most active members of the PFUJ and APNEC to the authorities with the assurance that the movement would collapse within days. However, when labourers, farmers, and students joined us and the movement spilled out from Karachi Press Club into the streets, the government lost its nerve and accelerated its propaganda. They resorted to the official media and rightist publications. Our peaceful movement was accused of being a threat to law and order and when their tactics failed to make a dent, they turned their wrath on to the traitors.

A special meeting was held at PMA House, which was reported on by Naeem Arvi in *Parbhaat:*

The gang of traitors once again shamelessly prostrated before the martial law authorities. An eye-witness to the meeting said that the operation in-charge responded angrily. 'We have already been embarrassed enough because of your advice. You are an incompetent and useless lot. You don't even enjoy the industry support. If things had not reached the present state, I would have thrown you out of here. Are you sure things will cool down after the arrest of these activists?'

'Yes, yes. This political movement launched by Barna will die. We are confident of that. Just begin the arrests,' they responded in unison.

Three days later, a major operation was launched on the night of 11 August. In the first sweep, Mahmood Sham, the editor, and Ashraf Shad, the executive editor of the weekly *Mayar*; Musa Jee Deepak, general secretary of Herald Workers' Union; Riaz Ahmed, general secretary of Javed Press Employees Union; and, Lalarukh Hussain, reporter of the daily *Sun*, were arrested. During these arrests, the police violated all norms of decency and privacy of the victims which was not surprising as it was the work of those trained by the British colonial administration. Riaz's frail mother was dragged to the doorstep and Lalarukh was arrested from her bedroom, which the police entered through a window. Her husband was also arrested for no reason.

Zia ul-Haq panicked. Basic human rights were abused. Old women were harassed, homes were broken into, and decency thrown to the winds. There are no words to describe Lalarukh's arrest. Dragged away from her 11-month infant girl and thrown into jail, she became a role model of courage. The traitors made a devious move at this point, filing an appeal for her release on the grounds that she was a new entrant into the field of journalism and had been manipulated by the movement.

In a letter written from jail, Lalarukh dubbed this appeal an insult to her. She wrote, 'Newspaper workers are conducting a historic movement for their basic right of freedom of expression. If that is a crime, then I am equally guilty for committing it.'

She advised the Rasheed Siddiqui group and the self-proclaimed president of the PFUJ, Ali Kabeer, 'Rather than wasting your time making hypocritical appeals for my release, you will profit more by begging for privileges and awards from your masters.'

About her child she said, 'I am upset about my 11-month old daughter. She is innocent and oblivious to all that is going on. Imprisonment is acceptable to me. When the children grow up they will also support us and resist their rulers.'

On the third day of these shameless arrests, the daily *Jasarat* and the spokesman for the Jamaat-e-Islami predicted that 'Further activists are expected to be arrested'.

Obviously, who else could have been better informed!

WHERE IS AHFAZ UR REHMAN?

The government, notwithstanding the unlimited resources at their disposal, proved to be a pauper when it came to action and was incapable of breaking our resolve. Apart from stray opportunist regressive circles, the whole city was ours and our passion reigned.

As police forces increased in number at Regal Chowk, we targeted other localities. We courted arrest at Boulton Market, Lyari, Lee Market, and other neighbourhoods. Farmers, labourers, and students were in step with the journalists. It was an exemplary model of discipline and organization.

Those volunteering for arrest would suddenly appear on the road and make every effort not to be caught before they had shouted out their demands and conveyed their message to the crowds. Meanwhile, police violence intensified. Many colleagues were interrogated and then taken to a torture cell where they were treated with extreme severity. Some autobiographical accounts of victims are included in this book; others were not received. Some of those who suffered are no longer with us, such as Altaf Malik of *Musawat*, advocate Shamim Asghar, and, Hassan Zaheer of the weekly *Razdan*. The detainees were dragged by their hair, punched in the face, kicked and passed through torture devices installed at the special cells built for the purpose. They would be hanged upside down, submerged in water, hit on the soles of their feet with flat leather whips, and asked stupid questions under the glare of eye-piercing lights, not to mention the obscene language used and gruesome threats made. Our security forces have always comprised of masochists.

Notwithstanding such oppressive actions, our colleagues remained steadfast and highly motivated. Student, farmer, and labourer bodies remained in constant touch with us. Although lists of journalists were prepared, the authorities remained substantially ignorant about who these individuals were or where had they come from. They had no idea about anything and were never able to arrest those who came from outside.

Despite the lack of resources and living underground, we were efficiently organized and effective. Loyal supporters kept us informed which helped Raqeeb and me to formulate our strategy. Shamim Alam remained our messenger and evaded arrest till the end.

I also maintained telephonic contact with outsiders. Telephones were not common in those days and only a few of our hosts had a connection and it entailed a great risk. I used to don a cap, wrap a scarf around myself, and walk through dark streets to an acquaintance's house. It was dangerous as the police had established checkpoints and searched incessantly for Raqeeb and me. During the movement our real strength was indeed communications. It was imperative to mobilize out of town supporters to prevent any prospect of running out of volunteers.

We had in place a well-coordinated system of receiving and

settling labourers, students, farmers, and journalists from outside town. Our members would offer their own or their friends' homes to the volunteers. On the appointed day, they would board buses to pre-determined locations to offer themselves up for arrest.

As mentioned earlier, these volunteers were backed by those of our colleagues who did not court arrest but expressed their solidarity with us. The police had begun to arrest them too. They included Mahmood Sham of *Mayar*, *Aman* photographer, Moinul Haq, Hassan Zaheer, assistant editor of *Razdan*, and, a student leader Aqil Lodhi (now an active lawyer).

As was expected, most of the owners of private newspapers opted for the path of shameful expediency and opportunism. The doors of official media were closed to us and to our press releases. News coverage by *Sadaqat*, *Hilal e-Pakistan*, *Aman*, and the weeklies *Al Fatah* and *Mayar* began irritating the government. That is why they were repeatedly targeted and penalized. Their declarations were cancelled under the PPO and security deposits were demanded from them. They were denied official advertisements and newsprint and were also restricted through press advisories. The active editors of these publications were also arrested.

When the movement ended, we discovered that the rightist journalists and traitors amongst us, while enjoying refreshments at the offices of Inter Services Public Relations, advised, 'Why have you not been able to arrest Ahfaz ur Rehman? He is the secretary of the Federal Action Committee of the PFUJ and knows everyone. He is employed by *Musawat*. His head is in the skies and he styles himself as 'Major'. His arrest is essential.' That piece of advice undoubtedly had an impact. Hassan Zaheer, Shamim Asghar, Altaf Siddiqui, and others were intensely tortured and asked a single question: 'Where is Ahfaz ur Rehman?'

They were strong men. In any event, what could they say? They didn't know by whereabouts. They were brutally beaten until they became unconscious. When they regained consciousness, the same question was repeated: 'Where is Ahfaz? Tell us and our car will drop you to your home.'

That was not all. In their search for me, they raided and harassed several of my friends' and relatives' homes, but in vain. Police went to my in-laws' house where my wife told them that I was not there. They barged in anyway in the face of resistance and they were not accompanied by women police.

They believed Ahfaz ur Rehman to be a cunning character, whose arrest would immediately bring the movement to its knees. It was wishful thinking on their part. Even if I had been arrested, the movement would have continued because every PFUJ member was a leader. The loyal comrades who organized the most important civil rights movement in Pakistan's history were after all trained by Minhaj Barna.

ARRESTS IN THE RAIN

It was 14 August when India was divided. A movement had succeeded and a new state was born. It was 14 August once again.

Maintaining the sanctity of that date, we took an interesting and important decision for the next batch of volunteers. We selected the Quaid's Mausoleum for them to court arrest. Two much respected colleagues, who were also members of this batch and had earlier suffered whiplashes in Lahore, were Ahmed Ali Alvi and Khawar Naeem Hashmi.

The police somehow got wind of our intentions. A heavy police contingent was deployed and every visitor to the mausoleum was checked. Our supporters reached there covertly and suddenly the entire venue resounded with slogans: 'Long Live Pakistan!'; 'Long Live the Quaid-e-Azam!'; 'Release Arrested Journalists, Labourers, Farmers, and Students!'; 'Restore the Freedom of the Press!'.

Saleem Shahid of *Imroz*, Multan; Mohammad Omar Meher

of the Sindhi Hari Committee; and, Abdul Fatah Memon of the Labour Federation, Larkana accompanied Alvi, who led them. He had just begun his speech when the police dashed up and surrounded him.

Iqbal Jafri, a young man who had endured severe lashings with a smile, was scheduled to court arrest six days later, i.e. 21 August. We are proud of him and Khawar Naeem Hashmi, Nasir Zaidi, and Masood Khan who will live in our hearts forever.

At the joint session of executive committees of the PFUJ and APNEC on 16 August, a public rally was announced which was to be held at Karachi Press Club. It was in support of our eight-point demands and in protest against extreme violence unleashed on our comrades. We wanted to tell the world about the raids on the homes of our colleagues, the harassment of their families, and the torture that they had been subjected to.

After the announcement of this public convention, 16 August became a symbol of fear for the authorities. In all probability, the press club was declared an enemy of the state. Police contingents and vehicles surrounded the club early in the morning; their formations resembling a battle order. Some reporters said the order was to 'crush them'.

The main entrance was also cordoned off. Police questioned and intimidated anyone entering or leaving the club and did their utmost to derail the convention. However, notwithstanding the hostilities, Zafar Rizvi, a PFUJ leader, presided over the rally. Several leaders addressed the gathering, including Zahid Hussain of Workers Organizing Committee, who is now a well-respected senior journalist. The most important thing was that the press club was full.

Police employed devious machinations to arrest the late Sabihuddin Ghosi, who was later elected president of the press club. He had gone underground. The informants amongst us told the authorities that it was he who had drafted our press releases, although this had been done by other colleagues. In any event, the news media was not permitted to print news about us. Warrants for his arrest were issued and the police tailed him, and raided several places to capture him but failed. Then they resorted to an underhand ruse. They raided his apartment late at night, harassed his family, and took his brother into custody. Their parting threat was that if Ghosi did not show up, the entire family would be thrown in jail.

This was deplorable conduct. We were all prepared to undergo all manners of hardships but the mistreatment of families, especially women, was intolerable. Ghosi therefore presented himself for arrest at Regal Chowk on the morning of 17 August. Meanwhile, another active member, Ghulam Nabi Mughal, was arrested from the *Hilal-e-Pakistan* office on the basis of intelligence information by an informant.

What occurred on 18 August can be gathered from the following report in *Parbhaat* (Al Fatah Publications), in its issue of 25 September:

The warriors of journalism announced that they would offer themselves for arrest on 18 August at a major Imambargah in Kharadar area. It rained heavily that day and all the link roads were flooded. Regardless, large crowds had gathered to receive the crusading journalists. Police also strolled around anxiously. Because of the roadblocks, the Action Committee directed the backup batch of volunteers to court arrest at Regal Chowk. In the torrential downpour when the volunteers presented themselves for arrest at Regal Chowk, a huge mob built up, zealously shouting slogans. In the midst of all of that, Aziz Siddiqui, senior assistant editor of *Pakistan Times*; Ghulam Abbas of *Jang* (Quetta); Shafi Mohammad Kalhoro of the All Pakistan Workers Federation; and, Habibullah Panhwar of Larkana Labour Federation were taken into custody.

The times were in our favour, as we proclaimed:

Chain us, shackle us, whip us, lock us in dark dungeons, deprive us of livelihood, murder us economically and physically; we will not retreat. You must have discovered after using all your arsenal and oppressive tools that you cannot break our resolve, or defeat us. Your arrogance is destined to be squashed.

TWO MONTHS; 245 ARRESTS

The government had erroneously assumed that our movement would fizzle out in days. That did not happen. It not only survived but also garnered the support of all the freedom-loving segments of society. Several politicians advised the government to accept the journalists' demands but power and arrogance supervened, and oppression continued; however, we were steadfast. Press workers, the labour classes, and the unity of the students created a formidable bastion of resistance against oppression.

We continued to mobilize and organize the volunteers. Notwithstanding the need for caution, I was unable to resist the urge to see the arrests with my own eyes. On three or four occasions, with a cap on my head, a scarf over my shoulder, and wearing crumpled clothes, I ventured out to locations where volunteers offered themselves for arrest. However, the arrest of Hafeez Raqeeb, who followed at a distance, meant that at least one member of the Central Action Committee had been rounded up. I witnessed the energetic slogan-chanting volunteers with glowing faces and glittering eyes, and their passion and enthusiasm filled me with joy. Our faith in victory was reinforced. I always adopted covert methods to witness those memorable moments. Raqeeb was the only other person who was aware of this. I would decide the time of my expedition at the last moment. Had the volunteers or other supporters recognized me, it was possible that some inadvertent error could have jeopardized my freedom. They could have become emotional and begun chanting slogans which could have led the authorities to me.

Although these excursions were kept extremely secret, somehow Barna learnt of them and wrote a letter to us on 20 August which said:

Be very careful about your security. The locations of courting arrest should be filled with as many sympathizers as possible from amongst the students, labourers, and newspaper workers, so that in case the conservative elements create trouble, we should be able to respond in kind. However, those who are running the movement from underground should not go there.

We were all soldiers but we did not require weaponry. The melody of peace and songs of resolve were sufficient weapons to defeat the adversary. The press club was our centre but in the interest of caution my name was never mentioned there. My code name was 'Major' but I don't know who invented it. There were spies in the press club as well, who informed on us. I was caught unawares once. Raqeeb and I were staying at the home of Kaiser Hasni in North Nazimabad (courtesy, senior journalist Mohammad Ali Siddiqui), and Irshad Rao was to meet me to convey an important message. We suspected that the *Al Fatah* telephones were being tapped. He was only told that we were in Nazimabad. He had the number and called me one night.

'How are you, Major?' After some trivial exchanges about family and other things, he said, 'Long time no see. We should meet.'

'Alright ...'

'OK then, Hassan, see you ...'. I could not understand why I had suddenly become 'Hassan'.

'I don't understand ...' I said.

'Hey, buddy ... Hassan ... Hussain ... Hassan ...'

Suddenly, 'Al Hassan Coffee House' flashed in my mind. It was a popular cafe located in the vicinity. I reached there at the appointed time but we did not enter the coffee house. We spoke to each other in a street close by.

Iqbal Jafri, who had been whipped in Lahore, was among those courting arrest on 21 August. The morale was still high. The following day our very likeable friend, Hamraz Ahsan (famous journalist and writer from Lahore, who moved to London afterwards), and Zia Awan of Progressive Students Alliance, Karachi University, were also there.

Habib Khan Ghori was secretary of Karachi Press Club and preceded me as the general secretary of the PFUJ. He was an important figure and it was necessary for him to court arrest as an inspiration for others and indeed, his house had already been raided. It was best for him to be arrested in public rather than in private in a cloak and dagger operation. I sent him a message through Shamim Alam and he courted arrest on 25 August after prayers at the Jamia Masjid, Saddar.

Police brutality was intensifying by the day. Their men would jump on our colleagues, and punch and kick them before herding them into vans. Many were seriously injured. A prominent example of street violence was the case of Mohammad Zahid of PPI, a journalist from Bahawalpur. Zahid was a stout youngster. He was arrested in early August and could have returned to Bahawalpur if he had wished so. That notwithstanding, he again offered himself for arrest on 13 August. This time, he was mercilessly bloodied by torture and forced to sign a damaging statement. Senior journalist Habib-ur-Rehman, senior vice chairman of APNEC, Peshawar was also arrested twice. This was the passion and commitment which served and spurred the movement. When such news reached other cities, it boosted the spirits of our colleagues there and motivated them to volunteer and join us in Karachi.

By the end of August, 186 newspaper workers, labourers, and

students had been arrested. During that period, rumours began circulating that some pragmatic official circles were trying to persuade the martial law rulers to negotiate with the genuine representatives of the press workers because they sensed our determination and solidarity. Those who supported this included important names such as Ghous Bakhsh Bizenjo, Asghar Khan, Akbar Bugti, Shah Ahmed Noorani, Sher Mohammad Marri, Meraj Mohammad Khan, and Begum Bhutto. The most important statement came from the head of Qaumi Ittehad, Mufti Mahmood, who pressed the government to reinstate the sacked journalists and press workers of the National Press Trust, and paved the way for talks with the genuine leaders of journalists.

The PFUJ's secretary general, Nisar Usmani, welcomed the proposal and announced that they had been in favour of talks and stood by that policy from the outset. This development baffled the opportunistic segment of journalists who were threatened with the prospect of going out of business. They were said to have mobbed Mufti Mahmood.

The reigns of the martial law government were in the hands of Jamaat-e-Islami, and the traitors who had their full backing were set on convincing the government not to hold talks with the 'Barna Group'.

Anyhow, the government realized the reality of the situation and the strength of this faction, and so began looking for ways to extricate itself from the pressure they were exerting. As the snow was beginning to melt on the mountain peaks, initial contacts were made with Nisar Usmani.

The heat of the battle in the plains continued. Karachi was in the grips of an intense confrontation. On 11 September, some more journalists courted arrest in the Chakiwara area. This batch comprised Sher Afgan and Mahmood Zaman of *Musawat*, Lahore; Salman Lund of the Sindhi Hari Committee; and, Asifa Rizvi of the Mazdoor Kissan Tulaba Rabita Committee.

The late Asifa was a courageous and determined woman. She was always at the forefront of every battle in defense of democratic values. She, along with Hamida Ghanghro, waged an epic struggle in Patfeeder Kissan Tehreek. They were probably the first Sindhi women to be arrested in any Balochistan movement and were incarcerated in Machh Jail.

The 'proud' police came to Chakiwara in 16 trucks, accompanied by 10 Suzukis of their colleagues in civvies. They were armed with tear gas and guns. They were abusive towards the crowd that had gathered to welcome the journalists. The crowd became infuriated very soon and began pelting stones after which many were arrested.

On 12 September, volunteers and their supporters were subjected to a brutal assault in the Kulry Lyari neighborhood. The mob was ruthlessly tear-gassed and subjected to a baton-charge. Samuel Masih, a *Musawat* photographer, was severely beaten up. Forty people, including Siddique Raho of the Sindhi Hari Committee, were rounded up. Some were immediately sentenced to a year-long rigorous imprisonment and 10 lashes in summary military courts.

On the 55th day of the movement, Lee Market became the venue for courting arrest. This batch included Rahim Bux Jatoi (*Imroz*, Multan), Khalil Khatri (SNSF), and Abdul Salam Unnar (Sindhi Hari Committee). Police reached the venue six hours beforehand. A heavy force of plainclothesmen surrounded the entire area. Our batch of volunteers was seized before they could get out of their taxi, herded into police vehicles, and transferred to the jail. This brought the number of arrested volunteers to 245.

The ranks of the volunteers began shrinking. I was in touch with Barna. When the situation became difficult, I considered it necessary to inform him. With a dull heart, I sent him a message saying: 'The supply line is thinning out … May I court arrest in a couple of days?' I had no idea what Barna would decide after receiving my message. The next day it became evident.

A LIST OF THOSE IMPRISONED

Let's pause here for a moment and glance at the list of those who made sacrifices for this unparalleled movement. This is not a complete list of journalists, labourers, farmers, and students who courted arrest but mentions the batches up to 12 September, according to the 15 September issue of the weekly *Zulfiqar* (Al Fatah Publications). There might be discrepancies in dates and details.

18 July 1978
1. Minhaj Barna, *Pakistan Times*, Karachi.
2. Rahim Bux Jatoi, Sub-Editor, *Imroz*, Multan.
3. Zahid Sammoon, Sub-Editor, *Aftab*, Hyderabad.
4. Kaiser Mehmood Butt, Representative, *Itemad*, Quetta.
5. Ahmed Khalid, Sub-Editor, *Musawat*, Lahore.

19 July 1978
6. Amir Ahmed Khan, President, Sun Employees Union, Karachi.
7. Zafar Alam Sarwar, Sub-Editor, *Pakistan Times*, Rawalpindi.
8. Agha Bakar, Sub-Editor, *Tameer*, Rawalpindi.
9. Achhi Memon, Representative, *Musawat*, Larkana.

20 July 1978
10. Hashmat Wafa, Sub-Editor, *Imroz*, Multan.
11. Ali Rizwan, Newspapers Employees Union, Faisalabad.
12. Waheed Baghi, *Hayat*, Lahore.
13. Shabbir Husain, *Musawat*, Karachi.

21 July 1978
14. Amjad Sultan, *Musawat*, Lahore.
15. Hassan Jatoi, Sub-Editor, *Aftab*, Hyderabad.

16. Urs Mallah, General Secretary, Hilal-e-Pakistan Employees Union, Karachi.
17. Omar Farooq, *Musawat*, Lahore.

22 July 1978

18. Zubair Ahsan, *Musawat*, Lahore.
19. Masood Ahmed, President, Jang Employees Union, Quetta.
20. Tahir Najmi, General Secretary, Aman Employees Union, Karachi.
21. Agha Arbab, General Secretary, Faisalabad Union of Journalists.

23 July 1978

22. Mushtaq Shah, President, Sadaqat Employees Union, Karachi.
23. Talib Rizvi, *Musawat*, Lahore.
24. Sabah-ud-Din Saba, *Musawat*, Karachi.
25. Mohammad Soomro, Representative, *Musawat*.

24 July 1978

26. Shabbar Azmi, Sub-Editor, *Musawat*, Karachi.
27. Iftikhar Ahmed, *Musawat*, Lahore.
28. Mohammad Ayub, *Azad*, Lahore.
29. Faqeer Mohammad Shahid, *Musawat*, Karachi.

25 July 1978

30. Noor Mohammad Noor, *Jang*, Quetta.
31. Abdul Rehman, Jawaid Press, Karachi.
32. Sikandar Ali Rind, President, Shah Karim Press Club.

27 July 1978

33. Rana Naz Iqbal, Lahore.
34. Zeeshan Ahmed, *Sun*, Karachi.

35. Nisar Ahmed, Shahdadpur Union of Journalists.
36. Ahmed Ilyas Abro, Sanghar.

30 July 1978
37. Wali Mohammad Wajid, Chief Reporter *Imroz*, Multan, Assistant Secretary General, APNEC.
38. Rashid Abbasi, President, APNEC, Peshawar.
39. Sardar Qureshi, Sub-Editor, *Hilal-e-Pakistan*, Karachi.
40. Ghulam Rabani, *Musawat*, Lahore.
41. Manzoor Husain, Awami Rabta Committee.
42. Insaar Baig, Government College, Nazimabad.

31 July 1978
43. Qalandar Bukhsh, Muttahida Mazdoor Federation.
44. Akram Qaimkhani, National Students' Federation.
45. Rehman Anjana, *Musawat*, Lahore.
46. Maulana Bukhsh Bhutto, Sukkur.
47. Habib-ur-Rehman, Vice Chairman, APNEC, Peshawar.

2 August 1978
48. Nasir Zaidi, *Nawa-e-Multan*, Multan.
49. Rehman Shah, *Musawat*, Lahore.
50. Bashir Bhatti, *Aala 101*, Sukkur.
51. Abdul Karim, *Sun*, Karachi.
52. Ali Mohammad Sadhu, Sindhi Haari Committee.
53. Saeed Ashraf Khan, Dow Medical College, NSF.
54. Ismail Fedra, Pakistan Workers' Federation.

4 August 1978
55. Jabbar Khattak, Sind National Students' Federation.
56. Masood Qamar, *Aman*, Faisalabad.
57. Ghulam Rasool, Sub-Editor, *Aftab*, Hyderabad.
58. Ghulam Nabi Rumani, *Nijaat*, Sukkur.

59. Malik Akbar, Mazdoor Tanzeemi Committee.
60. Mohammad Suleiman Lundd, Sindhi Haari Committee.
61. Mohammad Riaz Bhatti, *Musawat*, Lahore.

5 August 1978

62. Johar Mir, Member, Action Committee, Peshawar.
63. Abdul Waheed Sheikh, *Musawat*, Lahore.
64. Mohammad Yusuf Soomroo, *Aftab*, Hyderabad.
65. Mohammad Sarwar, Sub-Editor, *Musawat*, Karachi.
66. Kaleem Durrani, *Noujawan Mahaaz*, Karachi.
67. Baseer Khaaskheeli, Sindhi Haari Committee.

6 August 1978

68. Wahab Siddiqui, Editor, *Al Fatah*, Karachi.
69. Hout Laghari, Reporter, *Ibrat*, Hyderabad.
70. Mohammad Ghulam Jatoi, Representative, *Hilal-e-Pakistan*, Sukkur.
71. Mohammad Azeem, *Musawat*, Lahore.
72. Malik Haq Nawaz, Mazdoor Tanzeemi Committee.
73. Yaqoob Khorro, Sindhi Haari Committee.

7 August 1978

74. Rana Nayar Iqbal, *Musawat*, Lahore.
75. Nadeem Chishti, Sub-Editor, *Afaq*, Lahore.
76. Abdul Sattar Bhatti, *Hilal-e-Pakistan*, Karachi.
77. Mehboob Ahmed, Representative, *Al Fatah*, Mirpurkhas.
78. Shaukat Ali Palejo, Sindhi Haari Committee.
79. Ishaq Sulangee, NSF.

8 August 1978

80. Jawaid Siddiqui, Faisalabad Union of Journalists.
81. Rana Muhammad Rafiq, *Musawat*, Lahore.
82. Munir-ul-Deen Baber, Sub-Editor, *Musawat*, Lahore.

83. Rauf Bhatti, Makran.
84. Zubeir Rehman, Mazdoor Kissan Student Committee.
85. Abdul Razzaq Khusq, Sindhi Student Party.

9 August 1978
86. Altaf Malak, Reporter, *Musawat*, Lahore.
87. Riaz Muhammad Raza, *Musawat*, Faisalabad.
88. Fareed Khan, *Sun*, Karachi.
89. Siraj Ahmed, *Musawat*, Karachi.
90. Pir Baksh Karmati, Sindhi Haari Committee.
91. Abdul Khaliq, SNSF.

10 August 1978
92. Shakeel Qaisar, Sun Workers Union, Lahore.
93. Masood Qamar, Faisalabad Union of Journalists.
94. Noor Muhammad, Karachi.
95. Ali Muhammad Bhava, Sindhi Haari Committee.
96. Shafi Muhammad Kalhoro, United Workers Federation.

11 August 1978
97. Nasir Zaidi, *Al Fatah*, Multan.
98. Mehboob Ali, Sub-Editor, *Siyasat*, Bahawalpur.
99. Baseer Naveed, Sub-Editor, *Sadaqat*, Karachi.
100. Noor Muhammad Baloch, NSF.
101. Salah Muhammad Bhao, Sindhi Haari Committee.

12 August 1978
102. Mujahid Barelvi, Sub-Editor, *Mayar*, Karachi.
103. Qaisar Mehmood Butt, *Aitmaad*, Quetta.
104. Rafique Ahmed Chaudhry, Sun Workers Union, Lahore.
105. Muhammad Younus Memon, Mazdoor Tanzeemi Committee.
106. Allah Deeno, Sindhi Haari Committee.
107. Yusuf Zardan, SNSF.

13 August 1978

108. Ali Muhammad Khan, *Sun*, Karachi

109. Muhammad Zahid, PPI, Bahawalpur.

110. Shaukat Hussein, *Musawat*, Lahore.

111. Yusuf Lashari, Sindhi Haari Committee.

112. Muhammad Dawood, *Naujawan Mahaz*.

14 August 1978

113. Ahmed Ali Alvi, President, Jang Employees' Union.

114. Khawar Naeem Hashmi, *Musawat*, Lahore.

115. Saleem Shahid, *Imroz*, Multan.

116. Muhammad Umer Mehr, Sindhi Haari Committee.

117. Abdul Fateh Memon, Larkana Mazdoor Federation.

15 August 1978

118. Hassan Sangrami, *Musawat*, Karachi.

119. Somar, *Musawat*, Interior Sindh.

120. Ayub Azad, Lahore.

121. Ismail Udaasi, Sindhi Haari Committee.

122. Noor Khan, Muttahida Mazdoor Federation.

16 August 1978

123. Agha Arbab, *Roznama Gharib*, Faisalabad.

124. Muhammad Irfan, *Dawat-e-Amal*, Gujranwala.

125. Abdul Ghani Dars, *Ibrat*, Hyderabad.

126. Muhammad Ali Baloch, Larkana Mazdoor Federation.

127. Ali Murad Khoro, Progressive Sindh Federation.

17 August 1978

128. Habib-ur-Rehman, Senior Vice Chairman, APNEC, Peshawar.

129. Muhammad Siddique, Assistant General Secretary, Jang Employees' Union, Karachi.
130. Sabihuddin Ghosi, Reporter, PPI, Karachi.
131. Hussein Baksh, Sindhi Haari Committee.
132. Gul Muhammad Khushk, Sindhi Student Tehreek.

18 August 1978
133. Aziz Ahmed Siddiqui, Senior Assistant Editor, *Pakistan Times*, Lahore.
134. Abbas Ghulam, *Jang*, Quetta.
135. Shafi Muhammad, Workers' Federation.
136. Habibullah Panhoor, Larkana Mazdoor Federation.

19 August 1978
137. Jameel Ashraf Mulk, Sub-Editor, *Musawat*, Karachi.
138. Muhammad Khan, *Hilal-e-Pakistan*, Karachi.
139. Ali Gohar, Larkana Labour Federation.
140. Muhammad Ahmed Rizvi, NSF, Karachi.

20 August 1978
141. Jehanzaib, Sub-Editor, *Musawat*, Karachi.
142. Tahir Awan, Representative, *Al Fatah*, Lahore.
143. Ghulam Mustafa Bhutto, All Pakistan Cement Union Federation.
144. Murad Hussein, Sindhi Haari Committee.

21 August 1978
145. Iqbal Jafri, *Sun*, Karachi.
146. Masood Suleiman, *Musawat*, Lahore.
147. Jan Alam, NSF.
148. Rahim Hussein, Sindhi Haari Committee.

22 August 1978

149. Humraz Ahsan, Reporter, PPL Union, Lahore.
150. Aziz Ahmed Khan, *Musawat*, Karachi.
151. Zia Awan, Progressive Students Alliance, University of Karachi.
152. Muhammad Siddique Channa Ismail, Sindhi Haari Committee.

23 August 1978

153. Muhammad Masoom, *Musawat*, Lahore.
154. Anwar Ai, *Musawat*, Lahore.
155. Laluaqlani, Sindhi Haari Committee.
156. Saleem Baloch, NSF, Karachi.

24 August 1978

157. Ibadat Shah, *Musawat*, Lahore.
158. Muhammad Rafique Akhter, *Musawat*, Lahore.
159. Khaleeq Panhoor, Sindhi Haari Committee.
160. Ahmed Ali Soomro, NPSF, Larkana.

25 August 1978

161. Habib Khan Ghori, Secretary, Karachi Press Club.
162. Muhammad Saleem Sindhi, Representative, *Mayar*, Larkana.
163. Muhammad Hanif Soomro, NPSF, Larkana.

26 August 1978

164. Moosa Tair, President, Hilal-e-Pakistan Employees Union, Karachi.
165. Abdul Bari Khan, *Naujawan Mahaz*.
166. Muhammad Jaffer Haqwani, Sindhi Haari Committee.

27 August 1978

167. Meer Basheer Ahmed, *Musawat*, Lahore.

168. Muhammad Ali, *Musawat*, Lahore.
169. Wajeeh-ud-din, President, NSF.
170. Muhammad Suleiman, Sindhi Haari Committee

28 August 1978
171. Nasreen Zahra, NSF.
172. Muhammad Ismail, *Musawat*, Lahore.
173. Javed Akhter, *Musawat*, Lahore.
174. Deeno Shahani, Sindhi Haari Committee.

29 August 1978
175. Khursheed Anwar, Secretary, Musawat Employees Union, Karachi.
176. Yaar Muhammad Chandio, Representative, *Manama Tehreek*.
177. Ismail Hamiri, Sindhi Haari Committee, Badin.
178. Abdul Rasool, *Sindhi Shagird Tehreek*.

30 August 1978
179. Prof. Adil Bhatti, Sub-Editor, *Roznama Tameer*, Rawalpindi.
180. Muhammad Moosa Machee, Sindhi Haari Committee.
181. Saleem Balouch, NSF, Karachi.
182. Rafique Akhter, *Musawat*, Lahore.

31 August 1978
183. Abrar Rizvi, *Musawat*, Rawalpindi.
184. Muhammad Arif, Senior Sub-Editor, *Musawat*, Lahore.
185. Masood Anwar Palejo, Sindhi Shagird Committee.
186. Gul Mohammad Chandio, Sindhi Haari Committee.

2 September 1978
187. Zafar Ujan, Editor, *Awaz*, Karachi.
188. Raees Ahmed, *Musawat*, Karachi.

189. Abdul Hameed Farooqui, Secretary, Democratic Students Federation.
190. Muharram Meer Jannat, Sindhi Haari Committee.

3 September 1978

191. Muhammad Ejaz Butt, *Siyasat*, Jarawala.
192. Abdul Aleem, *Tehreek*.

4 September 1978

193. Syed Muhammad Sufi, Sub-Editor, *Musawat*, Karachi.
194. Ghazi Muhammad Ishaq Arabi, Representative, *Musawat*, Gujrat.
195. Shakeel Ahmed Paan, President, NSF, Hyderabad.
196. Khuda Bakhsh Rind, Sindhi Haari Committee.

5 September 1978

197. Masood Qamar, Representative, *Dawat-e-Amal*, Faisalabad.
198. Ibrahim, Sindhi Haari Committee.
199. Ali Muhammad, Student.
200. Jam, Sindhi Haari Committee.

6 September 1978

201. Abu Nasr Mulk, Staff Reporter, *Mashriq*, Karachi.
202. Ali Muhammad, Sindhi Haari Committee.
203. Sadiq Jar Choye, NSF.

7 September 1978

204. Ali Muhammad Jaat, *Tehreek*, Hyderabad.
205. Ali Muhammad Khan Kerani, Sindhi Haari Committee.

8 September 1978

206. Abdul Lateef Soomro, *Hilal-e-Pakistan*.
207. Altaf Ismail, SNSF.

208. Muhammad Baksh Rao, Sindhi Haari Committee.

9 September 1978
209. Rahim Bux Jatoi, Sub-Editor, *Imroz*, Lahore.
210. Abdul Qadir, Sindhi Haari Committee.
211. Khalil Khatri, SNSF, Sindh Medical College, Karachi.

10 September 1978
212. Muhammad Illyas Lakho, *Hilal-e-Pakistan*.
213. Muhammad Ali Sudu, Sindhi Haari Committee.

11 September 1978
214. Sher Afgan, Sub-Editor, *Musawat*, Lahore.
215. Suleiman Londh, Sindhi Haari Committee.

12 September 1978
216. Muhammad Zama, Reporter, *Musawat*, Lahore.
217. Asifa Rizvi, Mazdoor Kissan Talba Raabta Committee.
218. Siddiqi Rahu, Sindhi Haari Committee

In addition to these, about 40 persons were arrested in Kalri, Lyari for supporting the movement for freedom of the press, and these included non-volunteers. Wahab Siddiqui, Hassan Zaheer, Shehzad Chughtai, Moeen-ul-Haq, and Mehmood Sham were arrested while performing their duties at the arrest venues. Raja Hassan, Ameer Mohammad Rajpar, Nisar Ali, and Aqil Lodhi were arrested for their 'presence at the protest venue'.

The names of those arrested under Martial Law Order 12 are as follows.

1. Mehmood Ali Asad, General Secretary, Jang Employees Union.
2. Mehmood Sham, Chief Editor, weekly *Mayar*, Karachi.
3. Ashraf Shad, Executive Editor, weekly *Mayar*, Karachi.

4. Riaz Ahmed, General Secretary, Javed Press, Karachi.
5. Mrs Lalarukh Hussain, *Sun*, Karachi.
6. Moosa Jee Deepak, General Secretary, Pakistan Herald Workers Union.
7. Ghulam Nabi Mughal, reporter, *Hilal-e-Pakistan*, Karachi.
8. Shamim Asghar, Labour Organizing Committee, Landhi, Karachi.

These are the so-called miscreants, the enemies of the state, and the traitors whose voice was suppressed by using extraordinarily violent measures but history has reviled tyranny and honoured truth.

LONGING TO SOAR: AN URGE FOR MARTYRDOM

Gentle, playful sunlight filtered into the prison cell. It was one of those days when the great decisions which determined the course of history were made.

As I mentioned earlier, I wrote and informed Barna that the supply line for volunteers was thinning out and we needed to do something about it. The very next day, Barna announced that he would undertake a fast unto death. This announcement filled the press workers with enthusiasm and raised the spirit of all in Pakistan who treasured democratic values. However, it unnerved the government but those opposed to the strike continued to maintain that the hunger strike would make no difference.

In Khairpur Jail, Amir Mohammad Khan and Ishaq Solangi declared that they too would go on a hunger strike unto death in support of Barna's. Such action then spread to other jails.

Barna had announced that he would commence his indefinite hunger strike from 9 September but at the appeal of Nisar Usmani and other members of the Action Committee, it was postponed in order to give the government time to consider the implications.

The government however believed the delay to be an indication of weakness on the journalists' part. Barna's strike unto death began on 20 September.

From Khairpur Jail, Barna had despatched a letter to the president and chief martial law administrator, Zia ul-Haq, in which he wrote: 'It has now become clear as daylight that the government is being openly obstinate. It wants to suppress through violence the just movement of journalists which is fully supported by workers, students, and the enlightened public.' He also referred to the partiality of the minister for information who, a few days earlier had proposed a meeting with the fake PFUJ representative on the official media. In conclusion, he wrote: 'My hunger strike will continue until all our demands are met.'

The detention of Barna and Ameer was extended for another month. The day Barna began his hunger strike, the crusaders of journalism courted arrest at Sindhi Hotel (New Karachi). Their morale was sky high.

It is important to relate an event of 19 September at the Bahawalpur Press Club to fully expose the machinations of the traitors. The brave journalist of Bahawalpur, Mohammad Zahid, who had been brutally tortured while in jail, was being lured by the coterie of traitors. They had even published a fictitious statement allegedly by Zahid in their favour. Zahid's speech was published the following day in *Musawat*, Karachi, in which he said: 'The torture has further raised my morale.' He highly commended Barna and condemned the traitors. 'Minhaj Barna, Nisar Usmani, and Ahfaz ur Rehman are our real leaders. They have always raised their voice for truth and righteousness. They can go to the gallows but under no circumstances can they compromise over the interests of journalist community.'

On 19 September, we received the sad news concerning our brave colleague, Nasir Zaidi, who endured a nine-month prison sentence plus five lashes for his participation in the Lahore movement.

He was in Sukkur jail and was very ill. As he was suffering from cataracts, doctors had to bandage his eyes. His mother had to go through many problems to obtain permission to visit him. When she saw her son in that condition, she fainted. Two days later, an important member of the movement, a staff reporter of *Musawat*, Karachi was captured.

Notwithstanding these shocks, the valiant activists of the PFUJ and APNEC marched forward courageously under Barna's leadership. Now, numerous prisoners in Sindh jails, including journalists, farmers, and students also joined the fast unto death. This phenomenon spread across six jails, from Khairpur to Karachi. The strikers were thrown into unlit cells with a small quantity of water. Straw-fans were snatched from them and electricity was switched off. Our comrades illuminated the dark cells with the glow of their resolve.

The government propaganda accelerated with the launching of hunger strikes. A shameless press note was issued by the Sindh government which denied the ongoing hunger strikes. In response, the People's Action Committee issued a proclamation which termed the press note a falsehood and an indication of the failure of the government. On 22 Septmber, Hafeez Raqeeb, secretary general of the APNEC and a member of the Central Action Committee, who had been underground with me, published a statement in the newspapers to the following effect: 'The government has imposed a confrontation on journalists. There is no possibility of improvement in the situation until the government restores the terminated journalists and press workers, and releases those arrested during the movement for freedom of the press, including labourers, farmers, students, and intellectuals.'

CANDLES OF RESOLVE AMIDST DARKNESS

They were dark little cells infested by flies during the day and by mosquitoes at night.

Barna and Ishaq Solangi's condition was deteriorating. A period of 120 hours had passed since the beginning of the hunger strike. No one was allowed near their cell. Khairpur Central Jail doctors sent a report to the authorities stating that Barna's pulse was abnormally fast and he had become weak. Solangi's condition was bad too and he was experiencing fainting spells.

In Karachi Jail, the condition of Riaz Mohammad Raza, Habib-ur-Rehman, Zia Awan, Qaiser Butt, Jan-e-Alam, and Rab Dino Chang was also critical but they did not receive medical facilities. Similarly, in Sukkur Jail, Javed Siddiqui and Johar Mir were also reported to be in very poor health. The headline in the 23 September edition of *Musawat*, Karachi screamed: '72 Hours of Fast until Death, Barna Lost Weight!'

The report stated that despite their physical weakness, their morale was high. Barna said in a message: 'God willing, the truth will soon be victorious. Our procession has reached its destination. We have only been locked in dark cells; we are ready even to be hanged because our struggle is for the glory of the pen.'

In view of Barna and his companions' weakening health, the PPP general secretary of Khairpur district pleaded that the government immediately accept the demands of the journalists. As anticipated, the request fell on deaf ears.

Our colleagues in Sukkur Jail were also fasting till death. The action was spearheaded by Shabbar Azmi, Javed Siddiqui, and Johar Mir. Later Sabahuddin Saba and Wahab Siddiqui joined them. The jail administration did its utmost to conceal this but the news leaked out.

When the hunger strike entered its fourth day, the number of those fasting unto death in Karachi had reached 14. Zia Awan,

Rabdino Chang, Rahim Bux Jatoi, Jamil Malik, Iqbal Jafri, Adil Bhatti, and Ali Mohammad Mallah joined those who had begun fasting with Barna on the 20th. Soon, this number was going to rise.

A SPATE OF UNCEASING RAIDS

The police were raiding numerous places in search of me. The press club and the *Musawat* offices were under tight surveillance. Their informants were scattered throughout the city but were continually unsuccessful. On a couple of occasions, they raided a hideout just after we had fled. It later emerged that they showed a *Musawat* clip bearing a photograph of me to various shopkeepers and asked if they had seen this 'criminal'. Back then, I was living in Federal B Area, where they conducted a search. They also raided my sister's home in Mehmoodabad, several old friends' places of residence, and also questioned other relatives.

My in-laws lived in North Nazimabad where my wife, Mehnaz, was temporarily staying. They carried out a raid there, searched the place, but found nothing. In reality it was just a formality because they were aware that I was not there. Interestingly, this incident was reported in the 24 September 1978 edition of *Musawat*.

Meanwhile, editors and senior journalists from over 25 national newspapers and magazines issued a collective statement in which they expressed concern about the ongoing fast unto death strike undertaken by Minhaj Barna and his colleagues. They appealed to the chief martial law administrator for immediate intervention to resolve the underlying causes for this hunger strike. Criticizing the administration's attitude in their statement, they rejected the view that the movement had political motives and said that none of the demands were political. In their statement they also appealed to Barna and his colleagues to end the hunger strike, and to create a conducive environment in which the government would consider their demands.

Prominent signatories of the statement were: Basheer Ahmed Rana (*Sadaqat*, Karachi); S. G. M. Badruddin (*Musawat*, Lahore); Khalid Alig (*Musawat*. Karachi); Ameenuddin (*Ailan*, Karachi); Afzal Siddiqui (*Aman*, Karachi); Basheer-ul-Islam Usmani (*Tameer*, Rawalpindi); Fazal Adeeb (*Jurrat*, Rawalpindi); Rashid Zaidi (former editor *Hurriyat*, Karachi); Shaukat Siddiqui (distinguished author and journalist); Dr Feroz Ahmed (Pakistan Forum); Fahmida Riaz (monthly *Awaz*, Karachi); Dr Ahmed Hussain Kamal (*Qiadat*, Hyderabad); Wahid Basheer (*Al Fatah*, Karachi); Shehnaz Ahad (*Mayar*, Karachi); Rasul Bakhsh Palijo (*Tehreek*, Hyderabad); Mahmood Javed, Hussain Naqi, Mussarat Jabeen (former editor *Akhbar-e-Khawateen*); Zaheer Kaashmiri (distinguished journalist and poet); Abdul Waheed Khan (distinguished journalist); and, Ajmal Dehlvi (editor *Aman*, Karachi).

In the meantime, numerous writers, poets, and intellectuals also issued a joint statement expressing deep concern that due to pressure exerted and misleading advice given by certain elements with vested interests, the long-drawn protests for the rightful demands of journalists were not being addressed. Instead, a policy to crush them is being pursued, which is inappropriate and inhumane. It is the duty of the government to address and resolve the issues raised by any segment of the society without making it an issue of pride or ego. They went on to demand that the government, without further ado, should accept the demands of journalists and press workers, release those under arrest, and immediately reinstate the Press Trust employees who had been fired. The signatories of this joint statement were: Shaukat Siddiqui, Sultana Meher, Mohammad Ali Siddiqui, Farhad Zaidi, Sibte Hassan, Shafi Aqeel, Hassan Abidi, Prof. Mumtaz Hussain, Shahzad Manzar, Syed Anwer, Hameed Kashmiri, Pekar Naqvi, Wahid Basheer, Rasheed Patel, Hassan Abid, Mohammad Saeed, Afsar A'zar, Ghazi Salahuddin, Ijaz Rahi,

Haji Adeel, Naqash Kazmi, Rafiq Chaudhry, Fehmida Riaz, Khalid Alig, Qamar Abbas Naeem, Iqbal Mehdi, Abu Zia Iqbal, Gohar Taj, Kaif Siddiqui, Saeeda Gazwar, Anwer Sen Roy, Naeem Arvi, and Anupa Hyder.

The statement of the CPNE, an association of newspaper editors, was encouraging but their appeal to end the hunger strike unilaterally was not acceptable. Barna responded, 'It would have been more appropriate for the president of the CPNE, Mohammad Ahmed Zuberi, to press the government to withdraw its arbitrary measures that forced the journalists into the struggle.'

By the end of September, our movement would have completed two and a half months. We had to suffer all kinds of hardships and difficulties during this period. At the time of the CPNE appeal, there were over 250 journalists, workers, and students in jail. It would have been so much better had they shown greater resolve and courage. However, like the newspaper owners body, APNS, the editors association also yielded to expediency. The autonomy of the APNS had also gone because all the owners had become editors and controlled both the organizations. The institution of independent editors had just vanished.

A few days after Barna's hunger strike began, the Joint Action Committee and People's Struggle Committee announced a drop in volunteer arrests and the beginning of protest rallies.

On 24 September, on behalf of the movement I announced, 'Journalists will not beg the government out of frustration. The movement will succeed with the support and backing of the people. The preachers of oppression, lies, and injustice will face defeat.' As the secretary general of the Action Committee, I appealed to all segments of the population: 'At this critical historic moment, please fulfil your responsibilities by carrying forward the sacred struggle of the APNEC and PFUJ which aims at promoting democratic principles in this unfortunate country. The government is set on being obstinate due to which our colleagues are compelled to resort to fasts unto death. A regressive ruling party has closed all doors to mutual dialogue.' The government was also warned in this statement: 'Don't be optimistic; we are fighting for basic rights and the ultimate victory is ours.'

Why was I so confident that we would succeed? Several reasons can be given but I would like to stress only one: the movement was backed by the resolve from which it sprang and which drove it. That resolve was our ultimate weapon.

This message was received from Karachi Central Jail by the incarcerated ladies, Begum Shafqat Tanveer Mirza and Farkhanda Bukhari (Lahore), and Asifa Rizvi and Nasreen Zehra (Karachi). They requested the APNEC and PFUJ Action Committee and People's Struggle Committee for permission to fast until death. They sought to keep pace with their brothers in arms. What passion and bravery!

EID IN JAIL

As Eid approached, some leaders of the National Alliance (NA) appealed to the government to release those imprisoned and to resolve the issue peacefully but the government was not willing. We celebrated Eid in various jails of Sindh. The government had presumed that the movement would fizzle out in a matter of days.

We however proved to be more resilient than they had expected and wore them down. On our part, we faced a difficulty too. Our numbers were small and therefore we were aware that we could not provide volunteers to court arrest for a considerable length of time.

Barna's hunger strike had lasted 224 hours on 29 September when he was covertly transferred to Sukkur Jail under the cover of darkness. They tried to keep the event secret but somehow we found out and the country as a whole learnt about it through the following day's newspapers. Before his transfer to Sukkur, Khairpur's deputy commissioner, Jamil Siddiqui, came to Barna's prison cell. He threatened Barna of the consequences of his not ending his fast and that if he didn't do so a glass of glucose would be forced down his throat. When Barna refused, the DC instructed the jail doctors to force-feed him. The resident doctor replied that given Barna's condition, using force could be lethal. The DC said, 'So be it. Let him die.'

Frail and emaciated, Barna argued in his characteristic style. 'Kindly do not exceed your authority. According to the jail manual, the final decision about force-feeding rests with the medical officer. You should fulfil your responsibilities rather than meddling with those of others.' He also said he would write to the home secretary about the DC's action.

Barna had been under pressure to end his fast during the preceding days. A number of different officials visited him in his cell to persuade him. The DC retreated after the verbal confrontation. When Barna asked for paper and a pen to write to the home secretary, he was given excuses.

The day this incident occurred, Hamraz Ahsan, vice president of the Punjab Union of Journalists, and a certain Mohammad Ibrahim Soho, distinguished leader of the Sindhi Shagird Tehreek, began their fast unto death in Karachi Jail. This brought the number of those fasting-unto-death volunteers to 29 from 26.

Meanwhile, a Students' Action Committee was formed by the office-bearers of progressive student organizations in Karachi with the objective of offering effective and positive support to the struggle of the newspaper workers. The convener of the action committee, Qazi Abdul Ghani, held a press conference where he criticized the government's attitude and commended the journalists. He assured the journalists that progressive students would support the brave journalists in every way possible.

'SHOULD THEY DIE, SO BE IT!'

The first of October brought disturbing news. Barna had fainted. He was administered an IV drip but refused any form of medical assistance as soon as he regained consciousness. His weight had decreased by 25 lbs. We also began receiving news about the callous attitude adopted towards him. Naeem Arvi reported the situation in the 6 October issue of *Zulfiqar* (Al Fatah Publications):

> During the initial couple of days, he was locked in a small dark cell. Strict measures were taken to prevent anyone from meeting him. Human values were shredded by silence about his rapidly deteriorating condition. When his condition went out of control and he was unconscious, glucose was administered intravenously. When he regained consciousness, he pulled out the drip and said, 'Those who give their life for principles, are not afraid of death. Worshippers of truth are born in every era, who keep the flag of righteousness high and look into the eyes of death with a smile. We, the humble workers, will follow the footprints of our predecessors and write a new chapter of sacrifices with our blood.' Barna's other companions on hunger strike followed his example.

Even during that time of hardships, the band of traitors did not refrain from their scheming, although the government had become disenchanted with them and had discovered that a majority of the journalist community loathed and despised them. However, they enjoyed the complete patronage of the information minister, who was a member of JI. He refused to talk to the real PFUJ and APNEC representatives and was determined to crush them. One traitor commented on the hunger strike: 'It is good; the snake will be killed without breaking the stick.'

The band of traitors was infuriated by Mufti Mahmood's suggestion that discussions be held with the true representatives of journalists. He was so severely criticized for this that he quietly got himself admitted to a military hospital for toe surgery. In the meantime, the information minister met the PFUJ and APNEC journalists on his retainership and under the guise of a Third Wage Award, gave the impression that he was resolving the issue.

EIGHT OCTOBER: VICTORY AT LAST

It was a cold foggy day. A restlessness pervaded the streets with lengthening shadows of gloom as the thought of the demise of our colleagues afflicted everyone. In these circumstances, Usmani came to Karachi from Lahore and Raqeeb and I went to see him at the *Al Fatah* office where Irshad Rao was also present. We deliberated about all the issues before us. I suggested we prepare our last press release to commend and thank all the newspaper workers, labourers, and students while simultaneously announcing that in this last phase of the struggle, all three of us (Nisar Usmani, Hafeez Raqeeb, and I) would offer ourselves for arrest at Mazar-e-Quaid the following day. This press release would not signal the end of the movement. Our colleagues were still on hunger strike; the movement was ongoing but it would mean the end of the street protests. I drafted the press release.

Usmani disagreed with me but I did not insist. Later it was revealed that a well-known bureaucrat and intellectual, Yousuf Jamal, had contacted Usmani on behalf of the government and talks were about to commence. Our fasting colleagues' condition was deteriorating by the day. I have already mentioned what the traitors wished; we for our part were not scared but extremely concerned about the fate of our colleagues. In those circumstances, there arose a significant question: could we abandon Barna and our other colleagues to the mercy of murderers?

We also heard that the government had prepared for talks

when Barna began his hunger strike. Some even claimed that the government had begun to consider talks when our movement left the press club and took to the streets in August but Rasheed Siddiqui and company had come in its way. They were afraid that if Barna came out of jail, they would be abandoned by whatever small number of people they had succeeded in gathering around themselves. They therefore pleaded vigorously that no talks be held with the 'Barna Group'. However, when the hunger strike crossed its second week there was intense pressure on the Zia government from those wedded to democracy and a harsher tone was adopted by the international press. Some conciliatory government representatives contacted Usmani and Raqeeb. Eventually, an agreement was reached between the government and the Central Action Committee announcing the release of all detainees and the restoration of employment of the journalists whose services had been terminated. The radio broadcast regarding this included an appreciation and tribute by the Action Committee to the courageous struggle of the newspaper workers.

By that time the fast unto death protest had entered its eighteenth day, the condition of the volunteers was precarious. Barna, who was the oldest among them, was emaciated and in a semi-conscious state. All our hunger-striking colleagues continued to suffer the after-effects of their ordeal for a long time into the future.

The news brought a wave of jubilation for journalists throughout Pakistan. 8th October was the victory day. Our struggle had forced a dictator to his knees. In Lahore, he had tried the charade of negotiations with fake representatives but this time around, he was compelled to negotiate with and settle directly with our Action Committee. This was our greatest success.

We congratulated each other as all our demands were met. However, the government did not restore the employment of four individuals, including Barna's. The name of the other three had not been announced by then. Nevertheless, the eight-point demands, the foundation on which this great movement was launched, were accepted. This was a great success.

The helicopter of the Sindh martial law administrator, Major General Ahsan Abbasi, landed in the compound of Sukkur Jail. He met Barna, informed him about the agreement, and asked him to end the fast. I imagined the smiles and joy that that piece of news must have brought to the faces of the courageous strikers.

Looking back at those events today, I wonder how we were able to achieve all of that in the face of a brutal military dictatorship.

It had been a long battle divided in three phases (protracted war, to employ military terminology). The protesters began by courting arrest on 3 December 1977 in Karachi when Zia ul-Haq's dictatorial government had been in power for just four months. Then began the process of courting arrest in Lahore which extended from 30 April to 30 May 1977, and our colleagues imprisoned for a long time in eight Punjab jails were whipped and tortured and exiled from the province.

Only a month and a half later, a new front was opened in Karachi. For 84 days, the volunteers courted arrests in various areas of the city and were sent for incarceration to six Sindh jails. Again, they were subjected to hardship and torture but bore it with stoicism and idealism. Most senior journalists, intellectuals, brave young women, farmers, labourers, and students embraced our goals and shared our pain.

Our days of hiding were ending. I reached the press club and headed to Hyderabad from there. I had to inform my colleagues in Hyderabad Jail of the developments. I spent the night in the office of National Centre, the director of which, Johar Hussain, was delighted to see me. When he had been secretary general of the National Students Federation, I was a member of its executive committee.

'You guys have achieved wonders!' he said.

The following morning Ali Hassan, a senior journalist working for the BBC, accompanied me to Hyderabad Jail to convey the message to our colleagues.

The season of the return of the caged had begun!

A VICTOR'S SMILE

The morning of 13 October was brighter than usual. Energy infused Karachi's train station. Laughter echoed, colleagues embraced each other, and slogans were raised. It was a huge congregation of newspaper workers, students, farmers, and labourers. Every face beamed as the great leader of the movement for the freedom of press, Minhaj Barna, boarded the Chenab Express and was expected to shortly arrive in Karachi.

It was a lovely sight as everyone held flowers in their hands. Following Nisar Usmani's lead, we, the members of the executive committee, were there to receive Barna. Everyone's faces exuded happiness and satisfaction. The difficult times were not over but the anxiety had decreased.

Although, the railway officials had been informed, the others present wanted to know who was expected. At around 9 a.m., we sighted the Chenab Express. The station erupted with slogans the moment the train halted. 'We Live With You, We Die With You Minhaj Barna, Minhaj Barna!'; 'Long Live Leader of Journalism, Minhaj Barna!'; 'Long Live the Freedom of the Press!' The frail figure of Barna disembarked. He was smiling and it was surely a victor's smile.

Everyone was eager to see him at close quarters and crowded around him. Barna waved in response to the slogans. Usmani stepped forward, embraced, and garlanded him. Everyone else held flowers and rose petals, cameras flashed, and the train station exuded the fragrance of flowers.

Barna had to leave for the press club immediately where a horde of press workers and devotees of democracy awaited him. This was the very same press club where the great war for freedom of the press had begun on 3 December 1977, and now, on 13 October 1978 was welcoming its soldiers returning from the front. Their faces were dusty, clothes in tatters, and their bodies worse for wear.

THE TALE OF A MOTORCYCLE

A number of interesting incidents occurred during the movement. One of them was directly linked to a shining new motorbike I had fondly bought on instalments two months before the movement began. After the hunger strike commenced at the press club on 18 July, I was simply unable to go home. I arrived at the press club on this bike and walked a path that led me underground. In this way, both the bike and I, so to speak, vanished.

During the initial days of the movement, my companions and I had to change our locations frequently. At the time, we were staying at Aleem Pathan's house but it was time to move on again. Ashraf Shaad brought a vehicle for Usmani, Raqeeb, and Nasr Malik, and I had my bike. We began our journey after sunset but we were not told where we were headed.

Ashraf's friend Shamsi's house was in Nazimabad. When we reached the Habib Bank SITE area, Ashraf suddenly stopped the vehicle and I stopped too. He approached me with a worried look on his face.

'Partner, your bike's registration number is listed with the police and they are searching for it.' He was concerned that this would endanger those who were going to shelter us. He gestured towards Habib Bank.

'Let's leave it in the parking area. The bank manager is a friend; I will pick it up tomorrow morning.'

The idea did not appeal to me but there was nothing else to be done. I parked the bike, locked it, and handed him the keys. A few minutes later we arrived at our new safe-house.

Ashraf never went back to collect the bike and after a couple of days, it began to arouse suspicion. The bank staff contacted the police who carted it away to the police station in a truck. When they investigated, they traced the number to the showroom in Saddar where I had bought it, and the person whose name it was in. The PRO of that company was a friend, Saeed-uz-Zafar, who narrated the story to me subsequently. They told the police that 'Ahfaz ur Rehman, a journalist, was paying the instalments for that bike.' On further investigation the police discovered that I was a 'dangerous' wanted man. They handed the bike over to the CIA.

Anyhow, by that time I was so engrossed with the movement that I forgot the bike. When things began normalizing I asked Ashraf who had no knowledge of the matter. Zafar filled in the details. I called an acquaintance in the CIA, Kazim Raza, who was a senior official. We had known each other from Urdu College where he had been my senior and very popular. He came on the line, and when I introduced myself I heard a loud laughter.

'Brother, where are you?'

'In the press club.'

He laughed and said, 'Of course, at the press club, now that things have calmed down. Buddy, you have caused me a great deal of humiliation.' I remained silent.

'These soldiers have showered me with more filthy abuses during the past three months than I have heard all my life. They abused in Punjabi, Urdu, English, and other languages, reproaching us for not being able to capture a single individual. I pushed my guys hard all over the city in search of you but couldn't track you down. Where were you?' I joined his laughter.

'Kazim *bhai*, you realize that I was not in any one place. I switched places and stayed in many homes. There was no single magic house where I hid.'

He insisted on a meeting, perhaps wanting to vent his frustration. I went to his office where he received me warmly. He ordered tea and we began conversing. He wanted to hear my story. The movement had concluded successfully; there was nothing to be secretive about. I related what I had been doing and narrated some incidents. Then, when I inquired about his activities, he related what he had been up to in the preceding months.

'These scoundrels were amazed about how you guys could organize a movement of this magnitude. How you managed to garner the support of students and workers. They presumed that the total number of journalists could not exceed 3,500; how was it possible to run a countrywide movement? They gave me a hard time. They wanted me to counter it. Their own military agencies were also very active.'

According to Kazim Raza, martial law officials were astonished that when a nationwide organized political party like the PPP had retreated, how a bunch of journalists could continue running a movement.

'Although Barna was constantly badmouthed, they used to be very abusive towards you because you were leading the Karachi movement. They asked us who this Ahfaz ur Rehman was. They were very surprised when they learnt that you are a young man. However …' he leant forward, '… there were a couple of meetings where they did abuse you but also admitted that you were a very brave man.'

That was a pleasing compliment because nothing could be more flattering than to have an opponent appreciating your courage! However, hundreds of members shed their blood to nurture the movement, sacrificing everything for a noble cause.

Anyhow, I did not get the bike back but the company did as it was registered in their name. I asked Saeed-uz-Zafar to get it back for me, who said, 'Those people were mad at me for helping a "dangerous" man buy the bike. The police made my life miserable and called me to report to the station every now and again to berate and threaten me. He has not even paid the instalments regularly, they said. We are not giving him the bike.'

I was therefore left mourning the loss.

A CONTINUATION OF CONSPIRACY

Our struggle had succeeded but at a considerable cost. There are few parallels in Pakistan's history to the barbaric violence let loose on newspaper workers, labourers, farmers, and students. Innumerable volunteers were physically and mentally tortured in 'mysterious' CIA torture cells. They were blindfolded and transported to unknown locations where they were tortured for 10–12 days at a stretch. One volunteer from Sindh, whose name I am unable to recall, died a few days after being released. A Lahore colleague, Altaf Malak, never recovered from the ailments he developed due to the treatment meted out to him by his captors. Those who remained on hunger strike for up to three weeks suffered a variety of ailments for years afterwards. Barna was among the worst sufferers. His liver function never returned to normal.

True to its character, the government made full use of its paid agents in the newspaper industry. An impression was created that the movement had been politically motivated to consolidate the PPP. Such propaganda however had little effect. The coterie of traitors continued to be promoted by the government even though it feared the strength of the APNEC and the PFUJ. Three of these traitors were nominated as workers' representatives on the Wage Board. The objective was to maintain the reputation of the traitors by tempting the workers with economic incentives.

There is a background to the issue of the Wage Board. When APNEC announced that it would hold its two-yearly convention in Faisalabad, the four traitors on their part announced that they would also hold a parallel APNEC convention in Faisalabad. To help make the latter convention successful, the government had nominated three of the four traitors to the Wage Board just two days earlier. The depth of the government's involvement in this issue can be gauged by the fact that the guest of honour at the parallel convention was Labour Minister, Zahoor Ilahi. He came and spent his entire time criticizing the courageous struggle of the newspaper workers and their leader, Minhaj Barna. Only a handful of unions were represented at that convention, whereas the office-bearers of 40 newspaper unions, from Karachi to Peshawar, participated in ours. Through a resolution of this convention, simple and reasonable demands were presented to the government: remove fake representatives from the Wage Board and hold a nationwide referendum to determine the bona fide representation of newspaper workers to enable the true situation to emerge. The unelected government was, however, determined to continue to patronize the unelected individuals. This undemocratic action by the government which frequently referred to 'the sanctity of law' was not confined to the newspaper industry alone but was also extended to all the other industries. Their 'special interest' in the newspaper industry stemmed from both the resistance they faced from effective organizations like the APNEC and PFUJ whose members were ever willing to make all manner of sacrifices and also because of the far-reaching influence of the media.

When the Wage Board began functioning, all the newspaper workers jointly decided to boycott it; neither to appear before it, nor submit any written recommendations.

A SIGNIFICANT COMMUNICATION

Dear Mr Rao,

Despite my best efforts to evade arrest, I was eventually trapped. It transpired that when I left Shamim Alam's home I was probably tailed. I was surrounded near Water Pump and was forced to stop at gunpoint. Making the excuse that I needed to park my motorbike, I asked them to go to my flat where I concealed the documents I had on me. Later, I changed my clothes and accompanied them because Barna's letter to Ahfaz which you handed me was in the pocket of the trousers I was wearing. I was escorted to the CIA centre after midnight where Kazim Raza interrogated me in the morning. His key interest was to find out Ahfaz's whereabouts. They said that no one else had been able to provide that information.

There were a lot of other questions, such as: where does the money come from apart from that provided by Ashraf Shad? How is it spent? Where do people stay? How are farmers contacted? Who brings them to you? Where is Raqeeb and where does he normally live? Who attends the meetings? What is discussed when you meet Ahfaz? Who is attending the meeting at Al-Azam scheduled for the 22nd? What is to be discussed?

They were preparing to torture me to extract answers to these questions when Niazi entered and whispered something to Kazim Raza. He sent me back to the lockup. A short while later they sent me to jail. I am particularly worried about Shamim Alam because they began chasing me near his home. Anyhow, you can figure out how I answered these questions. However, it is very significant that they know the details of all the meetings of both the Action Committee and Struggle Committee. The extent of their intelligence surprises me.

Please tell Ahfaz to completely stop his movement and confine himself to one hideout. According to them, the warrants for Usmani and Raqeeb have been cancelled but they want to find Ahfaz at all costs. They are being pressurized from above to apprehend him. Akram Dharija is also being pursued relentlessly because of the farmers' issue. However, there was no mention of Shamim Alam or Kamran in the hour and a half questioning session. My name has however been floating around in every precinct. From DSP Asad Jahangir to Asad Ashraf, everyone has been in hot pursuit of me and Ahfaz. This was revealed not only during the CIA interrogation but also in jail where all the other detainees said that SP Altaf Siddiqui questioned every police station about Ahfaz. At the moment, Shamim Alam and Ahfaz are in danger. They must be kept safe under all circumstances; the Kharadar location must be abandoned immediately. These people were aware of the dates and proceedings of all the meetings which even I did not know. Those were the crucial matters.

The situation is very complicated in jail. Within a day, I have felt that class discrimination is very acute here. The farmers and non-journalist staff are isolated. The distribution of things is improper; finders are keepers. Misappropriation is rampant and mistrust is prevalent. People have curious attitudes. Three hunger-strikers are added daily but ordinary workers complain of not being taken into confidence on any issue and this is creating complications. I have been sentenced to three months detention under Martial Law Regulation 52. Probably, I will be transferred to Hyderabad as all those detained under MLR 12 are there. A military court will be in session in the jail tomorrow. Chances are that sentences will be passed and prisoners transferred accordingly.

There are 90 prisoners but the situation is very strange as the *Musawat* (Karachi) staff and some farmers and students are locked up in a single cell. The *Musawat* (Lahore) employees and some farmers occupy another cell. The rest of the detainees are completely separated; some of them even enjoy a superior style. If I continue to stay here, I will attempt to change all of this because it is harmful in every respect. The *Musawat* guys, both those from Karachi and Lahore, feel isolated. I will narrate the rest of the conditions later. My only request to you is that please, at all costs, deliver my second paper to Shamim Alam today. Please also hand him the keys to my flat so that he can deliver it there. Oh, yes, I would be grateful if you could send me some Capstan cigarettes as cigarettes are scarce in here.

Goodbye,
Altaf Siddiqui.

The Niazi mentioned in the letter was an important CIA official monitoring journalists. As we were very young and agile, we often managed to dodge him. Asad Jahangir later became IG Police and Asad Ashraf Malik held important positions too. Akram Dharija was an important labour leader. Kazim Raza was SP in the CIA. Shamim Alam has already been introduced.

FAR-REACHING TENTACLES OF INJUSTICE

The despicable tendency to imprison journalists under black laws and false accusations continued even after October 1978. The bureau chief of PPI Lahore was a courageous and exemplary colleague. Senior journalists Hussain Naqi and Khalid Chaudhry, sub-editor, *Musawat*, Lahore, remained in jail for a long time. Naqi was arrested for an article he wrote in *View Point*. In it, he revealed that the government had instructed its institutions to identify socialists. Interestingly, the editor and printer of this magazine were also arrested and released on bail a few days later. Naqi's bail, however, was delayed. He was placed in the notorious Shahi Qila, as was Khalid Chaudhry who was charged with manufacturing a bomb but remained in jail notwithstanding Amnesty International's intervention on his behalf. Masood Qamar, who had come from Faisalabad and was imprisoned in Sukkur jail, was released after a long period—an experience which he narrates in his prison diary.

Mehmood Sham and Ashraf Shad of the weekly *Mayar* were also tried for a long time under the Official Secrets Act. The publisher of the weekly *Parbhaat* (Al Fatah publications), its editor Wahab Siddiqui, its officiating editor Wahid Basheer, and printer Nasir Ali were also indicted under the OSA in May 1979.

The former president of the Multan Union of Journalists, Wali Mohammad Wajid and the chief editor of Al Fatah Publications, Irshad Rao, were detained under ridiculous charges and were released after much difficulty and a long effort.

Wajid was mistakenly arrested as Wajid Ali Shah, who was an active member of the PPP. He was not released even after the error was pointed out. When a delegation of eminent people went to the home secretary to seek his release, it was told that if Wajid gave up his trade union activities, he would be released. In other words, the government did not even attempt to hide its mala fide intentions.

It will not be out of context to mention another extraordinary incident which illustrates how the National Alliance leaders regarded basic human rights. Wali Mohammad Wajid and Mufti Mahmood were old acquaintances. When the Mufti was approached by common friends to help in the release of Wajid and informed him about the condition that he abandon trade union activities, Mufti Mahmood said, 'Let him give it in writing; what is wrong with that?'

The absurd, albeit shameful, charges levelled against Irshad Rao were that he intended to bring out a procession of naked women followers of the PPP! The reality was that the government was afraid of *Al Fatah's* consistency and criticism. To list the hardships that this institution had to undergo as a consequence of the government's confrontational attitude requires a separate article, even a book. However, here is a brief account of those adversities.

First, they were slapped repeatedly with demands for cash

deposits for articles published in the weekly *Al Fatah*. The owner of its printing press was constantly harassed. Government advertisements had stopped coming in. When these measures did not change the publication's critical editorial line, they resorted to the notorious Press and Publications Ordinance and cancelled its declaration. The government did not leave its workers in peace. Twelve magazines by this organization were closed down one after the other during the movement. It set a new record of courage in Pakistani journalism. Later, Wahab Siddiqui, Wahid Basheer, Zamin Shah (calligrapher), and Abdul Saleem were formally arrested for treason and suffered the tribulations and pain of long court cases and spells of incarceration although the International Commission for Human Rights had declared them prisoners of conscience. Siddiqui's case was slightly different. The Al-Zulfikar plane hijackers included his name in their list of prisoners who they demanded to be released. In this way he boarded that plane and spent 17 years in exile in Holland.

Similarly, the following publications were also strangulated: the daily *Aman; Sadaqat;* the daily *Tameer;* the daily *Hayat;* the weekly *View Point;* and the weekly *Mayar. Mayar*'s travails were no different from those of *Al Fatah*. In addition, the weekly *Nawa-e-Jang* was also among many whose declarations were cancelled.

Although the journalists from the major cities who were victimized have been frequently mentioned and lauded, those from the smaller towns, notwithstanding their equal suffering and sacrifice, did not receive the same level of acknowledgement. The truth is that during and after the movement, a large number of district correspondents were tortured in jails and lock-ups. An atmosphere of fear and terror was created. The government wanted them to report according to the government's perspective and to give an impression that the PPP was lacking in popularity. The *Musawat* correspondent in Larkana, Achhi Memon, was tied to a tree and beaten with a stick for 20 days because he refused to adhere to the 'sincere instructions' given by the authorities. He was released with a warning that he should never return to Larkana. Innumerable incidents like these are stored in newspaper files and people's memories.

Let us now consider the question of censorship. Everyone is aware that censorship is imposed during times of war and national crisis, and is imposed across the board to all newspapers and magazines. A great accomplishment of Zia ul-Haq's military rule was that censorship was imposed during peacetime. The most condemnable aspect was that censorship was only imposed on those publications which opposed the government and favoured democratic rule.

This measure exposed the ridiculous claim of the Zia government that it stood for freedom of expression. The reality was that in comparison to his predecessors, Zia did not have the strength to withstand criticism or opposition.

The clumsiness and absurdity of the censorship regime was unimaginable. Every news item that implied criticism of the government was deleted. Every article that exposed the government's contradictions was cut. The censored publications were not allowed to publish even a tiny photo of Zulfikar Ali Bhutto. No more than two columns were allowed for statements by Begum Bhutto and Benazir Bhutto. As a consequence, half the pages of censored newspapers used to be blank. This notwithstanding, the leaders of Qaumi Ittehad, especially those of Jamaat-e-Islami, made loud claims about the press being free in Pakistan. Can there be a more blatant example of hypocrisy and falsehood?

During this period, the opportunists of the Qaumi Ittehad (QI) played an extremely ugly role. Mahmood Azam Farooqui, minister of information, used the mass media to promote a particular religious school of thought. The newspapers and magazines of the opposition were stifled by innumerable restrictions. Although, the QI had promised to cancel the Press and Publication Ordinance and to disband the National Press Trust (NPT), when it came to power, they did quite the contrary, creating new tools to obliterate the opposition. A total ban was imposed on the opposition at the NPT newspapers, official news agencies, television, and radio. Government advertisements were closed to the periodicals of the opposition which were offered restoration of official business in exchange for unconditional support to the government. 'Press Advice' was practised with no restraint.

In this context, it is important to cite one incident. When Z. A. Bhutto was sentenced to be hanged, numerous national and international personalities made mercy appeals. The appeal of the former president, Fazal Ilahi Chaudhry, was significant but when the draft of his appeal was released to the newspapers, a Press Advice blocked its publication.

Part Two

1978 Freedom of the Press Movement

By Aurangzeb

It was the year 1978 and Zia ul-Haq's martial law was in place. It was the worst kind of dictatorship ever. Every word uttered by the military ruler became the law of the land. Basic human rights stood annulled and the worst kind of censorship was imposed so much so that even the verses of Quran were censored. Employees of the daily *Musawat* (Lahore), who had been targets of vengeful action by a self-styled martial law administrator, were in a terrible situation. Not only *Musawat*, but all other press institutions of the country were bearing the brunt of Zia's rule. In March 1978, the publisher of *Musawat*, Mir Jamil-ur-Rehman, editor Syed Badruddin, and assistant editor Zaheer Kaashmiri were arrested and sentenced to rigorous imprisonment by a summary military court. On 23 March 1978, *Musawat* (Lahore) was banned. After it was restored, *Musawat* (Karachi) was banned.

A few instances of the cruelties unleashed included the replacement of Khwaja Asif by Jameel-uz-Zaman as the new chairman of National Press Trust. This new chairman began an endless series of revengeful activities. His biggest target was PPL, where his first action was to terminate the services of H. K. Burki, the senior most reporter of *Pakistan Times*. Its editor, A. T. Chaudhary, was publicly abused and forced to resign as the chief executive of PPL. In Multan, Haroon Saad was imposed on the resident editor, Masood Ashar. Saad employed armed men to gain control of the daily *Imroz*, after which he forced about 107 workers out of the office of *Imroz* (Multan). These press workers then set up their camp outside the office. This resulted in a major strike in Multan. On 20 July, the editor of *Musawat* was arrested under a martial law regulation and forced to apologize before being released. On 5 August, Mahmood Sham, editor of *Mayar* (Karachi), was arrested by FIA under the Defence of Pakistan Rules and the Official Secrets Act. Minhaj Barna, president of the PFUJ and *Pakistan Times'* Karachi correspondent, was also terminated from service. The editor of *Urdu Digest*, Altaf Hassan Qureshi, was arrested under Martial Law Regulation 16 on 21 October. Editor of the daily *Hayat*, Nazeer Naji, was arrested on 24 October for printing an article of *Urdu Digest*. In May, the printing of *Musawat* (Karachi) was suspended because the government took over Peoples Foundation Trust which refused to publish it. Editor of the daily *Hayat* (Rawalpindi), Muzaffar Lodhi, was arrested on 2 November under Martial Law Regulation 13. He was accused of issuing a baseless report concerning Gordon College. Editor of the daily *Musawat*, Syed Badruddin, was re-arrested and on 8 November, Altaf Hassan Qureshi, Naji, and Badruddin were released. The PFUJ did not remain silent on these unusual incidents and it consistently protested against extreme martial law measures.

Under these conditions, *Musawat* faced severe difficulties. On Pakistan Day, *Musawat* was not published in Lahore and Faisalabad because the martial law administration had impounded the newspaper's printing press. The background was that it published the summary of Zulfikar Ali Bhutto's statement given in Lahore High Court whereas the court hadn't allowed it to be printed. The martial law authorities sent a show-cause notice to Mir Jamil-ur-Rehman, who was serving one-year imprisonment in Lahore. He was required to submit his reply within seven days. Later on, the martial law authorities deemed his reply unsatisfactory and impounded Musawat Press. This action rendered 300 workers of

Musawat jobless. Consequently, the PFUJ president Minhaj Barna sent an urgent telegram to the Chief Martial Law Administrator. Musawat Employees Union apprised the APNEC and PFUJ on the situation and demanded an emergency meeting of their executive committees for adopting measures to protect the welfare of the workers. Consequently, the meeting was called and a serious concern was expressed over the impounding of Musawat Press. It was decided to organize a nationwide movement for restoring the publication of *Musawat*. We demanded that government return the control of Musawat Press and release its editors and workers, withdraw the cases under martial law regulations, stop hostile actions against the trade union protests, and withdraw the vindictive measures taken against *Hilal-e-Pakistan* and NPT publications. Finally, it was declared in a meeting that if all these demands were not met by 22 April and all measures against freedom of the press were not withdrawn, the Joint Action Committee of the PFUJ and APNEC would decide the right course of action. Five out of the eight demands listed concerned the economic affairs of the press workers (which had been raised in earlier meetings), whereas three demands were about *Musawat* and other publications that were restricted by the government. The basic objective of these demands was to use common laws for addressing complaints against journalists and to withdraw all special laws. One organizational decision in this connection was that all newspaper unions across the country will observe a Demands Week from 9 to 15 April.

The PFUJ and APNEC decided that in case *Musawat* was not restored and the demands remained unmet, an agitation movement would be launched by courting arrests in Lahore from 30 April. In response, the Federal Ministry of Information invited the Action Committee to Islamabad for talks. The PFUJ's president Minhaj Barna, secretary general Nisar Usmani, and APNEC secretary general Hafeez Raqeeb presented their recommendations to the Secretary Information. After preliminary discussions, the recommendations were declared unworkable. The union leaders asked for counter proposals which were promised but never delivered.

Several rounds of dialogue were held between the PFUJ and the Ministry of Information concerning the restoration of *Musawat* and the release of all arrested workers but they did not succeed. In his early speeches, General Zia ul-Haq announced that freedom of the press would be protected but the newspapers would also have to play a responsible role. The PFUJ also propagated the same principles, therefore, a solution could have been found on this basis. In one meeting, the government representatives said that the issue of *Musawat's* restoration could be resolved according to the point of view of the PFUJ and APNEC but some conditions had to be met. Barna and Usmani were asked to guarantee that subsequent to the restoration of *Musawat* and release of workers, their behaviour would be 'in line with government policies' and the newspapers would refrain from writing about sensitive political matters. The workers' representatives took the stance that they could not bear responsibility for any condition concerning a newspaper's policy; however, they could serve as mediators between *Musawat* and the government. This could not be agreed upon and the negotiations broke down. The government assumed that by these guarantees, the tone of newspapers would improve and at the same time, it could meet its objective of imposing restrictions without inviting domestic and international criticism.

After the dialogue with the government failed, the Action Committee of the PFUJ and APNEC announced its agitation campaign on 30 April. A day earlier, the government issued orders for Barna's exile from the province. He was taken in custody and put on a plane to Karachi.

The movement for the restoration of *Musawat* continued. The first group of volunteers started their hunger strike on 30 April. From 1 May, just when the film show at a cinema theatre on

McLeod Road ended and the crowds of moviegoers filled the streets, suddenly five of our members appeared and began raising slogans. At some points, they were showered with flowers and then they proceeded towards *Musawat* offices. Plainclothes men pounced on them, gagged them, threw them in police vans, and drove them to unknown locations. It was eventually known that they were taken to Camp Jail, Kot Lakhpat Jail, and later shifted to other jails in various cities of the province.

In order to participate in this movement, journalists and press workers from across the country came to court arrests. On 13 May, Masoodullah Khan, senior sub-editor of *Pakistan Times*, Iqbal Jafri from the daily *Sun*, Khawar Naeem Hashmi from *Musawat*, and Nasir Zaidi of *Nawa-e-Multan* courted arrest and were sentenced to flogging by a military court. This news spread all over the world within moments and was widely condemned inside and outside the country. During the UNO session, Agha Shahi, former ambassador of Pakistan to the UN, was severely criticized. On the appeal of the International Journalists Association, a two-hour symbolic strike was observed in all countries where newspapers were published to mark their solidarity with the struggling Pakistani journalists.

We came to know later that it was a conspiracy hatched by a group in Punjab Union of Journalists. They advised the government that by taking such measures, it would be able to intimidate the journalists and they would refrain from resorting to agitation, resulting in the end of this movement. That is why rumours had started circulating beforehand that those arrested on 13 May would be flogged. In spite of the imposition of martial law, a strong public reaction was seen against this punishment. The head of Tehreek-e-Istiqlal, Asghar Khan, said that these punishments were wrong and inappropriate and that such measures should be reserved for moral violators, not for those struggling for human rights. Mufti Mehmood said that lashes should be for the criminal thugs. The secretary general of Jamiat Ulema-e-Pakistan, Abdul Sattar Niazi, said that this punishment for journalists and intellectuals struggling for their rights was sad. The president of Tehreek-e-Istiqlal Punjab, Mian Mehmood Ali Kusuri, condemned it and demanded restoration of *Musawat*, *Al Fatah*, and *Mayar*. President of PPP Sindh, Ghulam Mustafa Jatoi, said that such measures had injured the dignity of Pakistan. In a meeting of Lahore High Court Bar, flogging was declared an inhumane act and the use of handcuffs on journalists was condemnded in a resolution. It was also demanded to withdraw court cases against all journalists. The resolution was tabled by Abid Hassan Manto and Abdul Basit.

The military government could not achieve its objectives. Similarly, the small group of conspirators in PUJ also faced humiliation because contrary to their opinion, the cruel and merciless punishments did not discourage the protesting journalists at all. From 14 May onwards, more supporters gathered to welcome those courting arrests. The number of volunteers from across the country, offering to be arrested, increased and so did the termination of NPT journalists and other press workers. The purpose of these measures was to intimidate those individuals from the Trust who were willing to participate in the movement. Consequently, fourteen senior journalists from PPL were fired. This included Aslam Shaikh, Aziz Siddiqui, Saleem Aasmi, Masoodullah Khan, Mohammad Ilyas, Habib-ur-Rehman, Naseem Anwer, Zia-ur-Rehman, Dost Mohammad, Aftab Ahmed, Shafqat Tanveer Mirza, Hashmat Wafa, Mukhtar Hassan, and Rahim Bakhsh Jatoi. On the other hand, the conspiracies of the minority group of PUJ also continued which was led by Zia-ul-Islam Ansari and supported by senior vice president, Mahmood Jafri, and general secretary, Rasheed Siddiqui. They started to widen the ideological divide in the union and urged the government to stall dialogue with protesting journalists since Minhaj Barna was a Leftist.

A conspiracy was designed to this end and PUJ president, Riaz Malik, was arrested. His arrest would automatically elevate

Mehmood Jafri to the presidency and enable him to announce the end of the movement. In pursuance of this scheme, the police carried out night raids on the homes of Riaz Malik and some other office bearers. The following day, Jafri appeared on television and announced the culmination of the movement. Nevertheless, the process of courting arrests continued. Later on, the government restored *Musawat* in order to save face. Meanwhile, the Joint Action Committee of the PFUJ and APNEC announced ending the Lahore movement and began their groundwork to launch the second phase of the Karachi movement.

Stories of Torture
From Lyallpur to Landhi Jail

Masood Qamar

General Zia's rule was the darkest for Pakistan. Loudspeakers were installed in public squares and stadiums so that people would hear the screams of those being publicly flogged. All across Sindh, the jails were full of students, political workers, writers, intellectuals, and journalists. Newspapers came out of the printing press nearly blank. Those who still did not refrain had heavy padlocks placed on their doors with keys disappearing in khaki pockets. Despite all this repression and tyranny, streets and public squares brimmed with agitation. Under these circumstances, the Pakistan Union of Journalists and non-journalist newspaper workers' organization, APNEC, called for a protest against the closure of some newspapers and magazines. The protest eventually turned into a historic movement. Lahore was where the movement began.

[*Masood Qamar has erred here. The first phase of this movement started in Karachi on 3 December 1977, when Musawat (Karachi) was shut down. The second phase began in Lahore on 30 April 1978 because Musawat (Lahore) was banned. The third phase kicked off on 18 July against the closure of Musawat (Karachi), during which Qamar was incarcerated in Karachi and Sukkur jails. Since the details are mentioned in this book, I did not feel the need to edit it.—Ahfaz ur Rahman.*]

Journalists from all over the country started converging at Lahore in large caravans. The Lahore Press Club on Mall Road was their destination. At that time, the president of Lahore Press Club was Abbas Athar. He was neither supporting the martial law regime nor the protesters. Why he did that is another story altogether. The APNEC had recommended including the labourers, farmers, and students in the movement for freedom of the press. However, the PFUJ did not approve of it.

[*These groups were included in the third phase of the movement and their inclusion marked an extraordinary development in the international history of journalism.—Ahfaz ur Rahman.*]

Four journalists would offer themselves for arrest every day. Processions were brought out all over the world in support of the movement but Zia's regime continued to ignore the demands of the journalists.

One fine day, four journalists entered a military court and told its head that they were not going to surrender, will emerge victorious in this struggle, and that they were ready to hear the court's judgment. They were told to wait outside the court and then summoned a while later. The head of the military court announced his verdict of a nine-month rigorous imprisonment, plus five lashes each, against journalists Nasir Zaidi, Iqbal Jafri, Masoodullah Khan, and Khawar Naeem Hashmi. The sentence was not only announced but also carried out immediately. Only Masoodullah was spared the lashes due to his health; the other three were tied and flogged right inside the jail compound. This news spread all over the world and generated strong opposition. Afterwards, the next phase of the movement started in July 1978 in Karachi.

It seemed that we had arrived prematurely in Karachi as there was a long queue of volunteers ready to court arrests. Karachi Press Club was the best press club in the country at that time. A strange ambience prevailed over there. Volunteers were arriving in droves from all over the country to offer themselves for arrest. One group sang poems of Faiz, Makhdoom Mohiuddin, Majaz, Sahir, and Nazim Hikmat, while another highlighted the life of

Che Guevara. Yet another group was mulling over the lack of unity among leftists in Pakistan. It was a prelude to revolution. Wearing their typical ajraks and caps, farmers from the interior of Sindh arrived jubilantly.

Every evening, a group of volunteers consisting of a journalist, a newspaper worker, a student, and a farmer would assemble under the canopy of the protest camp erected inside the press club. They would sing revolutionary songs and make speeches until the police rounded them up and took them away. All of it would happen inside the Karachi Press Club. Mine was the last batch to court arrest and Johar Mir's (from Peshawar) was the first that did so at Regal Chowk in Saddar.

My companions included a press worker from *Dawn* newspaper, a farmer from Sindh, and a student from Democratic Students Federation, Lahore. The police came around eleven o'clock at night, took us to the nearest police station, and then we were transferred to Landhi Jail two days later. It was during lunch that we were transferred to the prison at Landhi. We joined our comrades to savour dusty bread and watery lentil curry with red pepper flakes floating on it. Nevertheless, the ambience inside the prison was that of a Sufi carnival. It certainly did not seem like a jail.

Our group leader in the jail was Shabbar Azmi of *Musawat* (Karachi). We received a batch of four arrested volunteers every day. One night, a Sindhi peasant complained about a severe, relentless stomachache. We called the guard in desperation and asked him to inform his superior. An assistant warden showed up two hours later. He looked at the ailing prisoner and said that such things happen and there was nothing he could do until morning, crudely telling us that no one is going to die until then. He was yet to finish his utterance when Shabbar slapped him across the face. The rest of us were about to come forward but then some guards took the warden out of the cell. When the door opened, all of us rushed out and started chanting slogans. We declared that we were not returning to the cell until an ambulance was called and the sick farmer was taken to a hospital. They had to comply.

In the morning, our breakfast was reduced to half a bread and the same reduction in quantity was maintained while serving us lunch as well. All of us decided to go on hunger strike to protest against the jail administration. Shabbar, Wahab Siddiqui, and I were summoned in the jail superintendent's office where he apologized for the incident of the previous night. However, we could certainly tell something was wrong.

A MAJOR ATTACK

Two days prior to Eid-ul-Fitr, a police contingent entered our prison ward around ten o'clock at night and announced the names of about a dozen prisoners from Lahore, including mine, and declared our release. All of us refused to leave until the release of our other comrades and the fulfillment of our demands. The police was fully prepared to coerce us into submission. They held each of us from our arms and legs and we were carried to the jail superintendent's room. Eventually, Shabbar said that there was no utility in resisting at that moment. After being escorted outside of the prison, we were pushed in a truck and driven away. We had no idea where we were being taken. Screams of torture victims at Shahi Qila echoed in our heads. Press releases of prisoners hanging to death with belts were churning in our minds. The truck ride finally came to a halt.

The doors of the truck were opened an hour later. We disembarked and were surrounded by guards. I caught a glimpse of a signboard reading 'Hyderabad Railway Station'. Meanwhile, an SP arrived and told us that we were being exiled from the province of Sindh.

'We have informed the railway officials. You can collect your tickets and leave the province before sunset.' He said this to us and all of them left.

Qaisar Butt, another journalist from Lahore, and I headed towards the Hyderabad Press Club. We were famished and had run out of cigarettes. After we narrated our story at the press club, the entire journalist community of Hyderabad assembled there in half an hour.

I called at the office of *Al Fatah* and informed Irshad Rao and Wahab Siddiqui about what had happened. I was aware that the telephones at the office of *Al Fatah* were being tapped. Irshad and Wahab indirectly told me to come back. I conveyed the crux of the conversation to Javed and Qaisar. The three of us decided not to return home as long as the movement lasted, whether we were released or exiled. Within a short while, the news of our exile and presence in Hyderabad Press Club spread across the city. A sizeable crowd had assembled outside Hyderabad Press Club. A man who was taking our photos suddenly went missing and it was safe to conclude that he had been picked up by the authorities. Around eleven o'clock at night, our colleagues put the three of us on a bus headed to Karachi. We noticed that a man with military haircut boarded the bus and sat behind us. We looked at each other and hid our faces with the newspaper. As soon as we reached city limits, this man disembarked. Actually, the times were such that anyone who would have stared at us for five minutes and had a military haircut would immediately be perceived as an 'agent' of the government. Anyhow, we felt that the information about our movement and estimated time of arrival in Karachi had reached the authorities. We quickly changed our shirts and started to plan the next move. Suddenly, Qaisar said, 'I don't think we are going to make it to Karachi.' He suspected that we would be apprehended at the next police checkpoint near Jamshoro. We all felt that it was quite possible. I don't know how and when the spirit of James Bond crept in me. Two stops before the Jamshoro checkpoint, I told my colleagues to leave the bus and led them towards the jungle in the pitch-black night. Twenty minutes later, we reached a railway track which we followed for about three miles before returning to the main road to catch another bus for Karachi. Two stops before Karachi, we left the bus again and took a taxi to reach a DSF colleague at Karachi University Hostel at around four o'clock in the morning.

We went to the office of *Al Fatah* and met Rasheed Rao the next morning. I could sense a degree of reluctance in my two companions about our decision to not go home as long as the movement continued. Anyway, they left for their respective cities while I prepared to court arrest the same evening at Regal Chowk, Saddar. In spite of all its efforts, the police failed to apprehend any volunteer before he surrendered himself. A location for courting arrests was to be announced. It was decided that two hours before, the volunteers would arrive in the vicinity and sit in a nearby café. As soon as crowds would start to build up, a small procession would emerge from Karachi Press Club chanting slogans for freedom of the press and against military rule. We decided that when the police would dash towards them, the volunteers would pull out banners and placards hidden in their clothes and approach from another direction.

I reached the designated spot an hour earlier along with my colleagues and waited in a teahouse. As soon as the small procession emerging from Karachi Press Club attracted the attention of the police, we headed towards the protest site and started to invite crowds by chanting slogans for freedom of the press.

We were back to Landhi Jail the following day. Shabbar was still the barrack in-charge. The prisons of Sindh were filling up with journalists, farmers, students, and political workers.

A day before Eid-ul-Azha, I was released along with others who had come from Punjab. I called at the office of *Al Fatah*. They sent a car to pick us up and bring us to the office. We found out that the jails were full with our people; however, we realized that soon we'll be facing a shortage of new volunteers for the next batch on Eid day at Bagh-e-Jinnah.

I was chosen. The governor, General Abbasi, and all foreign ambassadors were going to offer Eid prayers at Bagh-e-Jinnah. The volunteers wanted to court arrests at that location so that the news of our movement could reach the dignitaries from every Muslim country.

[*Raqeeb and I were members of the Action Committee and operated underground. We constantly re-evaluated our strategy according to the prevailing conditions. After a couple of days, we proposed that we should court arrests from other locations in the city instead of the usual Karachi Press Club and Regal Chowk so that the public at large could remain aware about our demands and support us in keeping the military government perturbed. Nowadays, press organizations gather ten or twenty 'protesters' and hold rallies at press clubs in almost all cities, and feel happy about it. The tradition of holding protests at public places has vanished. I don't know how to respond to this deterioration— Ahfaz ur Rehman.*]*

On Eid day, we ate *halva poori* for breakfast. We didn't want to arrive at the prayer ground too early; therefore, we stayed back and went a little late. Due to strict security arrangements for foreign dignitaries and the governor, we could not make it to the front rows of the prayer congregation so we took the back rows. Anyhow, as soon as the imam concluded the prayers we pulled out the banners and placards hidden in our clothing. When I shouted, 'Death to the Martial Law,' even my colleagues did not respond as all those around us were mostly government officials. Both my Sindhi colleagues did not speak either Urdu or Punjabi. Within a few seconds, I knew that my show was a flop. I signaled my companions to make a dash to the front row. We ran breaking the security cordon and stood in front of Governor Abbasi.

I had hardly shouted anti-martial law slogans for two minutes when security agents in plainclothes pounced on us and pushed us to the ground. They tore our banners and started to hit us. Close by, an unrelated group of volunteers from a religious party, carrying banners for collecting skins of sacrificial animals, was also rounded and roughed up despite their continuous reiteration of not being associated to us. No one heard their pleas in the commotion. After five or ten minutes of being roughed up, we were thrown in a jeep and taken away. Judging from the facial expressions of our captors, it wasn't hard to imagine what sort of treatment awaited us. That was the point when a terrifying degree of violence was let loose by the administration in Sindh.

As soon as the jeep entered the police station, a guard sitting behind me showered me with harsh blows. Then he held me by the collar and pulled me out. He was joined by a couple more guards who began to hit me with canes. I noticed that both my companions were not brought out of the jeep; they were instead driven away.

I was taken inside the inspector's office where I was thrown on the floor. A couple of men held my arms and legs and one of them whipped my back while shouting expletives at me, Bhutto, and Minhaj Barna. My screams pierced the roof but they did not stop. This continued for seven to nine minutes. Afterwards, one of them kicked me in the face and my nose started to bleed. When they saw blood dripping from my nose, they stopped the thrashing and held me up against the wall and subjected me to the harshest verbal abuse.

A while later, the SSP of the area also arrived. He greeted me with a few slaps across my face. Then they noted down my name and address before throwing me into a cell. I could hardly sit as my back was bruised. I leaned by the wall or tried to stroll. Some hours later, I was again brought to the inspector's room where he inundated me with his harangue and questions.

The SSP was mad at me, as was evident from his questions: 'Who decides the protest venues? How much are you being paid by the PPP? Why didn't you court arrest at some other place but my precinct?'

After about an hour, I was thrown in a lockup with eight or ten petty criminals. Around six o'clock in the evening, their visitors brought food for them. Usually a staff member of Karachi Press Club used to bring food for those in custody; however, no one came this time. A burly inmate invited me to join him for food and I accepted his offer right away.

By ten o'clock at night, all the inmates were snoring in various tunes. The door opened at midnight. A guard first pulled me outside, and then shoved me in another room. I could not understand what was happening when suddenly, I saw an army of ants and insects on the floor. Initially I swept them away by hand. Afterwards, I lit a cigarette to keep them at bay. After a while, the insects stopped bothering me. I tried to lean against the wall and doze off when I overheard a conversation between two men.

'I wonder when the military truck will arrive to take away this god forsaken journalist and relieve us.'

I felt like being buried in an ice block. It was very strange. Half of my body was shivering with cold and half of it was burning with heat. I took out a cigarette with my shaking hands. I began remembering the short stories written on torture cells. I thought about Sartre, Hassan Nasir's belt, and a press release about my suicide in the next day's newspapers. I called a guard and told him that I wanted to go to the bathroom. He pointed towards a pot in the room. I tried but couldn't use it as a substitute to the toilet.

My shirt was drenched in sweat. To control my fear and prove my bravery, I started thinking about future events. I visualized myself being cowardly and weak, and begging for mercy. I could see my children's faces appearing on the walls in a flash and then disappearing. I waited to hear the sirens of rescue vehicles which would take me out of there. The footsteps of the guard outside seemed to muffle my heartbeat. When I felt the heat of the cigarette reaching my fingertips, I squashed the burning cigarette with my fingers. I was visualizing being tortured in a military barrack, bravely shouting against the martial law, and laughing in response to the torture. Suddenly, a policeman shook my shoulder.

'What happened to you? Why are you laughing so loudly?' He asked.

I responded with empty stares to which he walked out while saying, 'You will stop laughing when the military truck comes.'

I dozed off with my back pressed against the wall.

It was in the morning when someone held me by the arms and made me stand. It was a morning stained by darkness and certainly not the one that we had been waiting for. I was ushered into the inspector's room where the SP was also present. They were preparing to take me to a magistrate's home. The jail was closed due to Eid holidays so no prisoner could either enter or be released. Therefore, it was imperative that I face a magistrate at his residence. The SP instructed to take me there by foot. As we began to walk, the guard whined: 'Why are we being punished for his sins? We will have to walk with him.' The issue was resolved by hiring a rickshaw. I was in handcuffs.

'Were you tortured?' The magistrate asked before signing the documents.

'Sir, this is a court and I shouldn't be in handcuffs. The blood on my shirt and the bruises can answer your question.' I replied.

He ordered to remove the handcuffs and asked me to sit on the sofa, telling the guards to wait outside. He also ordered tea for me.

'Son, you are young. Focus on your career, work hard, and earn a name for yourself in journalism. What kind of activities have you gotten yourself into?' He lectured.

'I can focus on my career and work hard only if the newspapers are published. How can I learn if the newspapers don't come out?' He smiled upon listening my answer.

'Are you into literature?' He asked.

'Of course, one cannot be a journalist without being literary.'
I replied.

He went inside his house upon hearing my reply and returned
with some papers.

'I wrote this poem last night. Since you are interested in literature,
will you read it?' The magistrate asked.

The opening lines of his poem made it clear that it was run
of the mill stuff; in fact, of a very poor standard. It felt like a
continuation of last night's torture but I kept my opinion to myself.
Soon after, he called the guards and instructed them not to torture
me anymore.

The guards gave me stern looks and complained about me as
soon as we returned to the police station. Then they started to
punch and kick me. I was thrown back into the lockup with the
same inmates for another three days before being transferred to
the Karachi Central Jail instead of Landhi Jail.

There were a lot of prisoners in every Pakistani jail during that
period but the one in Central Jail, Karachi housed the most of
all. On top of that, the prisoners of our movement made it even
livelier. Its barracks brimmed with political and journalist inmates.
One whole barrack was full of Dr Aizaz Nazeer's party. They
were in prison for bringing out the 1 May procession and had
been sentenced to whiplashes. They named their barrack 'Lyari
Commune'—a system introduced by French revolutionaries.

Every leftist party had a study circle in the jail. The largest study
circle was that of Dr Nazeer. I was accommodated in that barrack
on my request. After the revolution in Afghanistan had taken place,
Bhutto told the following to his attorney, Memon:

'Memon, wrap up your books because we don't need them
anymore. Now I have become indispensable for America and they
won't let me die after the Afghan revolution.'

However, the USA had made up its mind to deflate this balloon for which a sharp needle had been handed to Maulvi Mushtaq and General Zia. Alas, Bhutto could not foresee that. The jail brimmed with regular political analyses and all of us agreed that the revolution in Pakistan was just around the corner. About a week later, I appeared before a military court where I had a serious argument with its head.

'Keep quiet. Shut up! Do you think we will surrender before a couple of journalists like you?' He screamed.

'No, you can only surrender before General Arora.' I said.

Upon hearing my reply, he started to beat me inside the court and because he could not get the approval to award lashes, he sentenced me to rigorous imprisonment of one year.

My clothes had begun to stink and I had none except for what I was wearing. A colleague arranged a prison uniform for me. Two hours later, I was summoned by the jail warden and he informed me that I was being transferred to Sukkur Jail. I went back to bid farewell to my companions. Hamraz Ahsan slipped some money in my pocket for the journey which came very handy. When I was brought to the railway station, a Sindhi guard who was escorting me removed the handcuffs.

'I know you people have volunteered for arrest so I am sure you won't escape.' He said.

I disembarked on various stops on the way and freely moved around sipping tea and smoking. The officer in-charge did not like it but the guard had somehow pacified him.

Sukkur Jail is the most ghastly prison in Sindh. There is a jail within the jail. Every two or three barracks have been enclaved by strong masonry boundary walls. Wahab Siddiqui of *Al Fatah*, Javed Siddiqui from Lyallpur, and about two dozen journalists, students, farmers, and labourers were already there. We were scattered across three different barracks within the same compound. The same festive atmosphere prevailed here, as in other prisons across the country. Sometimes, the jail administration was so kind to us that they would provide us all sorts of little comforts including groceries. We would then cook the meals ourselves. At other times, they would be so harsh that our toothpaste and shaving kits were also snatched.

On one occasion around midnight, the jail staff raided our barracks, roughed us up, and took away all our belongings. They returned the stuff two days later but I had decided to grow a beard by then so that we wouldn't have to plead with the staff. By the end of my sentence, it was difficult to differentiate between my beard and that of Sikhs. A few weeks later, our leader Minhaj Barna announced his decision to fast until death inside the prison. Rasheed Siddiqui's group had failed in all its mechanizations to create a rift within the movement like it did before in Lahore. However, two groups had formed within our hunger strikers. One believed that since the military and civil administrations played deceptive games with us, we should also covertly eat a little during the hunger strike. Wahab, Johar, I, and some other colleagues strongly opposed the idea of cheating and stopped accepting food from the prison staff. We survived on water, tea, and cigarettes only. I have gone on hunger strike several times and according to my experience, only the first two or three days are the hardest. One does experience frequent headaches due to dehydration but that can be managed with some liquid intake. However, smokers have more difficulty.

Anyway, on the fifteenth day of the hunger strike, Johar and I were summoned to the jail inspector's office. I had grown too weak to walk steadily so I asked Johar to go ahead. The guard came back again for me and I went while being propped up by two guards. Nisar Usmani was sitting in the inspector's room. He updated us about the situation outside and told us that Mufti Mahmood was pressing General Zia to talk to us as the country was getting a bad name internationally due to the strikes. He said that the talks were expected to take place soon.

A few days after the meeting, jail official Manzoor Ilahi came with his staff and informed us that an agreement has been reached between the leaders of the movement and the government. Accordingly, all prisoners were to pack up their belongings and prepare for release except myself because I was still under detention. Naheed Afzaal of Tehreek-e-Istiqlal and a labourer from Karachi were also not released. On two earlier occasions, I had refused to go when I learnt that I was released without my companions. This time around, my companions refused to leave without me. However, the jail staff took all of them away. The festive atmosphere of the barrack with two dozen inmates had suddenly turned into a deserted place for me.

Eventually, all of my friends departed with moist eyes. Johar was sobbing. That separation scene is permanently etched in my mind. Back then, I did not know that whenever I would recall his name in future, this scene would come to life. My friends took everything away with them: the revolutionary songs of the night, the irritability which confinement inevitably causes, those political analyses, the dreams for a glowing future for the country, dirty jokes (my apologies), the faith and resolutions, and everything else. The only thing they left behind were tears and cigarettes of different brands.

There was an inmate by the name of Qazi in one of the barracks in our compound. He was in for committing a murder. During his stay in the prison, he committed two more. He used to send a large amount of money from the prison to his family. I can surely say that 40 per cent of the crimes happening outside are planned inside the jails. Same ratio of drugs and liquor are also sold inside. From good looking boys to young women, all sorts of prisoners are also sold in there. Their prices vary depending on festivals as well as on whether their services are availed inside or outside the prison.

On festive occasions, the prison gangsters would add intoxicants in a large bucket of water. They called it 'Red Fairy' and went around selling a glassful for PKR five to the poor inmates. They supplied women, liquor, and grass according to what the buyer could afford. Qazi was very friendly towards us. He used to fight off the guards whenever they misbehaved with us.

At supper time, I noticed that the prison staff brought us food in clean crockery instead of the usual stained plastic utensils. The food was good too, with generous helpings of meat and potato curry and sweet rice for dessert. I didn't understand this sudden change. The guard told us that from then on we would be supplied with groceries and a cook. Then they locked me in the barrack and went away. I kept myself from overeating as I had broken my fast that day. I ate cautiously, lied down, and dozed off into sound sleep after a long time.

Next afternoon, two guards came and told me that the jailer wanted to see me. Jail official, Manzoor Ilahi, sat behind a desk under a tree in the open ground. I was offered a chair. He pushed a cup of hot tea and a packet of cigarettes towards me which I already had.

He obtained some information about me and then started my brainwashing regarding the PFUJ.

'Have you seen how everybody left you alone? Nobody cares about others. Everyone went back to their comfortable beds, leaving you in the stinking blanket of this jail.'

Now I got the whole picture. The clean crockery and sumptuous food, everything started to make sense. Twenty minutes into persuading me against the movement, he said. 'Look at Javed Hashmi. He is your age and already a minister. You can also get there.'

I choked on my cigarette puff with his crafty argument and a guard gave me some water.

He pulled out a paper from his pocket and placed it in front of me. It stated that our movement took money from the PPP and was launched on the party's instructions. It further stated that the party leadership had promised to give us money but it did not give any to me or to my family, and that I was ashamed of my actions and sought forgiveness. I looked at the jailer after reading the paper. I could feel the sweat in my hair. He continued:

'If you sign this, I will get you the job of chief reporter in daily *Imroz*.'

'Mr Shaikh, I came from Lyallpur on my own to court arrest. Do you think I travelled all this way to sign this apology? I am grateful for the facilities you are giving me since yesterday which will probably be discontinued now.' I replied.

He signaled the guards to take me back to the barrack. Within two hours, the desk, chair, lamp, cushions, and the white bed sheets were removed from my cell.

The political workers, writers, and journalists who go to prison do at least one or two things. They write about national politics, pen their autobiographies, or learn gardening. After a couple of days, I requested Qazi to use his influence in getting me some seeds, especially for rose flower plants. I figured that working physically during the day would help me sleep soundly at night and escape those shadows.

Before I could get the seeds, the prison guards came and began to gather my belongings. It emerged that I was being transferred to another cell, probably in solitary confinement. However, the new barrack I was moved to was like a hub for political prisoners. It was a long barrack with about twenty inmates. It housed Rasul Bakhsh Palijo, Masroor Ahsan of the PPP (who contested against Professor Ghafoor of JI for National Assembly seat), Nasir Baloch (later hanged for hijacking an aeroplane; he was the grandson of Maulana Shabbir Usmani), Jan-e-Alam of Qaumi Mahaz-e-Azadi, Zubair Rehman of Dr Aizaz Nazeer's party (who is currently a columnist in daily *Express*), and journalist Razzak Qureshi of Sindhi Haari Committee. The ambience at the barrack resembled that of an ongoing party where political analyses, study circles, revolutionary songs, and gambling using matchsticks filled our days and nights. One day, through the newspaper that we had smuggled in, I learnt that my eldest daughter, Marium Masood, was born. I wanted to name her after one of our arrested colleagues, Lalarukh, but my family insisted on Marium.

Three months had passed since the end of the movement but the PFUJ had done nothing for my release. Zubair Rehman was suddenly released even though there was no petition filed in the civil courts. He then filed an application for my release through the late barrister, Wadud, in Sindh High Court. Rehman is an awesome character. After his release, he went around chalking slogans on every building in the city. He was taken into custody while he was writing graffiti on the wall of a police station. The police found out that he should have been in jail at that moment. It emerged that due to a mix-up, he was actually released by mistake so he was sent back to us in Sukkur Jail.

There was no response to my release petition from Sindh High Court for about three or four months. Then a date was fixed for its hearing but the prosecutor dilly dallied until my one-year sentence was almost complete. A day before my release, I was summoned by the jail warden and he informed me that the military government had extended my detention for another three months at the same jail. During this period, Hassan Sangrami used to come to the court and took very good care of me whenever I went to Karachi for a hearing. Barrister Wadud was fighting my case and he used to slip some money in my pocket during every meeting. I was finally released on completion of another three months. The one-year sentence was stretched to fifteen months. Instead of releasing me while in court, the judge hearing the case ordered for me to be released from Sukkur jail.

It seemed that upon my return to Sukkur, the jail authorities would find an excuse to extend my detention further. However, I was set free.

The narrative of the longest imprisonment for this movement, as compared to that of other journalists, ends here. I would have neither written this account, nor boasted about my hardships. However, during the recent attacks on newspapers and television channels, when some crooked journalists, anchors, and columnists said that the freedom enjoyed by the press today was not because of any struggle rather it was owed to General Musharraf's generosity, I was compelled to record it.

The era of General Zia swallowed our youth. His legacy of the Taliban is devouring our old age.

Prison Diaries
What Confinement? What Freedom?

Farhad Zaidi

A major transformation occurred in my life when I entered Kot Lakhpat Jail on 25 May.

Like many other inmates, I had become the 'prisoner with a serial number', and could be identified only with that reference.

When I look back at that time of my life, I see the iron gate of Kot Lakhpat Jail and a completely different world inhabited by human beings who are a little different from the rest of us. My imagination pierces through the iron gate. The hallway leading to the next iron door and beyond through the vast courtyard flanked by barracks. On its right, the imposing rocky walls of Barrack-7 begin. In this barrack, I spent the most interesting, educative, and eventful time of my life.

My eight roommates are still in that barrack. They are serving arbitrarily awarded sentences of rigorous imprisonment for demanding restoration of a few magazines and newspapers. A few moments earlier, they had warmly and lovingly bid me farewell. They came up to the prison compound to see me off and embraced me as if I had been their companion for centuries.

I can see (late) Aziz Siddiqui, who is slim, has curly hair, and intelligent eyes which peep through spectacles. He holds a pipe between his thin lips and exudes gentle fragrance of Iron Moor. He is quiet and principled. He was a senior assistant editor in *Pakistan*

Times (Lahore), and has a wife and two beautiful children. Siddiqui was arrested on 4 May and sentenced to rigorous imprisonment twelve days after. During the trial, he remained at Camp Jail and reached Kot Lakhpat Jail as a prisoner. He witnessed several journalists arriving as prisoners in Barrack-7 who were then taken to other jails of Punjab in Mianwali, Bahawalpur, Sahiwal, Faisalabad, and Jhang. There was a time when he was in the company of thirty newspaper workers. Gradually, all of them were transferred and he was left alone in this 18 by 35 feet barrack with only his sleeping mat and a blanket remaining. There was nothing in the barrack except a water container made of clay, a metallic plate, and a cup. He would toil alone all day and thanked the Almighty for two pieces of bread and cooked lentils. He was all by himself in the barrack during night time. His only visitors were the red-capped taskmasters who got the barrack cleaned by other prisoners. The only respite from this agonizing existence occurred whenever a certain friend managed to send him some books. His loneliness ended when a new batch of four newspaper workers joined him. They included Abdul Kareem (a machine operator of the daily *Sun*), Ali Hassan (a compositor of *Sindh Times*), Abdullah Jeo of *Dawn Gujrati*, and Nazeer Mohiuddin of *Musawat* (Lahore).

I joined them the following day along with Aslam Azad (a news editor from Karachi), Shamsuddin of *Hilal-e-Pakistan*, and Ziauddin of the daily *Ibrat*.

For the first time that night, I had eaten in jail as a Class-C prisoner. It was Thursday so we were served meat. Class-C prisoners were given meat twice a week. It was generally a small piece of meat floating in salted water and served with two pieces of bread.

I don't remember when I fell asleep. However, when I woke up, I saw Siddiqui and Kareem jogging in the sprawling courtyard. I joined them too. It was probably for the first time in fifteen years that I had woken up early and worked out. The rest of the day wasn't as cheerful as the morning mainly because we had nothing to do except talking and eating lentils. Thinking of those on death row made the day even gloomier. These cells were just a few yards away from mine. Z. A. Bhutto had also been kept there until a few days earlier.

We had arrived in the afternoon of Thursday, 23 May. On Friday morning, we sat on our mats and had eaten a mixture of wheat and treacle for breakfast. Mohiuddin announced that there would be no tea because the ingredients required to make it were not available. At times, I'd look at my colleagues and wonder how a common cause could transcend the barriers of language, region, and unfamiliarity. Most people who participated in the movement for freedom of the press had met for the first time. Yet, within hours, it seemed as if they knew each other for years. All of them volunteered to live together in a dark prison cell, disregarding their livelihood, because they could not bear injustice.

Such conscientious people can be found all across Pakistan. The more zealous sons were those who happened to be the first ones to come out on streets in the movement against injustice, and had their conscience glowing in the jails of Mianwali, Faisalabad, Jhang, Multan, and Bahawalpur. A branch of this tribe was incarcerated in Kot Lakhpat and another at Camp Jail, Lahore. Incidentally, the route adopted by all these tributaries—courting arrest around *Musawat's* Lahore office, then travelling to Civil Lines on a police jeep, reiteration of personal and professional details (at least on seven occasions), and finally entering the Gora Ward as detainee— was the same route we followed later. The Gora Ward of Civil Lines is a strange phenomenon as we learnt from responsible people. It is a 12 by 14 room, especially constructed for those white people who come to Pakistan to smuggle drugs and are caught. We had heard a lot about it before being incarcerated here. We presumed that it must be no less than a four-star facility. The reality hit us when we were brought there by 8 p.m. in the evening.

On the day of our arrest, the temperature in Lahore was 112

fahrenheit. There was no fan in Gora Ward. Some journalist friends had sent a pedestal fan from outside which had stopped functioning by the time we arrived. We took the experience positively and used it as a rehearsal for the actual prison life awaiting us.

In the first phase of this exercise, we experienced a sweat bath within ten minutes of our arrival. In the second phase, we received straw fans, mats, and bed sheets through the window which were our only link to the outside world. We also managed to get tea and food from our colleagues outside. They slipped these items through the cracks in the window. However, before we could have our first bite, someone called out the name of Khushtar Abbas and informed that the DSP had summoned him.

Khushtar left the room without touching the food so the rest of us also stopped eating.

I had seen Khushtar for the first time a few hours earlier when we were being registered for detention.

'Here! Come my darling!' Khushtar said.

I saw a middle-aged man in a sleeveless vest behind the bars as I turned in the direction of his voice. He seemed calm and happy. I learnt that he was Khushtar when I joined him inside. He was in the lead in arranging logistics for those participants of the movement who had arrived from different towns. When the police started rounding up journalists, he was also caught in a sweep and jailed for a month. Meanwhile, the authorities came to know that he owned a metal factory. Consequently, he was transferred to Shahi Qila for interrogation regarding whether he produced bomb shells in his factory. Then he was brought to Civil Lines the same day and we happened to meet.

Apparently, everyone who came to that prison before us wrote their names on the lockup walls. With great interest we read the names of our clansmen who had preceded us. Among them were Abdul Hameed Chhapra, Masoodullah Khan of *Pakistan Times*, Habibur Rehman of *Musawat*, Khwaja Nisar of the daily *Jang*,

Ashiqullah Shah of *Aftab Sindh*, Rehmat Ali Razi of *Azad Lahore*, Ibarat Ali Shah of *Musawat*, Sikandar Ali Rind Baloch, Abdullah Jiva of *Dawn*, Ghulam Mohammad and Shaukat Hussain of *Musawat*, Abrar Rizvi, Waseem Farooq, Usman Nasir, Zafar Qureshi of *Hurriyat*, Raoof Bhatti, Fateh Mohammad Bhatti, Qazi Mian Nazeer Ahmed (editor of the weekly *Azad*), Mohammad Ibrahim, Altaf Hussain, Niaz Ali, Syed Mohammad Sufi of *Musawat*, and M. Ilyas.

We didn't see the names of those three colleagues who were flogged: Nasir Zaidi, Iqbal Jafri, and Khawar Naeem Hashmi. But then, their names were etched in our hearts.

On the morning of the 24th, a sweeper covered us with dust immediately after we had washed ourselves. Meanwhile, we received tea and fried bread for breakfast through the cracks above the window. We were told that if one didn't have enough money or friends outside, one would not be able to eat breakfast as the police had no budget allocated for it.

While we occupied ourselves with breakfast, Khushtar remained busy filing two different appeals. The first one for sugar-free tea as he was a diabetic, and the other requesting them to send a barber. Alas, both his appeals remained unrequited.

Around 10 o'clock at night, we left Khushtar in the lockup as he had to be transferred to Shahi Qila. We sheepishly boarded the prisoners' van to attend a hearing at the military court. More than half a dozen guards escorted us and displayed extraordinary courtesies. They politely requested us to help them jump-start the van. We cheerfully obliged and came to know later that 135 journalists before us had the same honour of pushing that van in the recent past.

A few minutes later, we were standing in a sprawling compound of a building next to the racecourse adjacent to Bagh-e-Jinnah. We were made to sit on the grass under a tree and our protectors settled in a circle around us. Small groups of people around the place were talking among themselves. In the corridors behind them, vigilant military soldiers guarded the building which revealed that we were confronting military courts.

Our turn came about two and a half hours later. The major took five minutes to dismiss us after summoning us the following morning. Just before that, he had sentenced six journalists to six months rigorous imprisonment each. When they walked past us, we looked at their handcuffs with great interest. The smile and resolve on their faces was inspiring.

We ate the lunch sent by our friends, pushed the van again to jump-start it, and reached Camp Jail in fifteen minutes. The time was 3:30 p.m. and it was sizzling hot. The tiny room was crowded with mostly scantily dressed detainees occupied with endlessly greeting and embracing each other.

The 'air tight' prison van was ready the next morning with about two dozen under trial political and moral offenders. There was a Sikh among them who was most probably apprehended on smuggling charges. It might be of interest for the reader that except for Shahi Qila, journalists and political detainees enjoyed a higher status than other criminals. A political detainee told us that whenever the guards showed excesses, he would shout, 'We are political prisoners!'

This amounted to some sort of a warning for the guards not to underestimate them. Nine out of ten times, it worked. We adapted that warning for our use and decided to shout, 'We are journalists!' In so doing, we attained much more clout than the political prisoners. It was probably because the common man had more respect for journalists compared to other notables.

This time the van was parked near the former British High Commission building and the guards apologetically entered to handcuff us before taking us inside the military court. They performed the task properly by tying two detainees with one pair of handcuffs. My left wrist was attached to Aslam Azad's right one.

Similarly, Shamsuddin and Ziauddin shared common handcuffs. It was painful until we saw the Sikh in handcuffs plus shackles. Azad could not resist to quip and said:

'We don't like to wear handcuffs but are obliged to do so. After all it is the court's order.'

We disembarked in our handcuffs with the benevolent guards and entered the building's compound through a small backdoor in a single file. Journalists, political prisoners, and other detainees were segregated here. We settled on a rug in a veranda. From nine o'clock in the morning until noon, we enjoyed the sumptuous refreshments arranged by our colleagues, Shabbir and Iftikhar. We also received fruits and soft drinks from other political prisoners which they had received from their supporters and friends. Ghazi Salahuddin of *Dawn*, flanked by two guards, walked past us around noon. He was probably headed towards the bathroom. The ever happy but restless, Salahuddin, who was arrested a day earlier, felt reassured to see us. His smile stretched wider and eyes glittered more brightly behind his thick glasses.

'I have also written my name on the wall in Gora Ward. It is a very interesting and pure experience.' He wanted to say more but his captors did not allow him to.

After Salahuddin, my handcuffs-mate, Azad, also wished to go to the bathroom. He conveyed his desire to the guard, who instantly became awkward.

'Let's go.' Azad said.

'But I don't want to go to the bathroom.' I said.

'In that case, it will become a lengthy procedure.' The guard replied.

When I did not agree to accompany Azad, the guard reluctantly unlocked our handcuffs, borrowed another set from someone else, and escorted him away. We were handcuffed together once again when he returned.

We were summoned around 1 p.m. and herded to Major

Tahir's summary military court. After waiting outside the court, our handcuffs were separated. I was called in first. The major first took an oath in Urdu pledging that he will decide my case according to his conscience without fear or favour. For a moment, I thought I would be set free. Then he sat down and read out the charges.

'Farhad Zaidi, son of Ali Naqi Zaidi, resident of Karachi, you are charged with bringing out a procession at about 6:45 p.m. on 23 May 1978 on Montgomery Road near Gulistan Cinema without prior written permission of the Martial Law Administrator Punjab, thereby committing a punishable offense according to Martial Law Regulation No. 5.'

'I admit.' I cut the matter short.

The honourable judge threw a glance at me and told me to stand aside.

Now it was Aslam Azad's turn. The major repeated his oath, sat down, and read the charges. Azad admitted to his offense. Then Ziauddin and Shamsuddin were brought in one by one and the same drill was repeated. We were anticipating our sentences, however, we didn't know that the process of justice was not complete yet as witnesses had to appear.

We returned to the same veranda where we had been sitting since morning. Meanwhile, our lunch arrived. During lunch, we argued about the extent of the punishments and unanimously concluded that we would be awarded rigorous imprisonment for six months and no flogging. We were summoned again around 3:30 p.m. one by one. Azad and I were awarded six months rigorous imprisonment plus a penalty of PKR 3,000 each. Failing to pay the penalty would extend our prison sentence to an additional three months. Ziauddin and Shamsuddin were awarded only prison sentences.

I noted my feelings while coming out of the court. I was neither happy nor sad and thought that I had paid back some of the debt to a profession which had put food on my table for 24 years.

The environment at the threshold of Kot Lakhpat Jail was

very different from that of Camp Jail. Our names, addresses, and statements were registered but in a more decent manner. While handing us over, members of the escort vouched for our being gentlemen with the command to treat us well. Then they warmly said goodbye to us (on the verge of tears), wished us well, and left.

A few moments later, the four of us joined five more journalists in Barrack-7. They had not been transferred to prisons outside Lahore. It emerged that the transfers only took place when they had sufficient passengers to fill a lorry.

I took a bath on the morning of 27 May but couldn't find a mirror to comb my hair. In an apologetic manner, Aziz Siddiqui told us that there used to be one mirror to service two dozen inmates. However, one of the groups that had recently transferred to another prison had carried it along. In such a situation, we could only see each other's faces and not our own but Nazar Mohiuddin solved this problem. He fetched a tin of powder milk, held its bottom to my face, and said, 'This should do.' I looked at my face with mixed emotions of surprise and regret. Nevertheless, I managed to comb my hair.

As we got done with setting our hair, a prison porter entered the barrack with a large sack. He put it down and left quietly. Addressing us all, Siddiqui said, 'Gentlemen, your chore.' We went towards the sack and turned it over.

Although we had toiled with chores all our lives, it was the first time that a task walked to us in a sack. A huge pile of colorful, intertwined woolen balls of various sizes poured out when we opened the sack. Siddiqui coached us expertly and told us that we should pick single colour balls, unwind the threads, and put them aside for tying them end to end in order to make one long string. He had three-weeks of experience with the job.

Like the rest, I picked out pieces of short strings with the same color from the heap of wool. Meanwhile, Siddiqui added another instruction in view of his rich experience. He said that each one of us had to deliver two kilograms of the string. He further said that it could be tolerated if the workmanship wasn't up to the mark but the weight of the string would not be compromised upon. In the past, a gang had made a waistband for their trousers from this wool (as jail trousers were not issued with belts), which landed them in trouble. The matter was resolved with the instructions that the poor workmanship of newspaper men can be tolerated if there wasn't any shortage in the weight.

By the end of the day, after spraying the barrack and breaking a water container of clay, we were debating about what to have for dinner: jail lentils or bread and onions. Suddenly, the barrack door opened and three quarters of the jail officers and eighteen porters appeared. They came pushing hospital beds along with stained bed sheets and pillows. Some of them carried chairs, desk, and crockery.

An officer announced that we had been promoted to Class-B. Accordingly, we would start receiving rations from the next morning. A porter was also assigned to serve us. We spent the next two hours arranging our housewares and discovered that the hitherto spacious accommodation had shrunk considerably.

That evening, we ate lentils with onions and bread and then decided to have another round of tea. Aslam Azad declared that these developments indicated our chances of getting freed and then we played card games late into the night, seated around the desk on chairs.

Our inspection started early on the morning of the 28th with the arrival of the barber to trim our whiskers. Azad saved his skin by declaring that he had decided to grow a beard.

After finishing with the barber, and according to the warden's instructions, we bathed and changed into prison uniform. The uniform was a shirt and pair of trousers made of cheap cotton and produced in Multan Jail. They were a perfect fit for thin men of medium height. My shirt clung to my body like a pillow cover. It had two buttons which popped out because I couldn't breathe with them fastened. It also had a pocket somewhere between the neck and shoulder. I could feel but not see it. Anyhow, we managed to get ready for the inspection.

Two desks were placed in the vast prison courtyard. One was occupied by the jail superintendent and the other by his deputy who was shuffling papers. We were made to stand against the wall and ordered to remove our shoes. Before we could comply, the superintendent approached us and told us to keep our shoes on, informing us that since we had been promoted to Class-B, there was no need to go bare feet. That 'class discrimination' deprived us of the experience that the hundreds of our preceding scribes had availed. We were neither asked to sit on the floor nor to keep our heads down. We stood under the shadow of the wall and watched it shifting slowly.

The inspection began a while later. When I was called in, I stood in front of the superintendent who asked me some formal questions, enquired about my health, and dismissed me in a minute or so. My colleagues followed suit.

The following day did not prove to be any better than the days before it. It was the same sad morning, the same sizzling day, the same prosaic exercise of spinning wool, and the same issue of satisfying our hunger. It reminds me that as Class-B prisoners, we were allocated about 190 grams of meat, 125 grams of sugar, 250 millilitres of milk, and half a kilo of flour daily. Tea leaves, vegetables, salt, and a loaf of bread were also given. Three eggs were provided on meatless days. We were also provided with ten to fifteen kilos of ice which was a blessing in that hot weather. Perhaps, these quantities were more than what we needed so the issuing staff adjusted them before they reached us. In view of the constant ongoing disputes with the staff on the issue of food, we formed a Works Council and elected Abdul Kareem as its president, Nazar Mohiuddin as its general secretary, and Ali Hassan as its joint secretary to assist him.

We were assigned three orderlies for cooking in Class-B. All three were former soldiers who had been court-martialled for six months to one year.

Then one fine day we finally received medical care also. It so happened that one of our companions, Ziauddin Shaikh of the daily *Ibrat*, fell sick for two days. Aslam Azad of *Hilal-e-Pakistan* also suffered from a stomachache. Our attempts to bring them to the jail dispensary failed, however, medical care arrived in the barrack. A bearded compounder accompanied by a porter carried a tray of medicines on his shoulder. He listened to every ailing prisoner and gave him pills from the same bottle. Tours, inspections, and medical care were important events in jail. It hurt me to see how people longed for visits from their loved ones. Only three of us had relatives in Lahore, therefore, not everyone received visitors. However, even this could not continue for long as Class-B inmates were allowed only one visitor in a fortnight. Moreover, our relatives did not know how long we would be in Lahore before being transferred to other cities.

On 3 June, the orders for my release arrived. The movement of journalists had ended three days earlier. Some of my colleagues were preparing for a siesta after lunch while Aziz Siddiqui started to read the translated version of the Quran. Abdul Kareem was looking for partners while holding a pack of cards in his hands. I was receiving applause for uttering some fresh verses by Aslam Azad. Before I finished reciting my last couplet, a murderous warden barged in and enquired in Punjabi, 'Which one is Farhad Zaidi?' I asked what the problem was.

'Your release orders have arrived. Get ready in two minutes,' the warden informed.

I changed my clothes, picked up my bag, and accompanied him. All my journalist friends and toiling colleagues came up to the door to say goodbye. I hugged them all and exited with a heavy heart. I was sure that they would also be freed very soon. Nevertheless, I felt like I was being separated for a long time from the tribe I lived with for eternity. Perhaps everything changed in confinement, however, even prisoners did not lose their natural impulses.

The Prison Door Opened

Aslam Shaikh

[The late Aslam Shaikh was one of the most distinguished journalists of Pakistan. He was a principled and upright leader of the PFUJ who struggled all his life for freedom of the press. I had the opportunity of working with him in the PFUJ and then had the privilege of his company in China, where he was working with 'Illustrated China' and I was employed in the Foreign Languages Publishing House. He was a lively person who kept his colleagues in high spirits. He was an office bearer of Rawalpindi Union of Journalists and the PFUJ. During the 1977–8 movement, he was senior vice president and later the president of the PFUJ. This article was published in the weekly 'Parbhaat', which was one of the thirteen publications that were edited by Irshad Rao and Wahab Siddiqui after 'Al Fatah' was banned. It was serialized and its last part appeared in 'Al Zulfiqar'.—Ahfaz ur Rehman]

These events occurred during May 1978 when the plains of Punjab were breathing fire and four groups of press workers and journalists were converging on Montgomery Road in Lahore. They had arrived from Karachi and Khyber because *Musawat* offices over there had shut down. More than 200 of its employees had been rendered jobless and we were protesting against the closure of the newspaper. This was not due to *Musawat's* association with a political party but because Pakistan's working journalists, through their federal organization, the PFUJ, had for the preceding thirty years opposed such measures by the government irrespective of the ideological leanings of the victimized publication.

The form of protest that we adopted was harmless and non-violent. Hunger strikes or fasts until death were 'political crimes' in the eyes of the martial law regime. Consequently, 180 journalists and press workers were rounded up from 30 April–30 May. They included calligraphers, machine-men, compositors, and administrative staff.

My name popped up in a draw on the evening of 6 May. The other three were those of Shafqat Tanveer Mirza, assistant editor of the daily *Imroz*; Ali Ahmed of the daily *Sun*, Karachi; and Mohammad Siddiqui of the daily *Musawat*.

After bidding farewell to a huge crowd, we climbed into the police van.

The first stopover of this journey was the famous Civil Lines police station of Lahore. We spent a night over there. I was restless throughout, chitchatting with Ali Ahmed and Tanveer Mirza, reading 'The Crash of '79', but mostly staring at the walls of the cell.

Late in the night, I heard footsteps outside the lockup. A hand reached in through the iron bars and a whispering voice requested a cigarette to which I complied instantly. This person then said to me, 'May God fulfill your objectives.' He was the police guard on duty that night.

It was probably six in the morning. I stepped out of a closed van, wearing dirty clothes with handcuffed wrists, and stood before the most famous prison in Punjab: the Mianwali Central Jail. I was accompanied by six other journalists who are popularly known as the 'prisoners of journalism' today. We were surrounded by a police contingent that escorted us from Lahore, waiting impatiently for the main prison gate to open so that they could dispose of us.

We reached there after a long and tiring journey. We passed through the most backward western regions of the Punjab and were anxious to enter the jail premises to get some rest. The horrors of Mianwali Jail as narrated by our colleagues had vanished after arriving there. It appeared to be quite a decent place from the outside.

Actually, I breathed a sigh of relief after reaching there in the hope that it would be the last destination of the journey we had embarked upon on 6 May. It was 14 May and we had been travelling constantly for the last seven days.

A week earlier, after departing from Montgomery Road, Lahore, our entire day was spent in Jinnah Gardens, though I didn't get the opportunity to stroll freely in this lush green 'Hyde Park of Lahore'. We spent the whole day in the police van waiting for permission without which we could not enter the transit Camp Jail of Lahore as 'under-trial' prisoners. We whiled away time by talking to each other and for the first time realized the extent of the hardships that each of us was dealing with. A strange sense of guilt weighed my colleagues down. 'We are helpless,' they said. They spoke further and said, 'We are nuts and bolts of a rusted machine. We don't understand what is happening; why are you in handcuffs? What is your crime? May God protect you. Please write about us too. Our workload is increasing and our house allowance has been slashed.'

At last, around four in the afternoon, we received the orders to reappear before the military court on the thirteenth of that month. The same evening, we landed in Camp Jail, Lahore.

Chakki No. 10, which was specially vacated for us, was considered a relatively comfortable place for Class-C prisoners. Half a dozen cells were allocated to us journalists. In the remaining space, two workers and leaders of the PPP were staying, who were under trial in a bomb attack case. These included Khalid Chaudhary of *Musawat* (who took good care of us being an old occupant and privy to the world inside), and a very interesting member of former provincial assembly, Mr Awan. He arranged an interesting entertainment show for us on our first day. We sat on a blanket under an old banyan tree within the compound of the Chakki, where we were delighted to listen to Punjabi folk songs and ghazals of Faiz, and enjoyed the bhangra dance.

Before we could settle down in our new abode, we received orders to appear before the court for the hearing of our case. We were speedily awarded a sentence of six months rigorous imprisonment, in addition to a penalty of PKR 5,000. We were transferred to Kot Lakhpat Jail directly from the military court. Our personal belongings and books remained in Camp Jail, and our right to reclaim them was snatched from us. After our release, we received all that stuff on 8 June with great difficulty.

Kot Lakhpat Jail looked very imposing after our brief stint at Camp Jail. When we entered the jail premises for check-in, it felt like moving from Lahore Hotel to Hilton Lahore; especially because of Z. A. Bhutto, the air of VIP protocol was unmistakable. The whole facility was under siege. Even the civil administration of the prison was awestruck and more vigilant due to the security arrangements of the military. Despite great efforts, we were unable to catch a glimpse of the 'big criminal' of the Nawab Muhammad Ahmed Khan case, although there was only a wall between our compound and his cell.

The searing heat did not prevent us from enjoying the next three days at Kot Lakhpat. Our group of about thirty-five inmates lived under the principles of tribal socialism. We equally divided the prison food with the outside 'bounty' of cigarettes. We presumed that the rest of our term would be spent happily in that manner. Alas, only three days later on 31 May, we were ordered to move under a scorching sun. We were split into groups of seven and spread over facilities from Bahawalpur to Mianwali.

It took us fifteen hours to reach Mianwali from Lahore. The police van was apparently driven by a novice. We took a route through Faisalabad as seven of my colleagues had to be handed over to the Central Jail authorities in that city. The driver left a decent main road and sped cross-country on a perilous route to

Faisalabad in five hours where we insisted on having lunch. The poor guards were perplexed. They eventually agreed to feed us at a restaurant but on the condition of keeping one of our arms in handcuffs. That was my first ever evening in Faisalabad which pulled a large crowd when we sat down to eat our food at a small roadside restaurant. The spectators seemed to admire our effort with affection. We were energized after the meal and resumed our journey to Mianwali.

The mud-walled Mianwali Jail was about 105 years old. Mr Durrani, the jail superintendent, confided in us about a grave secret. He said, 'From Gandhi to Mujibur Rahman and Bhutto, several historic personalities of India and Pakistan have stayed here. On the night of 3 December 1971 when the war between India and Pakistan started on the western front, Sheikh Mujibur Rahman was here. Ilam Deen Ghazi was also hanged here.' After hearing all of this, we thought there must be something special about us to be sent here.

The matter of lodging remained a headache for the jail administration the entire day. On one hand, there was shortage of space, while on the other was the assumption that journalists were a 'dangerous' lot, therefore, they wanted to keep us in a corner where we had minimum possible contact with other inmates so that the secrets of this place could remain safe. They were also concerned about why we were sent as Class-C inmates, although we actually merited the 'Prisoners of Conscience' category. They did not have clear instructions about how to treat us which perturbed them. Anyhow, after a great deal of brainstorming, the superintendent selected a room that was slightly comfortable as well as somewhat secluded.

Our stay at Mianwali Jail lasted for about twenty-five days—from 16 May to 7 June. In a way, it is quite a short period; nevertheless, while we were there, it seemed as if we had been in that place forever. By the time we were released, we started believing that we belonged in the prison as we had made quite a place for ourselves in a population of about 2,000 inmates.

We spent two weeks in Class-C and the last week in Class-B prisons. The former was a more interesting place because we got the opportunity to meet several colorful characters. One such special personality was Khan Zaman Khan. He was a famous political leader of Mianwali and belonged to Jamiat Ulema-e-Islam (Hazarwi Group). With a white beard and a beaming face, he told us that he had spent a long time in those corridors; he was probably a regular visitor since 1928. A very imposing figure with a sharp tongue; perhaps, that is why he did not get along well with the law enforcers of Mianwali. He landed in jail repeatedly after brief intervals.

He had set up some sort of a home in a corner of his room, complete with a water cooler, which we also benefited from sometimes. He offered and led prayers five times a day, preceded by *azan* in his thunderous voice. Then all seventeen of us in that room would stand shoulder-to-shoulder behind him. Besides seven journalists, there were some murder suspects and a man serving his jail term for financial embezzlement.

Apparently, the management of our jails followed a manual. This 'constitution' was basically compiled by the British and amended on-and-off after Independence. However, practically, that ordinance which was written a century ago was hardly practised. While in Class-C, we yearned to read newspapers. It is a different matter that we had arranged to receive them from outside; courtesy of Khan Zaman Khan, who had established special links within the jail owing to his influence.

If you do not possess influence and clout, especially of the monetary kind, your position in Class-C prisons is worse than that of a slave. Those who can grease the palms of jail staff can have a lavish life even as inmates. For example, they don't need to toil as sentenced if they don't want to and can outsource their assignments.

Or, you can perform your chores in your cell instead of going out to the work area to complete them. You can also rest frequently by obtaining a sickness certificate.

On 27 May, when we were promoted to Class-B, the jail staff had a serious problem. Class-B prisoners were uncommon and therefore the arrangements for that class were also absent. However, we made it easy for the staff by requesting them to keep us where we were but provide the beds which Class-B prisoners were entitled to. Our request was fulfilled immediately. Then the superintendent summoned us to offer his congratulations as we were being moved into an upgraded cell, and to inform us about other facilities we had become entitled to. He started reading to us the various clauses in the manual according to which we were to be given eggs, meat, and a 'serf' to cook and serve our needs.

We thanked him profusely, and with hearts full of joy and happiness, returned to our colleagues with the good news. We all spent the next ten days in anticipation of our new perks, especially the chicken and fish meat. Eventually, we decided to register our concern with the superintendent. He summoned the jail storekeeper and instructed him to do the needful. We returned happily to our cell. A short while later, we were informed that orders for our release had arrived. Thus, the longing to relish chicken and fish in the jail remained unfulfilled.

The Saga of Struggle

Ali Ahmed Khan

I don't know where to begin this story from. For my own convenience, I have chosen to start from the day when Shabbar Azmi and Amir Mohammad Khan handed me the ticket to Lahore and instructed me to accompany Ghosi and Liaquat Ali of *Aman* newspaper on their trip. We had to travel the very next day. Shabbar was a sub-editor with *Musawat* since his college days and president of its employees union. He was also the president of Karachi Action Committee of the PFUJ. He is currently working as a news editor for the daily *Aman*. Amir has been living in Saudi Arabia for a long time now. He worked with the Karachi-based daily *Sun* and was elected secretary of APNEC, Karachi. Both of these individuals began to render sacrifices for democracy since they were students. The late Sabihuddin Ghosi served as a senior commerce reporter with *Sun*, PPI, *Dawn*, and others. He was elected to key positions a number of times at Karachi Press Club and KUJ. He always played an active role in the struggle waged by the PFUJ and APNEC.

The idea of going to Lahore was very exciting. It had been a long time since my last visit to that city. It would also provide me with an opportunity to meet old friends. I took the ticket from Shabbar's hand before he could change his mind. Ghosi readily agreed.

We were to leave Karachi via the Super Express on 3 May. I reached my office early in the morning, left my travel plans on the editor's desk, and went to Karachi Press Club. Ghosi was already there, talking about his trip with everyone as if he was embarking on a voyage to the moon. Babar Ayaz remains sober even when he is angry. He told Ghosi not to make noise for fear of alerting the 'informants' and risking being stopped before we reached the railway station. So we went back home to pack our bags.

Ghosi bought underwear on the way home because according to Ahfaz, it is handier in prison than a shalwar. Ahfaz had returned a day earlier after being exiled from Punjab along with Johar Mir, Zahid Sammoon, and Mohammad Riaz. They were detained at Camp Jail, Lahore. I gathered some belongings, ate food, and gave a motivational lecture to my wife about the movement. I also explained the situation to my mother.

I was expecting a cheering crowd, carrying flags to receive us at Lahore Railway Station but the situation over there was similar to that in Karachi. It stirred a realization about self-worth but then Ghosi came to the rescue. He said, 'My friend, is it necessary that someone should see us off and be present to welcome us? The important thing is that we have arrived at our destination. Now let's go to the press club; we will meet everybody over there.'

After taking a shower and changing clothes at the press club, we saw a harried and worried Altaf Malak. Late Altaf Malak was a senior reporter at the daily *Musawat*. He was elected to key positions in Punjab Union of Journalists and was very popular among the press community. He was arrested in Karachi during the third phase of the movement and was mercilessly tortured. He lost his hearing and his kidneys were also damaged, which ultimately resulted in his death.

Before we could gather the words to express our disappointment on arrival at the train station, he hugged us while sweating profusely. 'I have come running from the station; which gate did you exit from?' Altaf Malak asked.

Tahir Najmi led us to our lodging. It was probably somewhere near Islamia College in Gawal Mandi and was very depressing.

I had expected arrangements to be made in some bungalow in Gulberg. It turned out to be a room in an under-construction building with a bathroom without the door-lock and a tub full of water. There was an iron bed and a mat and the room was filled with about ten people merrily sitting on the floor and gossiping. They embraced us warmly as if we had returned after performing Hajj. Food and water was immediately arranged for us. Hafiz Basheer from *Musawat* suggested getting some rest after the meal and before proceeding to the 'front'.

'Who will be going?' I enquired. It emerged that the names of volunteers were declared at the last minute to prevent the information from reaching the police. Meanwhile, Khushtar, the owner of the house also arrived. I lay down on the iron bed. Before I could doze off, I sensed some commotion in the room. When I opened my eyes, I saw everyone getting ready. Shah Jee, who was probably a calligrapher in *Musawat* and seemed to be a man of few words, was very animated.

'Get up, sir! It is five o'clock.' Shah Jee exclaimed.

Ghosi and Liaquat were ready. I splashed some water on my face and went down the stairs. Some of us boarded tongas while others jumped on scooters, and then we all headed towards the 'crime scene'. We got off at a short distance from the *Musawat* office. There was a movie theatre nearby and we were told to sit in its canteen. After a while, a prim and proper and cheerful gentleman arrived wearing a kurta and Aligarh pyjamas. He was smoking a pipe and held a tin of tobacco in his hands. He introduced himself as Aziz Siddiqui, senior assistant editor of *Pakistan Times* in Lahore. He was accompanied by another gentleman, Saleem Aasmi, whose body language reminded me of a neighbourhood thug. Aasmi talked like a spymaster. Mohammad Khan of the daily *Sun*, Karachi, was also there and had demonstrated his temperament before his management skills several times. Today was our turn to see the latter.

When I came out of the cinema canteen, I saw contingents of police standing in front of *Musawat* offices and a huge crowd on the other side of the street. Old and young men and women, children, labourers, clerks, and some well dressed gentlemen, all were gazing at the teahouse right across the entrance of the cinema hall. A man came forward and put garlands around the necks of the four volunteers. He handed them banners with 'Long Live Press Freedom!', 'Restore *Musawat*!', and 'Long Live the Unity of Press Workers!' inscribed on them. The group headed to the *Musawat* office. The crowd began clapping and cheering with heightened fervour and zeal. The police immediately shuffled and proceeded to push the crowd back. 'Long Live Press Freedom!' A slogan burst out which echoed in the whole area. The police then moved towards the hunger strikers and tried to contain the bulging crowd.

I was determined not to shout slogans; however, I soon realized that my voice was getting louder. Ghosi, Liaquat, and the rest were caught in a frenzy. Some female students standing at the gate of the *Musawat* offices held banners and stepped towards the volunteers with flowers. The roofs of the surrounding buildings were full of spectators. A jeep approached us and a burly police officer with a few plainclothes men emerged. They did some quick paperwork and pushed the hunger strikers into the jeep in a manner that suggested a kidnapping attempt instead of an arrest.

Back at the place where we were staying, Hafiz Basheer suggested that it'd be better if we see the city of Lahore before departing. After breakfast, we went to Allama Iqbal's mausoleum, Shahi Mosque, and climbed to the top of its minaret for a view of the sprawling city. The vast area occupied by Jahangir's tomb revealed the secrets behind the narrow lanes of Lahore. We were too tired to visit Noor Jahan's tomb; nevertheless, we learnt that despite having all the qualities of a ruler, she spent her life as Jahangir's maid. She did not believe in freedom of expression, or if she did, it was only to the extent of not displeasing the emperor.

After watching the passionate youth chanting slogans in front of *Musawat* offices a day earlier, Noor Jahan's tomb or even her presence for that matter, could not have impressed us.

On our way back from Shahdara, we visited Data Darbar and saw its golden door and groups of beggars sitting around the premises. If Data was alive, he would have donated many such doors to the needy. I guess the golden door would have added to the grandeur of a private mansion in a posh neighbourhood like Gulberg but in the middle of all those beggars, it looked very anachronistic. Upon returning to the place where we had taken refuge, Ghosi received a message which said, 'It's your turn today.'

Preparations for another round of demonstrations began in the afternoon. Ghosi shaved his beard, wore a starched shalwar kameez, and carefully combed his hair. We came to know that Tahir Asadi, city editor of *Musawat*, Sher Afgan, the peon, and Afzal Khan of APP were going to accompany him. Gulistan Cinema was completely cordoned off. The police probably wanted to make the arrests before the volunteers even reached the office of *Musawat*. The crowd near *Musawat* office included old and young women. For a moment, I thought that the women will have to retreat. Suddenly, I saw four demonstrators coming towards me, all of whom were carrying banners. The crowd's enthusiasm began to soar and all that could be heard were slogans. Ghosi and Tahir walked leisurely towards the *Musawat* office and were able to reach there before the police. Both of them started to chant slogans loudly. The police jeep reached the venue. As expected, after performing the usual formalities, the plainclothes men rounded them up and fled.

Back at the press club, Riaz Malik commented on the situation. Wali Mohammad Wajid of the daily *Imroz*, who had also held central posts in the PFUJ and APNEC, was requested to address the gathering. He was a lively, upright, and renowned journalist and played a central role in promoting the movement. All of us dispersed once his address was over.

Wali Mohammad Wajid also joined us at the house where we were taking refuge. All of us sat on the rooftop and exchanged stories of new and old arrests. It emerged that a large number of volunteers in our country wanted to participate in the movement and were willing to suffer hardships for the cause of freedom of the press. The next morning, Hafiz Basheer came to take us for a stroll around the Shalimar Gardens. I readily agreed considering the uncertain circumstances when our turn to be thrown into jails could come anytime. As soon as we returned home after sightseeing, I received a phone call informing me that I was the next to be imprisoned. I packed my bag, changed my clothes, and left for this rendezvous with the police. Aslam Shaikh, Shafqat Tanveer Mirza, and Sadiq were already at the protest site. [...]

The daily *Musawat's* calligrapher, Aatif Shaikh, came in all of a sudden. It seemed as if he had come right after playing a tennis match. He had arrived in Lahore the same day along with Iqbal Jafri of the daily *Sun*, Khalid Saeed of daily *Mashriq*, and Sharafat of the daily *Sadaqat*.

Somebody informed us that the police was intent on baton-charging the protestors if slogans were raised. Someone else also said that the police would never allow the protestors to reach the office of *Musawat*. A gentleman instructed us not to chant slogans. There were more women protestors than usual. I saw Aslam Shaikh smiling frequently while he keenly observed everything. Sadiq, a machine-man at the Lahore office of *Musawat*, was very old but he appeared quite at peace amidst all this commotion. Shafqat Tanveer Mirza, who was an optimist, had so much faith in the future that he did not bother to think about the past or present. Holding a packet of Marvens in his hand and a cigarette between his lips, he appeared content during those moments. I. H. Rashid, Riaz Malik, Ijaz Rizvi, Naveed Butt, Altaf Malak, Hafiz Basheer, and others stood around. The police looked quite alert. An inspector scolded a sergeant. The sergeant then turned to a constable and took out all his frustration on him. A policeman was shoving the crowd when, suddenly, somebody started to put garlands around our necks. The crowd started clapping, which was a special signal, hence we started marching forward. I felt like a soldier given a charge on an enemy post. Just as I reached the *Musawat* office, people advanced towards me. Some carried flowers, while others wanted to shake my hand. Someone gently patted my head. As I turned to check who it was, I saw my mother. I was taken aback as she had tears of joy in her eyes. She saw me triumphing probably for the first time. My sister stood next to her with flowers and she also had tears in her eyes. I lowered my head to help her put the garland around my neck.

I resolved to choose the severance of my head instead of lowering it before tyrants and oppressors. I decided that the neck that held my sister's flowers will not bend for selfish desires and cowardice. I began to chant slogans with full zeal and fervour. In that moment, I felt like I had become invincible.

Soon after, a police van arrived and we were pushed into it. It moved so fast as if wanting to cover the distance of a lifetime in a few moments. In a short while, we were inside the Civil Lines police station.

In the lockup, I closed my eyes and tried to sleep—a state Wordsworth called 'the mother of fresh ideas', but I found that impossible. Perhaps I believed that the ideas we believed in were the most fresh and there was no room for revising them any further. Mirza continued reading Crash of '79. I told him to go to sleep as it was very late. He looked at me with a smile as if wanting to say, 'Good that the night is passing.' I lay down again and it was dawn after a while. I could not believe that the night had passed so quickly.

Shaikh and Sadiq also stretched and woke up. Shaikh tried to do some sort of a workout which was not very impressive. There was a serious lack of coordination between the various parts of his body, which looked quite odd. Breakfast was arranged by our friends who were outside. We got ready and wondered what was in the offing next. A hefty police official arrived and ordered us to prepare for appearing at the martial law courts. We gathered our belongings and were escorted to martial law headquarters in a truck. Something went on there for about two hours while we remained in the truck. We were not allowed to get down despite the hot weather. Out of desperation, Shaikh ordered four cold drinks and paid for twelve. This act thawed the stiff police guards for the rest of the trip. We pushed the truck to jump-start once again, and reached the summary military courts. There we saw a long queue of almost seventeen of our handcuffed friends. A long iron chain enjoined their handcuffs. It was a rather strange sight. They had woven many stories with their pens. They believed that they could fight nuclear powers with the might of their pen but never thought that those hands could be handcuffed as well. Such was the destiny of all obstinate people.

While going inside after our names had been called, we saw Hafeez Raqeeb, Nisar Usmani, and others shackled in the corridor. We tried to talk to them but the guards did not want further delays. We were taken straight to Major Mumtaz's courtroom. We stood before him like creditors and he bent his head over documents as if implying that he had not received his salary yet. He signed a paper and requested us to come three days later.

Soon after, we reached Camp Jail. It had a huge door with a board displaying its name.

It took a long time for the gate to open. After the paperwork, we were sent to 'chakkar', which in the local prison jargon is a large room or hub where inmates are brought before being sent further to 'chakki'. A chakki is a room where prisoners are kept. Ours was Chakki No. 10. Some of our colleagues, including Raqeeb and Usmani, were already there.

In Chakki No. 10, we met Saleem Aasmi, Aziz Siddiqui, Afzal Khan, Tahir Asadi, Sabihuddin Ghosi, Mohammad Khan, Hashmat Wafa, Achhi Memon, Ijaz Mehmood, Hakim Ashraf,

Raqeeb, Arshad Khan, and others. We hugged each other as if we had gone astray from the caravan and had suddenly returned. Arif Awan and others from the PPP, as well as the bomb-case accused were also there. The news of the arrival of four more journalists spread throughout Camp Jail, Lahore.

In the absence of Usmani and Raqeeb, Afzal Khan performed the duties of the chef and Aasmi was the temporary commander. The latter charge was duly transferred to Aslam Shaikh on his arrival. The idea was to return the powers to Usmani and Raqeeb on their return from the courts in the evening. However, that evening never came. The roll call commenced and prison doors began to shut. I moved with Ghosi to the same cell where other friends from Karachi were kept.

Mirza, Shaikh, and Siddiqui joined Hashmat Wafa and Afzal Khan. The warden, Sajawal, proceeded to lock the cell doors but our friends who had gone to seek justice from the military court had still not returned. Moments later, the following announcement was made from the adjacent cell where Sher Afgan and Tahir Asadi were kept.

'Brother, we are all victorious!' This voice firstly echoed throughout Chakki No. 10 and then spread far and wide.

Sixteen journalists were sentenced to six to twelve months of rigorous imprisonment plus PKR 3,000 to PKR 10,000 in penalties.

The first night in Camp Jail seemed like it would never pass and we would not see the dawn ever again.

The toilets at Camp Jail were not only inadequate but also very outdated. The ritual of bathing was also very strange. Everyone bathed in the open as if nobody was watching.

On our third day in Camp Jail, someone called the names of Ghosi, Mohammad Khan, Naseem, and Habib-ur-Rehman. All of these men got ready in haste while instructing other colleagues to send so and so stuff to Kot Lakhpat Jail in case they were not released. An emergency meeting was called under Shaikh, and those summoned were instructed to apologize if they were intimidated and forced to do so.

All of them returned by evening and it emerged that a brigadier had browbeaten and threatened them to sign an apology in the presence of a magistrate; however, each one of them came back to the jail.

On 10 May, all except those who went a day earlier were summoned. A truck awaited us outside as we were being handcuffed in groups of four. When we arrived at the military court, a herd of friends started to gather around us. Some carried food while others brought buckets of water.

The court of Major Mumtaz summoned all of us once again and our handcuffs were removed. Our crimes were read out by the prosecutor and witnesses called. After listening to them, we wished we had committed all those crimes—at least we would not be going through the proceedings without having violated any law. I don't like to scribble more on the attitude and proceedings of the military court especially when Mirza's response sums it up so well.

'I pray to God that you and the entire prosecuting staff may earn promotions.'

We left the court and the Major went to another room to answer a telephone call. Moments later, we were summoned once again. This time a captain read the statement and ushered us out. Afterwards, the prosecutor summoned us and noted details of our jobs, salaries, and family members. That was worrying for me because my salary was PKR 1,100 and my family members seven. This was such a small amount that I thought it would possibly induce some measure of pity in their hearts, resulting in a lighter sentence for me as compared to my comrades. I even expected an outright order for my release. I prayed to God not to humiliate me with a punishment that wasn't equal to that of my colleagues. I assume that He was in a gracious mood as I was awarded a rigorous imprisonment of six months in addition to PKR 3,000 in penalty.

Shaikh and Mirza received a six-month rigorous imprisonment with PKR 5,000 in penalties. Sadiq was awarded a three-month rigorous imprisonment. By the time we came out of the court, other batches of our colleagues had also been conferred with similar honours (except for Achhi Memon's and Saleem Asmi's groups).

'How much do you have to pay in penalties?' Ghosi asked me very anxiously. When I told him that I got the exact same of what he had got, he seemed very pleased. He took out a cigarette from his pack and struck his matches to light it for me for the first time.

Aasmi, Siddiqui, and Mohammad Khan were sad because they were summoned the next day for the award of their punishments. Once this was over, we were made to sit in a truck and on Mirza's suggestion, we chanted loud slogans for freedom of the press.

Twenty-five people had gathered in our barrack and there was just no space left. Usmani intervened to resolve this matter and told us that the barrack facing ours would also be opened for us. After having tea and snacks, Usmani went and sat in the terrace of the other barrack. Our toil arrived in the shape of tangled wool yarn bundles, which we had to unravel. We finished the task around eleven and started preparing for lunch.

In order to beat the hot weather, we placed wet blankets on the fence. Each one of us was given two blankets—one for sleeping and the other to rest our head on. By three o'clock, the blankets were as dry as if they had never been wet. However, as the shadow of the barrack grew larger, we took shelter in it. We took tea. A couple minutes later, the warden arrived as usual, conducted our head count, and locked us in the cells. The white kurta that I had worn for Eid prayers when I courted arrest had turned brown and was torn. Usmani asked someone to give me a kurta from his jail issue. He told me that each prisoner was provided with two pairs of uniform and I would get mine soon. A while later, some bread and a bucket full of cooked lentils arrived. It was quite strange because the real Islam was practised in jail: everyone received food, clothing, and shelter. The slogan for these three things had toppled the royal rule of Ayub, ended Yahya's government, and landed Bhutto in Kot Lakhpat Jail. I thought that if I ever got the opportunity of advising the government, I would recommend turning the entire country into a jail so that people could surely receive two pairs of clothing, meals, and shelter.

The following night, Hakeem Mohammad Ashraf, Achhi Memon, Ijaz Mehmood, and Arshad Khan joined us. They were also guaranteed bread, clothing, and shelter. It was Friday the next day so the entangled wool bundles did not come. A barber was called in who trimmed our hair, clipped our nails, and tidied our moustaches and beards. Keeping blades was not allowed in jail, lest some desperate captive decided to use it for slashing his wrists. Ropes were also banned for the same reason. In other words, safety of life was also ensured. The jail was quite organized keeping in view the ideal model of a social welfare state.

A day after, a medical check-up and inspection was carried out. One gentleman, who probably belonged to the PPP, was also whipped. We saw him walking in a manly manner to the hospital instead of being taken on a stretcher. I thought, for all those amenities in the jail, fifteen lashes was a small sum to pay.

After returning from the hospital, we helped older inmates with their toil. We were about to hold our leisurely assembly after lunch when Usmani and Raqeeb were summoned. They returned with the information that we were being divided and transferred to different prisons. Soon, the editor of *Musawat* in Lahore, Badruddin, and a Punjab Assembly member, Mian Ehsanul Haq, arrived. They had received the information about our transfer.

Aslam Shaikh, Afzal Khan, Sabihuddin Ghosi, Hafeez Raqeeb, Sher Afgan, and Hashmat Wafa were being sent to Mianwali, while Tahir Asadi, Atif Shaikh, Khalid Saeed, and Rana were shifted to Lyallpur Central Jail. We lost two big singers, Afgan and Asadi, which was a major punishment. However, this did not prove to be

Prison Diary

Zafar Qureshi

[*Senior journalist Zafar Qureshi was one of the most active workers of the PFUJ. He worked at several newspapers in Pakistan and then moved to the USA where he published a popular magazine 'Pakistan Calling'. A good and true friend, he was elected Secretary, Karachi Press Club and held important positions in the PFUJ before leaving for the US. This article was published in the weekly 'Mayar' of 17–24 June 1978.*]

I left Karachi on 15 May and reached Lahore the next day after a delay of only three and a half hours. On 17 May, I courted arrest for the cause of a historic movement for press freedom and the restoration of *Musawat* in the midst of thousands of slogan chanting supporters. From the charges filed against me later, I learnt that I had violated Martial Law Regulations 5 and 33. I am not going to talk about what that is and how it relates to citizens because my comments might also result in yet another violation of some regulations. However, based on my sojourn in one lockup and four prisons, or four and a half jails, I collected the following statistics: the prisons in Pakistan house 50% political prisoners, 25% uniformed deserters, and 25% criminals. Moreover, the condition of the jails is also terrible. Approximately 1,100 inmates were kept in prisons with a capacity of 600. 1,700 inmates inhabited jails with a capacity of 800, and about 1,500 were locked in those with a capacity for 1,050.

After spending the night of 17 May in the lockup of Civil Lines he readily agreed and even suggested his favourite restaurant for lunch. It was probably close to the site where an Indian jet was shot down during the 1965 War.

The customers at the restaurant were horrified to see so many handcuffed individuals walking in. However, as soon as they found out that we were newspaper workers, a crowd gathered around us. The restaurant owner was astounded but as soon as he learnt that we were going to pay, he was very happy. He probably did not expect to sell his day's cookery so quickly. A cigarette stall nearby also had a heyday. The tab for the feast came to PKR 100. I don't know how Raqeeb arranged that sum.

We reached Sahiwal Jail around 9 p.m. where we dropped Shah, Jatoi, Butt, and others, and drove on towards Multan.

There was a hole in the floor of the van. We initially viewed it as a manufacturing defect but as we would soon discover, it was there so that we could urinate. However, we could not avail the 'facility' as the ride was very bumpy and the van was filled beyond capacity. I asked a guard to stop the van when I had to urinate. He led me by a chain to a roadside corner like I used to lead my dog, Tommy, when I would take him for a walk.

Everyone was fast asleep by the time we got near Multan. The guards were also strewn on the floor like dead bodies in a battlefield.

I always wanted to see Multan. We entered the city after midnight because the ASI lost his way, consequently, making frequent stops for directions. People were unable to differentiate between the central and district jails. It took us two hours to find our destination. Some prisoners were delivered after another half an hour's wait at the prison gate, and then we headed towards Bahawalpur Central Jail.

I started peeping through the screen in an attempt to see the rural side of Punjab as I had watched in Punjabi movies. Alas, there were no damsels like Mumtaz or Aasia, nor virile men like Sultan Rahi and Mustafa Qureshi. All that was there were shy girls and women wrapped in dirty chadors, toiling in front of their houses, and men leading their oxen to the fields. I wish our real villages were as cheerful and lively as those shown in Punjabi movies. Soon after, the sun appeared and cigarette smoke was replaced by dust and heat.

The guards and everyone else woke up while Mirza was still asleep. The van stopped when we reached Bahawalpur. There was probably a zoo nearby as we could hear a lion roaring. The ASI asked Mirza if he would like to go straight to the jail or shower first. Mirza told him that it would be nice if the shower could be arranged but breakfast was more important. Our next stop was the Police Lines area where a police band was playing for drill. There was a field toilet at some distance and Ashraf ran in its direction as soon as he saw it. Meanwhile, a newspaper hawker appeared. He was carrying the dailies *Imroz, Multan,* and *Mashriq.* The other newspapers were day-old issues from Karachi and Lahore. Front-page news in *Imroz* revealed the flogging of four journalists in Kot Lakhpat Jail: Khawar Naeem received three lashes, and Iqbal Jafri, Nasir Zaidi, and Masoodullah Khan received five lashes each.

Othe than me, everybody else bathed and changed in the Police Lines bathroom. We went to a roadside eatery where the ASI and other guards joined us with gusto and ate halva poori for breakfast. We saw a boy and persuaded him to carry our letter to Majeed Gill, president of Bahawalpur Union of Journalists and member of the PFUJ's executive committee, to inform him about our arrival.

A short while later, the prison door opened and we were summoned inside for a thorough search. Among other things, our razors, eatables, and books were retained by the jailers. The jail superintendent, Ranjha, was a very pious old man who assured us that our stay would be fine. He called a warden and instructed him to take us to Barrack No. 20 and advised, 'Please don't write back anything from the jail; it upsets us.'

While we followed the warden, everyone saluted us as if we were inspecting the facility. We were surprised by this reception until we discovered that our arrival was anticipated. Inside the barrack, there were arrested PPP members in large numbers. Our reception at the jail had not ended when the order to shift us to Barrack No. 19 came. The barrack almost emptied within moments. There was a black-plum tree in the courtyard opposite to our barrack, and death cells along the boundary wall. This was the beginning of the third phase of our prison tour where we witnessed life in its raw form.

I immediately went and sat under the black-plum tree. As I looked around, I noticed Mirza was busy informing PPP members about national affairs. I availed the opportunity, crossed my legs, and started to meditate.

Ali Ahmed's writing style is alluring. Only returning him to jail could have compensated for the misdeed of his leaving it unfinished.—Ahfaz ur Rehman

Prison Diary

Zafar Qureshi

[*Senior journalist Zafar Qureshi was one of the most active workers of the PFUJ. He worked at several newspapers in Pakistan and then moved to the USA where he published a popular magazine 'Pakistan Calling'. A good and true friend, he was elected Secretary, Karachi Press Club and held important positions in the PFUJ before leaving for the US. This article was published in the weekly 'Mayar' of 17–24 June 1978.*]

I left Karachi on 15 May and reached Lahore the next day after a delay of only three and a half hours. On 17 May, I courted arrest for the cause of a historic movement for press freedom and the restoration of *Musawat* in the midst of thousands of slogan chanting supporters. From the charges filed against me later, I learnt that I had violated Martial Law Regulations 5 and 33. I am not going to talk about what that is and how it relates to citizens because my comments might also result in yet another violation of some regulations. However, based on my sojourn in one lockup and four prisons, or four and a half jails, I collected the following statistics: the prisons in Pakistan house 50% political prisoners, 25% uniformed deserters, and 25% criminals. Moreover, the condition of the jails is also terrible. Approximately 1,100 inmates were kept in prisons with a capacity of 600. 1,700 inmates inhabited jails with a capacity of 800, and about 1,500 were locked in those with a capacity for 1,050.

After spending the night of 17 May in the lockup of Civil Lines police station, we were transferred to Camp Jail the following day. The cheerful jail staff warmly 'welcomed' us, and to prove their conventional pleasant nature, instructed us to sit down in rows of two in their harmless shrieking voices. In the Camp Jail, we were accused of several crimes. After registering us at the entrance and completing the paper work, two cells in Chakki No. 10 were allocated to us and we were kept in the same prison cell where murderers of a child had been locked up earlier. Chakki No.10 was called the boys' cell as it was reserved for underage detainees and had been vacated for us. Several leaders of the PPP and about eight to ten of those involved in bomb attacks were kept there.

The mission statement of this Chakki could be roughly translated as 'eat freely and bathe naked' (*khullay khhao, te nangay nahao*). Therefore, we put off our clothes and started feasting on the food our colleagues already detained there had arranged for us. After devouring the food, we met our neighbours. The detainees in the bomb attack case came from affluent families and narrated their ordeal of torture and interrogations.

We rolled on the floor laughing after reading the slogans on the prison walls which sounded like scrolls on a typical Iranian teahouse. For instance, one slogan read, 'The best man amongst you is the one who obeys the ruler of the day.' Another said, 'Humility and humbleness obliterate many evils.' Our stay in Camp Jail was brief and despite the numerous restrictions imposed on us, we tried to make it pleasant. Since there were no proper toilets, we had no choice but to use open latrines.

Camp Jail was a transit jail for us. We were transported to summary military courts where the disposal of cases took different durations of time for different inmates although they were all charged with the same offences. Some were decided instantly, others took hours, and even days. When there were delays, we had to wait in the corridors or lockups handcuffed in pairs. If the guards were in a good mood, they would provide us with water and refreshments;

if not, we would spend that time starving until our return to the jail. On the day of the hearing of our case, we spent over seven hours in suffocating heat inside a closed police van. The reason was that they wanted to decide the cases of Action Committee members Hamraz Ahsan, Ali Akhtar Mirza, I. H. Rashid, Ijaz Rizvi, and Riaz Malik. They had been in detention for almost a month; however, they could not be fired from their jobs before being sentenced. They were all awarded one year rigorous imprisonment in addition to a penalty of PKR 10,000 each. They were then sent to Kot Lakhpat Jail with us where about fifteen of our colleagues were already being held.

We arrived at Kot Lakhpat Jail around eleven o'clock that night. Usually, prisoners did not check in after five o'clock in the evening; however, an exception was reluctantly made for those who were sentenced by summary courts.

The first *mulahiza* that we experienced was at Kot Lakhpat Jail. We were given prison uniforms and beddings. Donning our uniforms and holding the bedding under one arm, we lined up under a shed near the entrance where the ground had been sprinkled. We were ordered to remove our shoes, spread our beds, and sit down with our heads bowed. A desk with a tablecloth and chair had been placed in front for the jail superintendent. Some registers and pens were kept on the desk. The ritual was that the superintendent would arrive with a platoon of wardens and carefully look at all detainees who were to be called one by one afterwards. The accused was expected to stand straight and respectfully respond to every question in a loud voice. In case he moved or attempted to scratch his back, the wardens on his either side did not hesitate to kick him. One of our colleagues committed such an error and had his arm twisted so severely that he spent the next two days in agony.

Despite all the preparations, the superintendent did not show up. We surmised that we would be transferred soon. In the jail hospital, we met a senator of the previous government. After introductions, I said, 'We are criminals under all governments.' He looked embarrassed and replied, 'Our biggest mistake was adopting an excessively harsh attitude towards newspapers.'

Many stories circulated about Bhutto in Kot Lakhpat Jail. By the time we arrived over there, he had been transferred to Rawalpindi. It was a mere coincidence that the death cell he was kept in was next to the cell we were locked in. We could see his cell from ours. One of the wardens told us that the security measures instituted during Bhutto's stay were extreme. Scores of personnel were always on duty on the roof of the cell and even the wardens were not allowed to go near it. Another warden told us that Bhutto cared a lot about his party workers. Once, when Benazir came to see him in jail, he told her that there were several PPP supporters locked in here and she should try to meet some of them.

Early on the first day in Kot Lakhpat, we noticed two noisy birds hovering over Bhutto's former cell. We needed the counsel of the wardens to understand the phenomena. It emerged that Bhutto used to feed the birds his leftovers from the previous night's meal and breakfast. Besides these two birds, there were dozens of crows contending for the leftover food which spurred fights and extreme noise every morning.

This bird show was a regular feature not only during the three days that we were there but it continued for some time afterwards, as our colleagues told us.

DISTRICT JAIL FAISALABAD

As we finished our breakfast of roasted chickpeas and treacle, a warden came to inform us that except for Aziz Siddiqui, we were all being transferred to various jails across Punjab.

When we arrived at District Jail, Faisalabad after travelling for four long hours in a suffocating police van, the jail authorities refused to accept us. Their stance was that with a capacity for 600 inmates, the jail already had 1,200 including thirteen women; therefore, they could not accommodate another ten of us. Consequently, we were sent to the Central Jail, Faisalabad, where the situation was no different. We were brought back to District Jail, Faisalabad. After roaming about for eight hours, some space was finally made for us. Luckily, the cells over there had ceiling fans.

This mud building had many peculiarities. We contracted itches very quickly over here. When we refused to eat the badly-cooked lentils for the second time, the warden was astounded. He added some oil and spices to make it more palatable but it was still unacceptable. Meanwhile, we received a message from a labour leader, Charagh Din, and an MPA, Badruddin, stating that they would arrange our food for the length of our stay. Thus the issue was resolved.

The newspapers we received were always two days old which was very frustrating. What else could ten people living in two 8 by 10 prison cells do? The local, small town reporters were too intimidated by the authorities to visit us. We spent about four days over there which felt like four months due to the lack of work, scorching heat, and too many restrictions. On the fourth day, we were moved somewhere else.

CENTRAL JAIL FAISALABAD

Our longest stay was in Central Jail, Faisalabad. Six of our colleagues under the command of Tahir Asadi of *Musawat* awaited us there. The special barrack allocated to us the first day had previously been occupied by Sheikh Mujibur Rahman, Ataullah Mengal, and Khan Abdul Wali Khan. We saw Rahman's cell with great interest. The tree that he had planted in the courtyard had grown and inmates used its branches for exercise. Mengal's plant was still young. They tried to pack us in Rahman's cell but Asadi refused to use a death cell for his colleagues; therefore, we were provided with an alternate space in the barrack in which Mengal and Khan had lived. Our companions included about half a dozen leaders of the PPP, Rawalpindi. The following day we were upgraded to Class-B in the prison and moved to another barrack.

After a long time, we ate a sumptuous dinner offered to us by our hosts, Qeemti and his brother Sardar, who were serving life sentences.

[*Zafar Qureshi's diary abruptly ends here. I was unable to find a sequel to it.—Ahfaz ur Rehman*]

Reminiscences of 1977–8 Freedom of the Press Movement

By Shabbar Azmi

Our struggle for freedom of the press did not span over days but decades, during which we bore the brunt of imprisonment, loss of livelihood, and some of us were even flogged. Thousands of individuals participated bravely and did not give up on the cause of freedom of the press. Undoubtedly, the commander-in-chief of this struggle was Minhaj Barna.

I would like to mention some events and facts (not sequentially though) for the perusal of readers.

I was the president of Musawat Employees Union and APNEC Coordination Committee, Karachi. I went to Lahore frequently with Barna. We would visit various newspaper offices. We were being constantly watched and a vehicle equipped with wireless communication followed us everywhere. Wherever we went, it followed us. Barna would sometimes enter a newspaper office from the front door and exit from the backdoor. That perplexed the people who were watching us and a manhunt for Barna would soon ensue.

One day, we had an appointment with Zia ul-Haq's Information Secretary. We were waiting for him in Chamba House, Lahore. Nisar Usmani also accompanied us and had to see off a relative leaving for India. We didn't have a vehicle so Usmani approached a man in a surveillance car and said, 'The rest of my associates will remain here, please take me to the railway station and then bring me back.' He agreed.

The PFUJ always struggled in a steadfast manner for press freedom and job security. Press freedom is linked with civic freedoms. The pursuit of civic and press freedom bestowed on the PFUJ a status higher than that of a common trade union. Regardless of the nature of the government, whenever press freedom was endangered, the PFUJ raised an overwhelming voice and fought for the right of journalists. The First Wage Board Award was only for journalists. Under Barna's leadership, the PFUJ demanded that everyone associated with the press must get the award and he also struggled for it. He had the demand accepted and in the Second Wage Board, all newspaper workers received their rights.

Barna was cognizant of the fact that the size of the journalist community was small; therefore, he gathered all classes of workers in the newspaper industry and created APNEC. He was elected its chairman. Several movements were launched from these two platforms. Some senior journalists had objections but Barna's arguments were strong. In the process of expanding the trade union movement, he also led the creation of the All Pakistan Trade Union Organization (APTO). Barna was its president, Anita Ghulam Ali its vice president, and the elderly leader S. P. Lodhi its secretary general. Shamim Asghar was a leading figure in creating the organization and disappeared after his arrest in the 1978 movement. He was severely tortured while in custody. Asghar had close link with Ahfaz ur Rehman because Rehman was running the movement from underground and the police wanted to trace him through Asghar. When they failed to break Asghar, he was sent to jail.

After the formation of APTO, other trade unions also valiantly joined the protesting newspaper workers. They participated in congregations and courted arrest in the journalists' movement in large droves.

On the other hand, the role of Jamaat-e-Islami and its student wing, Islami Jamiat Tulaba, was most shameful. They spied for the police and used to gather at the venues where some of us were arrested and identified other participants for the police.

In 1973, soon after the publication of *Musawat* resumed, the daily *Jasarat* was banned. The PFUJ announced a strike in protest. Some people in *Musawat* were not in favour of the strike. Their stance was that the strike would bring *Musawat* in the line of fire. Rehman was secretary of KUJ and took a firm stand. He supported the strike because all of us were members of the PFUJ and duty-bound to obey its policies. He proposed a referendum which went in the favour of strike.

During 1974–5, several employees of *Musawat* (Lahore) were fired or transferred to inappropriate departments and cities. Abbas Athar was the editor. This was purely a vengeful move; therefore a movement was launched against it also. Journalists from all over the country converged in Lahore and courted arrests. Eventually, the administration had to withdraw its decision.

Soon after coming in to power, Zia ul-Haq banned *Musawat*. Its editor, Ibrahim Jalees, engaged in a great deal of effort to get the ban lifted. He met the Interior Secretary of Sindh, who told him to forget *Musawat* as it was not to be restored.

Jalees returned disheartened to the office. In a husky voice, he said, 'The secretary tells me to forget *Musawat*.' Hundreds of people depended on *Musawat* for their livelihood. He suffered a heart attack in the office, was transferred to the hospital, and died the following day.

The next day, a huge condolence meeting was organized in Karachi Press Club to mourn his death. A large number of intellectuals and newspaper editors participated. Ahfaz ur Rehman proposed not to bring out newspapers to commemorate the death of Jalees. The APNS showed reluctance first but then agreed. It was for the first time that newspapers were not published on the death of an editor.

The government had shut down *Musawat* but gave the impression that it was sincere with its employees and the measure had to be taken due to the editorial policy of the publication. They took over its printing press, the People's Foundation Trust, and renamed it as Sheikh Al Nahyan Trust. Irfan Ghazi, who belonged to *Jasarat*, was appointed as the editor. It was already agreed that the new administration would not retain the services of three individuals: Ahfaz ur Rehman, Abdul Waheed Khan, and Shabbar Azmi. A meeting was held in Barna's office and we conceded. However, our other colleagues did not agree to go back to work without us three as it was a war for freedom of the press. This pressure resulted in the withdrawal of the decision to appoint Irfan Ghazi as editor.

After the restriction on *Musawat* in December 1977, a protest camp was organized at Karachi Press Club where Barna and other colleagues started a hunger strike. One night, police vehicles arrived to arrest those on hunger strike. However, when the crowd raised slogans against martial law, they rounded up everybody. We were held in different police stations and transferred to jail the following day. However, the government had to restore *Musawat* due to mounting pressure.

Sometime later, *Musawat* (Lahore) was shut down and protests ensued. A protest camp was set up. They arrested Barna and exiled him from Lahore. The following day, a month-long series of arrests from *Musawat* offices began. On 13 May, three of our colleagues, Khawar Naeem Hashmi, Nasir Zaidi, and Iqbal Jafri were flogged. They presumed that such tactics could suppress the movement; on the contrary, it was further intensified.

Meanwhile a deterring incident happened. We used to send two volunteers from Karachi to Lahore every day by train; however, one day we could not get tickets so we sent them by air. On arrival in

Lahore, instead of proceeding to the journalists' camp at the press club, they went to join the government forces.

More than 150 people were arrested during this movement. Jails in Punjab were filled to capacity. Many, including Nisar Usmani, were awarded sentences of rigorous punishment.

It was the third phase of the movement and the first day of the hunger strike at the Karachi Press Club camp in July 1978. The famous Lahore-based journalist and intellectual, Shafqat Tanveer Mirza, called to inform us that he was coming along with his wife to court arrest. Shuhrat Bokhari's wife, Farkhanda, also accompanied them. What a wonderful group of comrades that was!

Those arrested in Karachi were first sent to the Central Jail and then to Landhi Jail, and then transferred to other cities. Journalists were usually kept together but Tahir Najmi's case was odd. He was sent to Nawabshah Jail where he spent two-and-a-half months without any other press workers.

Those imprisoned in Karachi decided to bring out a newspaper, *Zinda*. Jameel Ashraf Malik became its editor and it was produced in jail. We used to distribute it among visiting journalists and sometimes the entire content was reproduced in next day's newspapers.

Johar Mir was with us in Sukkur Jail. He was fond of eating well so he decided to cook biryani on Eid day. Somehow, a cooking pot was arranged; however, when it was placed on the fire, he realized that he didn't have a skimmer. He found some tree branches and tried to use them as cooking utensils but it didn't prove to be very effective.

Landhi Jail authorities told us that we were not allowed to offer Eid prayers with the others in the main congregation. They offered to send the prayer leader to our barrack for the purpose. We strongly protested and eventually were allowed to pray with the rest.

Mehmood Ali Asad was in Sukkur Jail when I arrived there. He suffered from cataracts and since there was no eye-specialist in Sukkur, the decision to send him to Hyderabad Jail was made. He requested meeting the rest of the inmates before leaving during which he informed us that we were running out of volunteers to court arrests. Therefore, it was decided to start hunger strikes until death. Barna was the first to start his fast in Khairpur Jail and was followed by his colleagues in other jails. We prepared a list of inmates at Sukkur Jail, which Asad posted from Hyderabad and it ultimately reached Karachi Press Club.

The procedure was that everyone would gather in the jail and according to the list, the volunteers would begin their fast amidst speeches. These names would appear in the newspapers and were followed up with the hour-count for each hunger striker. The jail authorities were surprised about how the news reached outside the jails. They suspected that someone among the prison staff might be collaborating so they transferred a few of them; however, the leaking of information did not stop. Actually, the schedule had been prepared beforehand and it was known to the outsiders.

Sardar Qureshi from *Hilal-e-Pakistan* was with us in Sukkur Jail along with his friend, Kareem Baloch, and he was always in the lead. He used to say, 'We will court arrests because it is the decision taken unanimously by all; we will have to obey it.' When we told him it was fast until death, he said it was wrong but since the decision was taken by all, it was compulsory for us to respect it.

One day, we decided to have some fun and told him that the fast until death is not working; therefore, it has been decided that one of us would set himself on fire every day.

'Set ourselves on fire?' He exclaimed. Then he said, 'It is not right but since it is the decision of the leadership, we will have to obey it.'

We wrote his name on three chits of paper and told him that he will have to draw one of it. He picked a slip, read his name on it, and said, 'This is wrong but since it is the decision of the leadership, I will have to obey it.' He was even ready for self-immolation; such was the level of commitment to the cause.

The late Wahab Siddiqi was in Landhi Jail. He had not married Fauzia Wahab then but his proposal was under consideration. When he was arrested, her parents said that he was a political man who went to jail, therefore, they did not want their daughter to marry him. Anyway, they did get married eventually. Alas, both of them are no longer with us.

There was another incident in Landhi Jail worth mentioning here. There was a frail security guard who was a former military man. The only English he knew was the word 'OK'. He was responsible for our headcount every morning. Our colleague, Sardar Qureshi, who was a jolly fellow, used to say to the guard that the army takes out the brains of its recruits and makes them utterly useless and that's what has happened to him also. After that, whenever we'd ask the guard if any such thing happened with him, he'd take a long pause and say, 'Yes, something like that did happen to me!'

The well-known Sindhi poet, Mujrim Laghari, was also with us in Landhi Jail. The jail superintendent liked to call him to his office and listen to his poetry. Our appetite had increased inside the jail so one day we asked him to request his fan, the superintendent, to increase our bread quota. He obliged, resulting in an increase of half a roti for each of us.

When the movement ended, all prisoners were released and we were very happy. This movement was a severe blow to the Zia government. We started several movements and always ended them when we wanted to and not because of external pressure. This was a great and historic movement. We have not witnessed any movement of such an extent and duration afterwards that was this well-organized. We will always be proud of it.